Praise for *Make Your Case*
by Tanya Acker

"Tanya Acker lays out a common sense approach to deciding when to go—or not to go—to court. *Make Your Case* is straightforward and an invaluable resource from someone with the legal insight to tell it like it is."

—Judge Judy Sheindlin

"Civil court can be your first line of defense or your last avenue to justice in our legal system. That's why it's important that you know the process, the players, and the politics. Tanya Acker's *Make Your Case* offers the kind of knowledge and insight you won't find outside of law school. A must-read for everyone because you never know when you'll need it."

—The Honorable Anthony Daniels, Alabama House Minority Leader

"Whether you want to get the guy next door to stop dumping his garbage on your lawn or vindicate your constitutional rights against the President of the United States, with *Make Your Case*, Tanya Acker has you covered."

—Rebecca Buckwalter-Poza, Award-Winning Attorney, Political Strategist, and Journalist (who sued the President of the United States and won)

"Do not go to court without first reading this book! Smart, funny, readable, and filled with information and advice that only someone who has seen court from many different angles can offer, *Make Your Case* prepares you for what to expect at every stage of the litigation process. After reading it, you'll know the questions you should be asking your legal representative—and yourself. I've spent most of my career teaching law, and I learned something from practically every page."

—Omar Dajani, Professor of Law,
McGeorge School of Law, University of the Pacific

"An extraordinary clinic for non-lawyers and lawyers alike on what realistically to expect when you're compelled to enter the uncertain, often scary, and frequently expensive arena of litigation. Tanya Acker's *Make Your Case* is an invaluable compass to help you get your bearings as you attempt a journey toward your 'win.'"

—Chad Hummel, Co-Leader of the national trial practice at
Sidley Austin LLP, Fellow of the American College of Trial Lawyers

TANYA ACKER

MAKE
YOUR
CASE

Finding Your Win
in Civil Court

DIVERSION
BOOKS

To Mom, Dad, Randy, and the Constitution.
You all are the greatest.

For more information, email info@diversionbooks.com

Diversion Books
A division of Diversion Publishing Corp.
www.diversionbooks.com

First Diversion Books edition, October 2020
Paperback ISBN: 978-1-63576-701-8
eBook ISBN: 978-1-63576-688-2

Printed in The United States of America

1 3 5 7 9 10 8 6 4 2

Library of Congress cataloging-in-publication data is available on file.

CONTENTS

CONTENTS

PREFACE

When the world shuts down, people in disputes with one another don't just automatically stop fighting and make peace. Some do, but many don't.

Many simply cannot. For many, a global pandemic, and the near shut-down of the world in an attempt to stem it, can make what were already difficult situations much worse. Expectations are frustrated. People are unsettled and redrawing their boundaries.

During that same period—now, as I write this—a broad coalition is engaged around an issue with which many of us have long been familiar: the fact that the world can be far more dismissive, officious, brutal, or deadly if you are Black. Many American and global citizens are grappling with questions about how well the "system" works or whether it even works at all. Brutally stark examples of how it does not always confer to everyone the presumptive benefits of freedom and liberty, or value African-American lives as highly as others, have led to an important conversation about fairness and how to ensure it.

This book presumes a lot, not the least of which is some basic faith in the civic institutions that are supposed to hold us together in times of crisis. It presumes that *just because I say so* isn't a valid basis for compelling or restraining behavior and that those civic institutions can play a useful role in keeping *just because I say so* at bay when we're not—let's just say—"being our best selves." A diverse group of people who have to share space, who aren't always inclined to see things in the same way, and who are laboring under pressures that will themselves make history, need to know there is a platform for resolving disputes that is more likely than not to play fairly. Court is one of those institutions, and having more information about court can help mitigate both blind faith and hopeless despair regarding how the process works. Either can be fatal to your search for justice.

I hope this helps.

INTRODUCTION

Our Eternal, Timeless Brawls

"I HAVE NO PISTOLS! LET HIM FIRE!
STAND OUT OF THE WAY AND LET THE ASSASSIN FIRE!"

—Senator Thomas Hart Benton to Senator Henry Foote in 1850, as Benton strode toward
Foote on the Senate floor in objection to Foote's remarks, and Foote pulled a gun on him.

What is something that all of us—blue, red, purple, or otherwise—
have in common? We file lawsuits. Millions of them.[1]

We can fight with each other over just about anything. Someone
lies or someone else thinks they did. Someone claims they're owed
money and someone else thinks they're being extorted. Someone's
circumstances change and they find themselves unable to do something they previously thought they could. Someone thinks they de-
livered a masterpiece and someone else thinks their nine-year-old
kid could have done better.

Plus, neither life, nor you, are perfect. You'll enter into an agreement and not think of everything. You will think you've covered all
your bases, but you may let some things slip, thinking that everyone
is working on the same page and toward the same objectives. Maybe
you'll be too easygoing about something, or believe that the pressures you're under require that you not "make an issue" of things

you ordinarily do. You won't always be on your "*let-me-make-sure-there-is-absolutely-no-way-they-can-come-after-me*" game. You'll be surprised when you thought everyone was on the same page and someone conjures a way to cry foul, or actually has a way of doing so.

And all of that is just on a good day. Add to that a near shutdown of the world because of a global pandemic and you get mathematical magic—an already infinite number of reasons for disputes somehow seems to multiply:

- Your state or local government issues a stay-at-home order, requiring that all but essential businesses cease operating. Your business is considered non-essential. You disagree.
- Your state or local government does not issue a stay-at-home order but your boss refuses to let you wear a mask at work. You think he's playing Russian roulette with your life.
- The lockdown prohibits you from joining other congregants in your church for in-person services. You believe the order is unconstitutional.
- The government denies you COVID-19 relief funds because your spouse is undocumented. You believe this is unconstitutional.
- Your parent was in a nursing home where a COVID-19 outbreak took place. No one at the facility told you anything in advance and you don't think they did enough to protect residents from harm.
- Your company is forced to close down so you're not getting a paycheck, which means you can't pay your rent. You may get several months' grace period, but it's not like you're going to grow new money after you haven't been working for months. Oh, and the landlord still didn't fix the pipes.
- When you closed down your business, you weren't able

to earn money to pay for the supplies you ordered. You don't need them anymore and the supply company won't take them back. You have neither the ability nor the inclination to pay for something you don't need.

Just a random sampling of the kinds of fights that can send people marching to the courthouse door—or, as circumstances may require, a video-conferenced version of one.

As often as people may think they want to go to court, they sometimes can end up there with little idea about how or why it works as it does; or what they might expect when they get there; or how they might try to make the best of things if for some reason they end up there unwillingly. Some may be disappointed when it turns out that the process isn't just about figuring out whether they're right or wrong, but also about making sure they belong in court in the first place.

Some may think court forbidding. Others may over-romanticize it. But what would we do without it?

We'd eat each other alive.

You know this is true. We don't share the same values, the same sense of fairness, or even the same ideas about what "fairness" means. We sometimes reject facts (this is especially true if they're offered by someone who we consider to be "on the other side"). Our passionate disagreements sometimes erupt into consuming near-hatreds (or just hatreds) and even if they don't become THAT bad, we still want a way to resolve them. We are a simmering cauldron of opportunities to fight.

While our courts aren't perfect, they're much better than the dueling grounds of the past. They're far better than being left to the whims and mercies of someone else's mood. While there is no doubt that resources give you a leg up, it's also true that when those with few to none have sought refuge from the arbitrary and unfair conduct by others, court is and has been their last (and sometimes, their only) line of defense. Court has been where people from all walks of life have sometimes been able to get a fair shake, even when other institutions didn't think them entitled to any fairness at all.

WHEN COURT COMES THROUGH

Sometimes court has failed us—like the time in 1857 when the U.S. Supreme Court ruled that African Americans weren't fully human.[2]

But sometimes court has come through beautifully—like the time when a formerly enslaved African American woman could bring a lawsuit to recover her child after human traffickers—slave traders—had sold him illegally.

She was born Isabella Baumfree but later changed her name to Sojourner Truth. After she escaped her own enslavers, she learned that one of her children was going to be sold from the New York farm where he was being enslaved, to an Alabama plantation. (The families of enslaved African Americans were often ripped apart. In spite of efforts to sanitize the institution of slavery, it was, in fact, an inhumane and barbaric business.) In 1828, however, New York had banned the slave trade, so the sale was illegal. Isabella filed a lawsuit to court to get her son back.

She won.

That wasn't the only time court came through for her. Later, when she was falsely accused of being a party to murder, she sued those who made the accusation and won $125 in damages.

Every kind of fight ends up in court—cases some think are important; cases some find frivolous; cases some think are light and funny and others that break our hearts. That certainly has been my experience on *Hot Bench*. Court is where people go for a fair shake.

Where would we be without it? Would we settle our fights by force—whether the physical kind or some other type? The "force" might be the kind that's imposed by impassioned and concerned citizens speaking out on social media or other platforms. Or it might be the kind that's wielded by packs of internet trolls.

"Force" sometimes may have its merits but it has its limits, too. What if your landlord could send a gang of thugs to force you to pay for damages in excess of your security deposit even though you claim those damages were only the result of normal wear and tear? Imagine what would happen if our disputes were decided by who received the most "likes"? If you lent money to someone, would you really want their repayment obligations to depend on the results of a Facebook poll? What if you were a generous lender who didn't have enough "likes"? What would happen then?

Where would we be if we didn't have some way of resolving our disputes that relied on something more than the whims and moods of the loudest and most insistent people? What would happen if you could only be assured of a just and fair resolution of your fight if your preferred political party, or your friends, or the people you know and with whom you have some acquaintance, were in power?

What happens if (when) they lose? Where will you be then?

If we don't have a way of resolving our disputes that we can trust, we're done. I know it's a *highly polarized time*. But hasn't it always been?

NINETEENTH-CENTURY FACEBOOK FIGHTS HAPPENED IN PERSON WITH GUNS AND CANES

In 1856, Representative Preston Brooks physically assaulted Senator Charles Sumner on the Senate floor with a cane, in response to a speech Sumner gave deriding the then-much-embraced institution of enslaving people. A few years before that, in 1850, Senator Henry Foote of Mississippi pulled a gun on Senator Thomas Hart Benton of Missouri—also on the Senate floor (noted in the epigraph above). In another instance, Senator Foote struck Senator John Fremont of

California in the face in the hallway outside the Senate chamber. They would have had a duel but friends intervened.

In the "good ol' days" people weren't trolling each other online. They were beating each other silly in person.

True, the difference between today and the "good 'ol' days" (not really that *good,* if you ask me) is that our fights can escalate more quickly than ever. We can dig in and hunker down with the click of a button (or the batting of an eyelash, if you've got those glasses). We can draw battle lines, recruit allies, and replenish our arsenals without even leaving the sofa. Every glance at our screens reminds us of why everyone else is so hazardous to our health. Not only do we fight a lot, but now we can fight *quickly.*

So, we need court. Resorting to shootouts was not always productive. Duels don't provide much protection from mistakes. Court provides us a basis for resolving our disputes with one another—a basis grounded in something more than someone's whim, or their mood, or whether we can shoot straight.

Still, court is a mixed bundle of upsides and downsides.

On the one hand, court can be a refuge from certain types of savagery, a place with standards and procedures for ensuring that your fight is resolved according to principles based on something more certain than someone's whim or mood, or whether they like you, or fear you, or anything like that. In court, you're supposed to be able to enjoy the benefit of rules that ensure we resolve our disputes in a reasonably civil way. It is supposed to work this way even when the person with whom you're fighting is neither reasonable nor civil. That's why you're supposed to be able to go to court—to get them to play fairly.

On the other hand, court is a place where savagery can run rampant. Maybe it's a lawyer or litigant who fabricates tales with the same ease that others breathe air. Maybe it's an opposing party who obstructs and protracts matters just because they can—because the system allows them so many opportunities to do so while doing very little to protect you. Maybe it's the fact that some of your *"ride or dies"*—your great friends, your allies, the ones who say they'll always "have your back"—decide that when it comes to testifying on your behalf, your back is on its own. Who knew you'd ever have to subpoena your "friends"? (The quotation marks are quite intentional.) Some "ride or dies" would rather take the bus.

Maybe it's just the unremitting toll that litigation takes on your peace of mind and your wallet, especially when you show up unprepared for what you'll have to do in order to wage war in court.

This book contains no secret sauce about how to win your court case, should you happen to be in one. How could it? I don't know you or your fight, or whether you even should be in one. Maybe the fight is a complete waste of your time. Maybe you're in the wrong, at least partially. Maybe your position will be absolutely and thoroughly vindicated. I have no idea.

As someone who has decided a multitude of cases in our *Hot Bench* tribunal, litigated them in private practice, and counseled people about disputes and the dispute resolution process, I instead want to debunk some myths, help you better understand why some things in court might work as they do, and give you a general understanding of the process so you can better organize your thinking around your fight if it ends up in court. People sometimes think that when it comes to proving their case in court, they can assume more things than they really can—whether it's about what they have to prove; or how they go about proving things; or how the law might analyze and dissect an issue that looks like one Big Heaping Mass of Problem. Some people may think that picking through that Big Heaping Mass of Problem will be easier or more straightforward than it actually is. Or, they may be too intimidated even to start.

When you're not in court, "winning" can mean any number of things. In the most straightforward of circumstances, it can simply mean scoring more points or winning some objective contest. In less straightforward situations, "winning" can mean ensuring your opponent, who may be your opponent for reasons only you can know or determine, doesn't get something they believe is important or valuable to them. You might take this view irrespective of its consequences to you, if any. Your sense of winning may be derived from seeing someone else lose, in which case you don't really gain anything except a sense of satisfaction in someone else's struggle. If you find that "someone else" particularly devious or troublesome, perhaps this gives you a sense that they'll be kept at bay in the future, depending on the ground you're trying to protect. Perhaps you think the lawsuit will teach them a lesson.

Plus, so many of our fights aren't *really* what we say they're about. We claim we're fighting about the economy when we're really just hashing out longstanding culture war enmities. We say we're mad about a friend's sharp tone when we're really annoyed they forgot a birthday. Sometimes, we want a referee to make sense of our fights and bring some order to them. Decipher them. Explain our position to "the other side." Make them "get it." Sometimes people show up in court with their Big Heaping Mass of Problem—a kindling of grievances and offense spanning any period of time—to which a flame has been lit, and they want the process to rescue their valuables from the ash. What they don't always realize is that they have to take a walk through the wreckage first so as to point out where the valuables are.

How you define your "win" will determine what you do or don't in the course of your fight; how hard you try (or not) to resolve it; and what objectives you set as your medium- or long-term ends. When you're fighting in other places, you can craft a version of "winning" that suits just about any objective you like. You can make up objectives as you go along or improvise upon them as you see fit. You have a lot of flexibility!

You don't have that much flexibility in court. Improvising and flying by the seat of your pants can cost you a lot of time and money. If you're not very clear on precisely the "win" that you're seeking and what it will take to get there, you can end up being held hostage by the process, or by the whims and caprices of someone else's anger, or even by the whims and caprices of your own. You may ignore opportunities to escape your kidnapper because you really want to punch him in the face first.

Court may be a refuge from unfair and unjust fighting in other places but when you're fighting there, it won't always feel very just or very fair. You may not get the justice you think you deserve. Even if you do get it or something close to it, you should have some idea of what getting there will require of you.

When you know how messy, difficult, time-consuming, and expensive court can be, you will do everything you can to avoid it. You will send emails confirming your agreements, clearing up confusion before people become too wedded to divergent paths. You'll read carefully the contract upon which you know to insist, since doing a little work beforehand can save you a lot of (more expensive and frustrating) work later. You'll save some voicemails. You'll take better notes. Maybe you'll think twice about loaning someone money; or think twice about not paying it back; or maybe you'll consider more carefully whether to reject unilaterally someone's demand that you correct a problem they claim you created. Since having your *day* in court can sometimes mean having your *years* there, you may be more inclined to explore whether there are other, more effective ways of solving your problem.

By the same token, you may *have* to be in court for some reason. You may have no other choice. If that's your situation, there is good reason to be overwhelmed or intimidated by the process because it can place enormous demands on your time and resources. Those demands sometimes can result from the automatic application of rules and standards that may be as unfamiliar to you as the lost languages of Atlantis.

I hope this book helps demystify the process. Having some idea of what court may require of you, of the many ways in which it may disappoint you, and of the ways in which it may nonetheless give you a break, can help you better prepare how you move forward with your court fight. There are so many things that can happen in court to blindside you; I just want to give you a sense of a few of them so you'll understand how uncertain (and sometimes counterintuitive) the process can be.

In the course of resolving disputes on *Hot Bench* and during other phases of my legal career, I've seen people be completely bewildered by court. They sometimes seem to think that proving things in court is like trying to convince your mother not to ground you for staying out too late. They can't believe that in the course of a court proceeding *someone can get away with saying that.* They can think it's easier than it is or, alternatively, retreat into a type of defeatism, overwhelmed by twists and turns that can be as slippery and elusive as Medusa's hairline. Slippery and elusive as those twists and turns may be, however, rules still apply.

While a lot of the material I reference here involves tactics and maneuvers that apply to cases more complex than those you might see on *Hot Bench,* they're intended to give you a flavor of what different court experiences may be like. I wanted to highlight the sorts of demands court can make of you as you seek its help. You have to help court help you. I also want to explain why some things happen as they do so that you don't feel like the process is a complete gamble. It's not a "complete" gamble because there are rules and controls on things that can give you some guidance. Still, it's something of a gamble.

Some of the anecdotes in this book are inspired by case experiences and interviews with lawyers (with names and details changed); some are composites; others are complete hypotheticals; some are based upon or inspired by published and unpublished court decisions. Don't get nervous—I'm not talking about you. If something feels familiar, just act casual and no one will notice. So many of the fights and problems people have are similar to those of others, existing perhaps on a different scale and with different characters, but born of the same types of protectiveness and, sometimes, animosities.

To be clear—I am *not* giving you legal advice. Nor am I offering any definitive statement about what the law *is* on a particular topic; this is not, obviously, a comprehensive primer or textbook. Any law can change or be interpreted differently in different cases, or across different jurisdictions, or even interpreted differently by different people. Some may not even apply in every jurisdiction. Some of the rules and/or outcomes that I discuss in this book may have changed or someone may have an interpretation or perspective on them that I haven't considered. Since I started writing this book, someone has challenged a victory; a proposition that stood for something may no longer stand; some smart or dedicated lawyer found a way to break open an exception; someone brilliant will refine a concept or a principle in a way that gives parts of our ever-alive legal process a makeover. This book is just the start of a conversation.

In short, this is simply my argument to you that court sometimes can be far more involved, counterintuitive, and uncertain than many people expect. Maybe if someone wanted to write a book called *Court Is All Smooth Sailing!* they could examine the caselaw of different jurisdictions and collect real life experiences that would allow them to prove that point. (Maybe.) My intention, however, is to address what is all too often a different experience—one where the lawsuit that someone thought was "simple" turns into a years-long affair that starts to drown out other living expenses. Legal bills can end up making food and housing costs feel like a cheap date, especially when paying your lawyers starts to feel like subsidizing a small nation. A lawsuit can expand like a monster, one that grows new heads each time one is chopped off.

At the same time, this book is also my argument in support of the idea that it is possible to make justice a real thing and to get it to work for you, and that some general familiarity with why some things in court may work as they do can help lay the groundwork for making that happen.

As complicated and troublesome as our relationship with our institutions can be, our relationships with each other are sometimes no walk in the park either. Everyone isn't always able to make a bully stand down. Everyone doesn't even agree about who the bullies are. Sometimes court can be an effective intermediary between us and those with whom we can't see eye to eye. Sometimes there are better options.

Yes, court can sometimes reflect the injustice from which litigants are taking refuge—but it can also be a place where justice sings and where you're reminded that you matter too, regardless of how many "likes" you have.

Court, like the world at large, has become a more just place since Sojourner Truth engaged with it—in part because of battles that many people fought there, in court. Still, both it and the world have work to do.

Good luck to us.

PART I

When the Fight Heats Up

By a little inquiry, she found which was the building she sought, went into the door, and taking the first man she saw of imposing appearance for the grand jury, she commenced her complaint. But he very civilly informed her there was no Grand Jury there; she must go upstairs. When she had with some difficulty ascended the flight through the crowd that filled them, she again turned to the 'grandest' looking man she could select, telling him she had come to enter a complaint to the Grand Jury. For his own amusement, he inquired what her complaint was; but, when he saw it was a serious matter, he said to her, 'This is no place to enter a complaint—go in there.'

—Dictated by Sojourner Truth,
Written and edited by Olive Gilbert,
The Narrative of Sojourner Truth (c. 1797–1883)

1

SO, YOU WANT TO
BRING A LAWSUIT

You're Over It. You Think
You're Ready for the Fight. But Are You?

You're going to court because you have a problem you want to fix. You want to make your opponent pay a price. You want to win your fight.

"Winning" in court, of course, means accomplishing the objective you set out to obtain—getting the judge or jury to agree with you. It can mean getting the other side to pony up or to back off, as the case may be.

But that isn't all it means.

It also can mean arriving at the finish line without having been bled dry of your resources. It means accomplishing an objective that still matters because you haven't blown everything up en route to getting it.

Spend some time thinking about your case before it starts. Try to anticipate some things in advance. Flying by the seat of your pants when you're fighting in court can be really expensive. Save your pants and plan ahead.

What You Should Know: A Brief Overview of Our Court System

You're "going to court." Where? Which one? What do you do when you think court is your next step for solving a problem?

First, let's have a brief overview about how the court system is organized.

Most legal cases fall into one of two categories: civil or criminal. There are separate court divisions for each.

Criminal cases are those instituted by a government for a violation of (you guessed it) a criminal act. Governments—national, state, and local—are in charge of prosecuting crimes, the idea being that they (not private individuals) are charged with guarding the public's interest in safety and security. It's why criminal cases are denominated *The People vs. Jon Alleged-Criminal*. "The people"—the citizens—are seeking to hold responsible Mr. Alleged-Criminal for his misconduct (via the prosecutor). (The "people" elect the legislators who create criminal legal codes and/or determine appropriate penalties. When those legislators criminalize something, they are ostensibly acting on "the people's" behalf.)

Civil cases, by contrast, are brought by private people on behalf of private interests, although they often advance public goals, too. For instance, if someone brings a lawsuit against their employer claiming their boss discriminated against them on the basis of race or gender (which is prohibited by state and federal law), they might be seeking personal compensation for themselves, but they may also be seeking a remedy that will benefit a larger group of people in similar situations. Many rules about how people interact with one another have come about because of civil lawsuits individuals brought in which they sought relief from something that was harming them very personally and directly.

Teresa Harris, for example, a retail manager for a forklift company, brought a lawsuit against her employer which changed the rules of the workplace for many. She claimed her employer called her a "dumb-ass woman"; that he suggested she negotiate pay raises with him at a hotel rather than at work; and that he asked her and other female employees to get coins from his front pocket. She argued in court that she had a right to be free from that kind of treatment at work. Her 1993 victory in the U.S. Supreme Court is why hostile work environments are now illegal in the United States.[1]

Federal Court

Most civil cases are brought in either federal or state court.

AGENCIES AND OTHER DECISION-MAKERS

In some instances, you'll have to first file a claim with the relevant agency or administrative body, such as the California Labor and Workforce Development Agency (for unpaid wage claims) or the U.S. Equal Employment Opportunity Commission (for workplace discrimination claims). If these decision-makers decline to investigate or issue an adverse decision, then you can take your case to court.[2]

The president nominates federal judges, which include U.S. Supreme Court Justices, and the Senate votes on whether or not to confirm them. They have their jobs for life.

Federal courts are courts of "limited jurisdiction." That means in order to bring your case to federal court, you have to have a claim that arises under federal law—a federal statute or the U.S. Constitution. A challenge to a state law on the ground that it prevented you from voting for an impermissible reason—such as race, gender, or age, which are protected by the 15th, 19th, and 26th Amendments, respectively—would be an example of a claim a federal court can hear. Also, federal courts have what is known as *diversity jurisdiction,* or jurisdiction between citizens of different states when the amount is greater than $75,000.[3]

State Courts

State court judges are usually either appointed or elected by popular vote, or a combination thereof. Many states organize their courts into different divisions; in my home state of California, for instance, the divisions include Criminal; Civil (Unlimited Jurisdiction, for cases over $25,000); Family; Juvenile; and Limited Jurisdiction (Small Claims). When you file your case, you'll complete a cover sheet that will determine the division to which your case is assigned.

The rules in each of these different courts may vary; for instance, in a civil case, you can bring a summary judgment motion, which allows you to get rid of a case that someone files against you before trial starts because it's clear from the discovery process that the other side doesn't have enough facts to make its case. In family court (at least in California), however, summary judgment isn't available.

CALIFORNIA FAMILY COURT—LET THEM FIGHT IT OUT!

According to the Judicial Council of California, the basis for disallowing summary judgments in family law cases is that those disputes almost always turn on questions of fact.[4]

If you think this can promote litigation amongst already angry people who are looking for reasons to make things as difficult as possible for someone who they may, at the time, hate, then I would agree with you. It does.

The cases we hear on *Hot Bench* are drawn from small claims courts, where the parties represent themselves. The procedures in small claims court are usually simpler and the process more informal than in civil courts where larger amounts are at stake. Depending on the nature of your case (and the amount you're seeking), the cost and time savings may make small claims court an attractive option, even if you end up suing for less money.

Arbitration

Arbitration is an alternative dispute resolution procedure that allows for parties to resolve their dispute without going to court. I'll discuss it in more detail in Chapter 11 as a way to avoid litigation (and some of the travails I mention during the course of this book). It is also being used increasingly as a means of resolving disputes in the first instance; many contracts, for instance, require employees, consumers, and others to arbitrate their claims *instead* of going to court. While you can in certain circumstances challenge the decision of the arbitrator in civil court, those circumstances are limited. Some of the grounds for vacating an arbitration award include 1) fraud or corruption in obtaining the award; 2) partiality on the part of the arbitrator; or 3) the award exceeds the arbitrator's powers.[5]

What You Should Know: You Can Lose Before You Even Get to Right or Wrong

When you're in the middle of a dispute with someone, you're usually focused on questions that are pretty basic. Who's right? Who's wrong?

In court, you potentially won't even get to those questions unless you do some advance work and answer others, first. If you don't, you could end up spending time and money in amounts that will make you sick before you even get to the issue of how right you think you are in your case. Making your case means more than explaining why you think you should win. It means being prepared to explain why you should be in court in the first place.

For purposes of this chapter, let's assume you are on the receiving end of some perceived injustice and you want to fix it. Someone has done something wrong. They owe you money. They damaged your property. They've reneged on a commitment. They've injured you. You don't just want to rant about it or spread outrage about it on social media. You want to fix it.

Court is where people go to solve problems, and to solve them in a way that is fair and equitable—according to rules that are supposed to apply to all of us and to which we're all supposed to be able to resort if we need them. It's not supposed to be a free-for-all. Court is not where anything goes and the winner is the one who knows how to make mud stick best. In court, we expect an orderly resolution. There are rules, which ostensibly are there to keep everyone in line.

But if you're not careful, some of those rules can be trapdoors that will drop you into a No Man's Land where you're spending money chasing issues that have nothing to do with proving how right or wrong you are in your fight. You can end up going broke—and still be no closer to resolving the fight that brought you to court in the first place.

What You Can Do: Interrogate Yourself, First

If you think court holds a solution to your conflict, ask yourself some basic questions first. You'll be glad you did.

"Who" Is My Opponent in this Fight?

When you're fighting in court, this is not as obvious a question as it seems.

Who did the bad thing to you?

Who are you going to sue?

Are they the same person?

Are you sure?

Sam is a contractor who made some big promises about how he could transform your kitchen. You hire him to do the job. The total cost of the project was $7,000. You pay Sam $3,500 upfront to buy materials and hire workers.

Sam was supposed to start the project the following week. Three weeks later, he still hasn't started the project and has stopped returning your phone calls. The police tell you it that it's a "civil matter" and they won't get involved.

What can you do? You, I'm assuming, are a generally law-abiding person who isn't inclined to "take the law into your own hands" because you have no interest in seeing your already troublesome problem get any worse. The police won't get involved because it's a "civil matter." Pursuing your larcenous contractor probably has to take a back seat to more pressing law enforcement matters.

Writing a nasty Yelp review isn't going to satisfy you. Complaining online isn't necessarily going to get you your money back. You want your money back. You don't want someone to think they can just get away with taking advantage of you. I don't think any of us would give short shrift to the need to stand up for ourselves in certain situations.

Unaware of any other (legal!) options, you decide to sue Sam.

You are the "plaintiff." Sam would be the "defendant." But is Sam the person you should be suing? Is Sam an independent contractor who you could sue as a private individual (e.g., *You v. Sam D., an individual*)? Is his business structured as a limited liability corporation or some other entity? Should you name that entity in the lawsuit instead (*You v. Sam D. Construction, Inc.*)? If Sam works for a company, who owns the company? Who is the person in the company to whom lawsuits should be directed—its "registered agent" for service of process?

You could, of course, end up just suing everyone and their mother but if they all fight back, you'd have to explain how and why they were involved. You could end up having a lot of costly explaining to do.

There is also some time pressure on you to figure all this out. You have only a limited amount of time to file your complaint before you violate the statute of limitations, which is the time by which a case must be filed after the event giving rise to it happens (this varies depending on the subject of your lawsuit and where you are bringing it).

If Sam is trying to avoid you, you can really end up spending quite a bit of time just trying to serve him. You'll have to file a *proof of service* with the court, which is evidence that the person or entity being sued actually received the complaint. (Once the defendant receives it, they typically have 30 days to respond. That, however, is just a *starting* point. Defendants usually can get more time if they need it. In fact, in some jurisdictions you have to provide a good reason for *not* giving them extra time if they ask for it.)

On the upside, you may have the opportunity to ask the judge for an extension if you need more time to complete service. Or, if the court dismisses your case because you either can't find Sam or you serve the wrong entity, you can ask the court for an opportunity to bring it again.

Asking for the chance to bring it again, however, isn't just a matter of calling the court and checking everyone's schedule. You would have to file papers with the court, which takes time (and if she has a lawyer, cost money). Then, you or your lawyer would have to be prepared to show up in court (time + money) on a day that works with the judge's busy schedule (more later on just how busy), to explain your position.

Then, you have to hope the judge agrees with you. If you have a good reason for missing the service deadline, the judge may very well give you another bite at the apple—but don't plan on a free bite. All of these maneuvers can take time and cost money when you're fighting in court. Time + money = a lot of expense, aggravation, and disruption in your life.

What happens if you don't know the names of everyone who you think should be held accountable? You should still file your lawsuit anyway. The clock is ticking and you'll want to bring your claim before the statute of limitations runs out. If you're not sure who to sue, you can file your complaint against a "John Doe" party and substitute the correct name when you determine who that is.

Don't be surprised if you end up spending a lot of time and money on issues like this. If the person you want to sue is taking cover under an entity with a complicated business or organizational structure, you can spend a lot of time figuring out precisely who to sue and how to get to them. You can spend a fortune before you even get to the question of who's right and who's wrong.

For instance, you may think Company A is responsible but perhaps Company A doesn't exist anymore. You sue its owner, Person Z, and he says because the company is organized as a limited liability company, for instance, you can't sue him personally. Plus the company is organized in Delaware. *Sue me in Delaware*, Person Z may say to you. *I don't live in your state. Come find me.* Does Person Z have control over and direct Company A? Are they functionally the same entity?

Or, someone may have done business as XYZ corporation for as long as you've known them, and now they're in bankruptcy because they treated a lot of people the same way they did you. You really want to get its CEO, Person C. Do you have any idea where they live? How are you going to serve them?

You can end up spending a lot of time fighting about just who the right defendants are before you even get to the meat of your case.

This is just the beginning. There's a multitude of other ways in which things can spiral out of control.

WHEN YOU WANT TO SUE THE GOVERNMENT

The United States government has *sovereign immunity*, which means you only can sue it under circumstances where it says you can. Some of those circumstances include certain tort claims and claims for civil rights.[6] States also enjoy sovereign immunity, which is limited by certain exceptions for tort and civil rights claims.[7]

42 U.S.C. §1983 allows private citizens to sue government officials for civil rights violations:

Every person who, under color of any statute, ordinance, regulation, custom, or usage, of any State or Territory or the District of Columbia, subjects, or causes to be subjected, any citizen of the United States or other person within the jurisdiction thereof to the deprivation of any rights, privileges, or immunities secured by the Constitution and laws, shall be liable to the party injured in an action at law, suit in equity, or other proper proceeding for redress, except that in any action brought against a judicial officer for an act or omission taken in such officer's judicial capacity, injunctive relief shall not be granted unless a declaratory decree was violated or declaratory relief was unavailable. For the purposes of this section, any Act of Congress applicable exclusively to the District of Columbia shall be considered to be a statute of the District of Columbia.

Counties and municipalities don't enjoy the same sovereign immunity as the federal and state government. They may be liable for policies that result in constitutional violations.[8]

The judicially crafted doctrine of "qualified immunity" protects government officials from liability for their official acts unless their conduct violates "clearly established law."

Defenders of qualified immunity argue that "claims frequently run against the innocent as well as the guilty," and "the expenses of litigation, the diversion of official energy from pressing public issues, and the deterrence of able citizens from acceptance of public office," require that officials have some protection from liability for their official acts. As the Supreme Court described the issue in one case, the fear of litigation might "dampen the ardor of all but the most resolute, or the most irresponsible [public officials], in the unflinching discharge of their duties."[9]

On the other hand, there have been calls to reform or abolish this doctrine on the ground that it allows a free pass for novel governmental abuses. For example, if a governmental official does something to you that you believe violates your rights but which no governmental official had previously conceived of doing to someone else or which isn't factually on all fours with some earlier alleged abuse, then there may be no "clearly established" law indicating that what happened to you is wrong. One judge described the doctrine as "letting public officials duck consequences for bad behavior—no matter how palpably unreasonable—as long as they were the *first* to behave badly."[10]

"Where" Do I Have This Fight?

Are you bringing your case in federal or state court? That will depend on the nature of your claim; where you and your opponent live and the amount in dispute. As discussed above, if your claim involves questions of federal law, or if it involves more than $75,000 and you and your opponent live in different states, you may bring it in federal court. If it involves mostly questions of state law, or if the federal questions are really secondary to the issues that arise under state law, then state court may be your proper forum. The rules and procedures in federal and state court can be different, and in certain cases, the parties can argue vigorously over which is the proper venue for a lawsuit.

Even if you know you are bringing your case in state court, you still have to know which one. In some situations, the question of "where" may be easy. If you're suing over a breach of contract, for example, the contract may specify the jurisdiction where any disputes are to be resolved. Perhaps the agreement has what is referred to as a "forum selection clause"—where the parties agree that any disputes between them will be resolved in a particular jurisdiction.

In the absence of contractual direction, you have to consider a few things. Where did the offense happen? Where do you live? What about the offender? If you want to sue someone who lives in a different state, you have to show they have some *minimum contacts* within the jurisdiction; you can't sue someone in the state where you live just because it's convenient for you, forcing them to travel thousands of miles from their home to litigate. You have to show their connection to the place where you want to sue them: maybe they have an office in the jurisdiction from which they frequently work, or they regularly solicit business and clients there. If you aren't suing the defendant in the right place, you can end up in a long, costly battle over just *where* the fight should be before you even get to the subject you're fighting about.

So, for purposes of your complaint you have to consider where the defendant is located. But as your lawsuit goes forward, you'll have to think about the location of your witnesses, too. Their location may not impact the jurisdictional elements of your case but it can impact the time and expense involved when you want them to appear and offer evidence or testimony in your case. Where do they live? Where's the evidence in your case? Who has it, how long is it going to take you to get it, and what will that cost?

> You are involved in an acrimonious dispute with your former business partner. The dispute is pending in California, where you both live and had incorporated your business. You allege that your former partner has engaged in various improper activities that have interfered with your ability to obtain your portion of the revenues from your now-defunct company.

So far this is easy. You and your former partner are both in California and the lawsuit is pending in the same location as the former business. But . . .

> Pimkew is a friend of your former partner's. Pimkew lives in Idaho, but you have reason to believe that she has information about some of your former colleague's attempts to interfere with the sale of business assets.
>
> You want Pimkew to appear in court and answer some questions.

She makes regular visits to California. During one of those visits, your lawyers are able to serve her with a subpoena.

All good? Nope.

Your former business partner (through their lawyers) asks the judge to quash—cancel—the subpoena on the ground that Pimkew doesn't live in California and is only an occasional visitor. The judge grants the motion. Pimkew, for now, is outside of the court's reach.

That's not to say that you don't have options. You could hire a lawyer in Idaho (the lawyer representing you in California wasn't licensed in Idaho) to enforce the California subpoena.* Then, you would have to cross your fingers and hope that the process server in Idaho could find Pimkew; you'd have to cross them again and hope that Pimkew complies with the subpoena. (Given that the very reason you wanted Pimkew to testify was to cross-examine her about some suspicious transactions, her voluntary compliance was unlikely.) You might end up in another court proceeding, seeking to enforce the subpoena: a black hole of time and money. You might "win" the opportunity to force Pimkew to face the music to some extent, but would that "victory" advance your cause in any material way, when what you're really trying to do is finish liquidating the assets from your now-defunct business and move on? You have plenty of other evidence regarding what you believe to be improper activities by your former partner—would pursuing Pimkew cost so much that it wouldn't feel like a victory at all? Are you eager to go down that road?

You're asking me this? you say, hypothetically responding to this hypothetical question.

---

* These are the rules that apply to California, for instance. The rules may be different in other jurisdictions. There is a lot to figure out when you're fighting in court, and you'll need to be familiar with the rules in your jurisdiction.

Would you like to have your appendix removed without anesthesia? you hypothetically respond to us. *What do you think? I'm sick of paying lawyers to chase down lawyers! I just want an end to this!*

You don't pursue the effort to obtain testimony and evidence from Pimkew. While you are eventually able to sell the assets from your former company and enjoy your portion of the profits, you spend a lot of money on legal fees trying to do so.

These may not always be your circumstances. There may be a situation where you need to pursue someone who is evasive, or to otherwise maximize pressure on your opponent. Do what your situation requires but just know what that will require of you. Don't expect it to be easy and don't expect the "right thing" to happen without your having to invest a lot of time and money in it.

Just these two questions alone—*who are you suing and where should you sue them*—can suck up a lot of time and money if you're not clear about them in advance. Litigants have battled over these issues for years.[11] Sometimes battles spring from a good faith dispute over facts (*e.g., do they really live there*), or they can result from someone forcing you to prove something they know to be true and don't have a good reason for contesting. Maybe they just want you to blow as much of your litigation budget as possible before you even get to the point of holding them accountable for whatever they did.

What You Should Know: There's an Upside to All of This

Don't get too disheartened by all of these procedural hurdles. Look on the bright side—be heartened! Ok, that may be a stretch but still, these procedures serve a useful function—especially in a time where it's easy to accuse anyone of anything.

When we fight with each other in other arenas—social media; political tribunals; cable news channels—it's possible to wantonly ensnare almost anyone in a claim of wrongdoing using whatever tactic can be conjured. Sometimes the accused doesn't even get a chance to respond. They can be tried and convicted before the daily news cycle is finished.

In court, by contrast, because you're seeking to use the power of the state to force your opponent to do something, both they and you are entitled to due process, which is one of the constitutional principles upon which our court system is based. Our courts only have jurisdiction over those who fall within their purview—they can't force people outside of that jurisdiction to show up and submit to court process. Due process means your opponent can't order you to travel back and forth across the land, subjecting you to out-of-state proceedings without a good reason and without affording you the benefits of certain procedural protections.

Making sure you receive the benefits of those protections takes time. Due process also means your opponent must have a reasonable amount of time to explain why they should be subjected to the weaponized machinery of the state and why they shouldn't instead be left alone. If litigants don't have the opportunity to present their positions in a meaningful way, then the outcome of their disputes would be little more than a sideshow determined by someone else's whim or mood. No one wants that. So yes, your opponent may need some time to respond. You, too, may need time to fire back at whatever it is your opponent throws at you. As painful as it sometimes may be, this time-consuming process offers some protections for all.

"When" Is It a Real Fight—and Is It Even Your Battle?

A court can't get involved in just any fight. There must be an actual "case or controversy" brewing. If you're seeking to challenge something that doesn't impact you, or to receive the benefits of some protections that aren't intended for you, then you may not have *standing* to bring the lawsuit.[12]

Plus, your problem must have materialized. It has to be *ripe*. If it hasn't happened yet, you have to show some already-existing-in-the-real-world facts justifying your belief that it likely will.

> You loan someone money on December 1, with an agreement that they are going to pay you back by April 30, with interest. As part of your agreement, you agree to waive the interest if they start paying installments before then.
>
> Over Christmas, you notice they are especially generous to everyone, except you.
>
> In January, they get a new car.
>
> In February, they're off on a fun vacation with some friends. They don't invite you. In fact, it seems like they're just avoiding you.
>
> You broach the subject of the money. They become angry and confrontational. They accuse you of harassing them!

Is your case ripe? The debt isn't due until April 30, and April isn't here yet. You might be able to argue that the other person repudiated the debt—or indicated that they no longer had any intention of paying it. *What are you talking about? This was a gift not a loan—go pound sand!*, they might say. That would be an example of repudiation. Unless they've indicated in some way that they've no intention of repaying you, however, your case may not be ripe. They may not have breached anything because nothing has come due yet.

> Your neighbor keeps trespassing onto your property and trampling your tomatoes. Sometimes he throws garbage on your property. He's posted inflammatory things about you and your home on the internet, plus, he started building a fence that encroaches on your property line.

Now, you have been injured. Now your case is ripe.

Remember, however, your case also must be filed by the statute of limitations that's applicable to your claim—which means you can't wait too long. This is yet another issue that people can spend a long time litigating before they even get to the subject that brought them to court in the first place. There have been cases where litigants have fought for years over statute of limitations issues. Yes, years![13]

Why Are You Having This Fight Anyway?

People give all sorts of reasons for going to court:

> *I want my money back.*
> *I'm tired of that person taking advantage of me.*
> *I'm tired of people taking advantage of me, generally. I'm tired of seeing bullies get away with things.*
> *I really want my money back.*
> *I want my stuff fixed. They ruined something special.*
> *If I let this one slide they'll think they can get away with anything.*
> *I'm fed up with this behavior.*
> *Did I mention that I want my money back?*
> *I'm going to hurt them the way they've hurt me.*
> *I want to take a stand.*

Only you (and whatever legal professional is advising you, if you have one) can determine whether the potential delays you will encounter will advance, undermine, or not have any significant impact at all on your objectives. Court may or may not be your best course of action; still, being aware of the potential length of the process can alert you to the need to take other (legal and appropriate!) measures to protect your interests while your case drags on.

Sometimes court may be your best or only option.

CLOSE TO HOME

A group of community organizations sued my home city of Los Angeles because its City Council used an unchecked, unreviewable power to block affordable housing projects.

Here's what was happening: before an affordable housing project could move forward, the city required what was known as a "letter of acknowledgment" ("LOA") from the councilmember in whose district the project was to be located. Councilmembers essentially could veto these projects by not issuing an LOA, which they could do for almost any reason whatsoever or no reason at all. Keep in mind that the people of Los Angeles passed, by a 3-to-1 margin, a measure that would authorize the construction of more low-income housing, construction that the LOA requirement regularly stymied.

(The Los Angeles Homeless Services Authority counted nearly 42,000 homeless people in the city on any given night at the time of this writing.)

While it's impossible to know what would have happened if the plaintiffs hadn't filed this lawsuit, one might be able to formulate some reasonable hypotheses by looking at how the interested parties previously tried to achieve their desired outcome. Advocates for affordable housing urged the city to reconsider the practice. Developers reached out, lamenting that the LOA requirement interfered with their ability to build affordable housing. Local newspapers urged the city to abandon the rule. No go. So, what would have happened in the absence of litigation? Probably a lot more of nothing.

(Full disclosure: I serve on the board of Public Counsel, one of the groups that sued the city over this tactic.)

In any event, the organizations filed a lawsuit. Subsequently, then-Governor Brown signed a bill preventing state-administered funding or tax credits from being awarded to cities with an LOA requirement.[14] The city then entered into settlement discussions and discontinued the practice. I think it's fairly safe to say that the filing of a lawsuit was a significant factor in encouraging that outcome.

You hire a wedding planner for your dream wedding. You pay her in advance. She's supposed to arrange for the caterers, book the DJ, get your wedding party situated—in short, do all of those things that wedding planners do.

She doesn't show up or she shows up late; she doesn't provide the DJ or he doesn't have your music; the caterers are serving pork belly wrapped in croissant and you're a gluten-free vegan. The wedding planner, however, takes no responsibility. *It's all your fault,* she says. *You were too busy checking your hair and makeup while I was looking for the almond flour.*

What happens if you don't sue her?

1. She keeps your money;
2. You can write a bad online review, but if you go too far or if she just likes to sue people, it might land you in court, anyway;
3. You can report her to the Better Business Bureau, or some other such group that oversees business activities.

Will any of these satisfy you? Maybe. Sometimes you can vote with your dollars, or with your (non-defamatory) suggestion that others take their business elsewhere. A lot of places thrive on recommendations.

Sometimes you may want more. Sometimes you may want to force a reckoning. Still, however much you may think you need to do that, make sure you know what it will require of you.

Of course, the differences between my two examples are pretty stark. One involves lawyers seeking to change a practice that impacts the public, while the other involves issues that are ostensibly more of a private concern. Lawsuits that seek to bring about policy changes sometimes involve a different calculus: they often have lawyers who, committed to the cause, are willing to work for free or at very reduced rates. Allowing the condition or circumstance the lawsuit challenges to persist would be an offense to the very reason they're in business. To groups like Public Counsel, which was among the lawyers who brought the case against Los Angeles, closed-door, unilateral vetoes of affordable housing projects when there are over 40,000 people sleeping on the streets every night is not a tenable situation. The "why" of that lawsuit is pretty clear.

The "why" of the wedding planner fiasco seems pretty clear, too. People don't like to get ripped off. Money takes work to earn and people generally don't like to part with it without a good reason. Plus, when people damage you financially, you can also feel hurt in other ways. There is an injury to your reputation; your principles (the *don't rip me off* principle being a big one); your sense of honor and fair play. A lot of civil lawsuits result from our wanting to preserve the sense that people can't just get away with treating us poorly. Most people don't like having simply to absorb the consequences of someone's bad conduct; they bristle at the smirk of the offender who thinks he got one over on them.

It's not just that the wedding planner owes you the money. It's the fact that she thinks she can get away with treating you like this and giving such short shrift to your special day. It's not just that your roof is caving in after the contractor was supposed to replace it—it's the fact that after doing such shoddy work, he has the nerve to try to blame *you*. People want someone to pay attention to their predicament. Even if they don't get vindication, they at least want some acknowledgment. They're tired of people blowing them off and treating them like they don't matter.

Court can be a powerful way to make people take notice of the problems they've caused. But before you embrace it as your only or best option, make sure you have some sense of what may lay ahead in the course of your battle. Have some sense of what chasing that satisfaction may require.

You might need to track that wedding planner down—find her before you can serve her with a lawsuit. You will have to collect evidence of your agreement if you want to have a good shot of convincing a judge that she breached it in some way. (I hope you have a contract.) If you need a lawyer, you'll need to find one. Then you'll need to pay that lawyer money to get up to speed on the issue and move the ball forward. When it's time for discovery (which I'll discuss in Chapter 6), you'll pay that lawyer to prepare you for deposition and then you may need to take time off work. (Don't expect your opponent to reimburse you for that time.) When people are fighting over money, for example, they should make sure to do some math with their lawyers first. It's uncertain math because your lawyer will do everything not to make you any firm promises about outcomes, but they sometimes can give you some ballpark estimates. Often, however, the fights that are "just about the money" are never really "just about the money." Sometimes people need to understand that they won't be able to get away with treating you like a serf on some medieval noble's land, and even that description of their conduct may be generous. Still, knowing what kind of money is involved will help you make a more informed decision, especially if your fight is "just about money."

It's all your call. Every fight is different and people can approach theirs for different reasons—you should just make sure you're approaching yours with as much information as possible.

You probably won't have the kind of powerful allies that the plaintiffs in the case challenging the city of Los Angeles' housing policy had. You won't have newspaper editorial boards on your side; prominent members of the business community clamoring for your justice; or top-flight lawyers willing to advance your cause for free. Most people don't. I've met a lot of people who go to court because they feel they don't have allies anywhere else. Sometimes they are right.

You can't assume that the person who makes a false police report against you will get prosecuted. The movers who withhold your property unless you submit to their demand to pay them more than you'd previously agreed, probably won't be prosecuted either. The businesses that take your money and don't do what they say they will, and who assume you're not powerful enough or vocal enough or "well connected" enough to hold them accountable, may thumb their noses at you before they send you a $5 gift card. People break the law, trample others' rights, and ignore settled obligations with impunity. The lack of resources with which to challenge them successfully may be one of the things that predisposes people to go to court. No one is paying attention to you anywhere else.

Don't expect the system to be naturally responsive to your efforts to "fight the bad guys." Sometimes it will feel like the system is there to let the bad guys keep having their way with you as much as they like.

"What" Are You Hoping to Gain? (And a Note About Your "Worth")

When you're fighting in other places, like in the comments on someone's social media page, by proxy with the talking heads on TV, or even in person with someone who has annoyed you, the subjects of your fight can be so formless and shape-shifty that it sometimes may seem as if you and your opponent aren't even fighting about the same thing.

We're not always forced to answer "why" we're fighting over various things, which makes it easy for some fights to drag on indefinitely. Even more rarely do those fights grapple with "what" people expect to get out of the conflict. Sometimes it seems they're just in it for the fight.

In court, by contrast, you have to put some boundaries or contours around your fight. You have to define what you want and be very explicit about it, and then you have to convince the decision-maker to give it to you. But you have to be very clear about what the *it* is. If you can't do that, then your fight will be over before it starts.

What you want from court is usually easy to figure out: you want to force your opponent to do something, or to pay you something, or to leave you alone and stop bothering you. You want to be vindicated, to be proven right, to enjoy the sense of justice that comes when someone who has treated you badly gets what's coming to them.

But what's coming to them? And what do you think should be coming to you? In your lawsuit, you are going to need to fit your broad sense of outrage into the narrower confines of a request for relief that a court can order. Court can't turn bad people into good ones, or force people to grow a conscience; it can, however, order someone to remedy the damages they've caused you.

Damages. You have to show not only that your opponent did something wrong, you have to show you were damaged by it. You will need to connect the dollars you're seeking to the harm you claim you've endured as a result of your opponent's conduct. The exception to this are punitive damages, which aren't intended to compensate you for harm but instead are intended to punish the defendant for conduct that was intentionally harmful, malicious, or grossly negligent. Still, many jurisdictions have held that punitive damages must bear some relationship to the compensatory award; some have even placed limits on the multiple by which a punitive damage award can exceed the compensatory award; in other words, if your compensatory damages are $100.00, you're probably not going to get $100,000,000 in punitive damages.[15]

What You Should Know:
Court Puts a Discount on You

Here is something else to keep in mind about fighting in court: the law probably doesn't value you and your time as much as you do. Courts have a very different standard of common sense and good manners than the rest of us. While most of us want people to use common sense and a modicum of courtesy when dealing with us; to be decent; to honor the Golden Rule; to act as if they were raised by humans rather than wild animals (no disrespect to the animals), court doesn't always hold people to that standard. Laws represent an effort to distill all of our various judgments into some reasonably definable standard, but there is a lot of behavior that "normal" people might consider unfair or outrageous about which the law simply says *so what?*

There's a presumption in our system that courts (all agents of government, really) can't start ordering anyone around or compelling behavior unless they have a good reason to do so. There are limits on what a court can even order others to do—which means there will be limits on how much of a bad situation you should expect court to fix. While we don't like jerks, we also generally don't like having other people in our business, just randomly and arbitrarily telling us what to do.

(True, there are people who might not mind that kind of regime, just as there were many who didn't mind being ruled by a king, but most of us aren't into that.)

If a court could force someone to do something just on your say so, regardless of whether you've shown that their behavior had any adverse consequence or impact on you, then court simply becomes an instrument for *you* to be arbitrary.

In other words, changing personalities and transforming moral compasses is a complex business. Ordering someone to stay off of your property and stop trespassing is not.

Terms and concepts you thought you understood may turn out to have entirely different meanings in court. They can embrace definitions that don't entirely comport with your common sense (you, as it turns out, went to Common Sense School) and notions of fair play.

You've hired a contractor to work on the second-floor bathroom of your home. He takes off a large chunk of the roof in order to complete the task. A heavy rainstorm has been predicted and announced on the news. The contractor neglects to put the roof back on, or to cover up the house, or to do anything to secure your property against the rain. The rain arrives as predicted in the weather forecast and destroys a significant amount of your property.

Is this outrageous?

Your insurance company refuses to pay out a claim because your policy renewal request didn't comply with one of the company's procedural rules. In fact, that rule is against the law in your state.

Do you think *this* is outrageous? Oppressive?

Since these matters didn't show up on *Hot Bench*, I had no say in whether they were or not. Courts considering cases involving similar facts, however, decided that those circumstances were neither so "outrageous" nor so "oppressive" as to justify emotional distress or punitive damage awards.[16] "Outrageous" in the legal sense doesn't mean, "I can't believe you did that to me" or "it's ridiculous that you didn't know better." Legal "outrageousness" means going "beyond all possible bounds of decency…to be regarded as atrocious and utterly intolerable in a civilized society."[17] It is a very, very high standard.

You never know what will happen in court but there are precedents that can give you some idea of how likely it is that you'll get the court to give you the relief you want.

WHEN IT'S THERE BUT NOT REALLY THERE

If you're one of those strange types of people who like to read cases and do legal research, you have to be careful about interpreting "precedents" too. Some decisions, even though written down and technically published in a court reporter, are nonetheless deemed "unpublished" by the court. In California, for instance, this means that even though they're publicly reported and they resolved the issues before the parties in that case, they can't be used to support your position in your case—even if the facts and legal matters at issue in your case are similar to those in the "unpublished" case. Unpublished decisions can't be cited in court.[18]

Some find this odd. One of the purposes of having legal decisions made available is so that people in cases similar to those previously considered by the court can have some guidance about what the law expects or provides in a certain situation. The earlier decisions are "precedent"—and it is reliance on precedent that allows for a reasonable sense of certainty or reliability in the system. The doctrine of *stare decisis* refers to the principle that courts should adhere to previously established law. That doesn't mean you can't ask a court to overturn precedent—sometimes courts, obviously—but they are not supposed to do so lightly. In any event, some have criticized the extent to which some courts have "unpublished" their decisions, as it deprives litigants and lawyers of valuable guidance in their case, and forces litigation of issues that could have been previously resolved or decided.[19]

In any event, just because you may have heard about a case with facts almost identical to yours, don't assume that case necessarily will control your outcome.

You and your lawyer will need to review the facts of your particular case, however, to determine whether they fall within the definition of bad conduct that warrants a remedy. Are you the victim of something outrageous? Something that violated a duty of care? You'll need to be able to demonstrate how and why.

What sort of fix or remedy are you expecting from court? What do you think court will accomplish for you, and are you prepared for what you must endure in order to get it? Recovering dollar amounts might seem straightforward enough but money is, in many cases, simply a symbol of something else people want to fix. Are you trying to fix something that court can control?

For instance: let's say you've got a neighbor who gives loud parties, to which he invites the public, and those parties result in litter; noise at all hours; and other tangible harms you can identify.

It might make sense to try to get a court order prohibiting your neighbor from opening up to public gatherings in this way. You're entitled to the "quiet enjoyment" of your property and while your neighbor certainly, as a property owner, enjoys certain liberties in the use of his, those of us who don't live on deserted islands will have to make concessions to each other from time to time in order to keep the peace. In fact, that's why people go to court in the first place—so an objective third party can strike the appropriate balance of interests when they find they are unable to do this on their own.

Part of that balancing of interests means that the punishment has to be proportionate to the harm; in a system based on rule of law, you don't feed someone to the lions because their kid broke your window playing ball. Ordering your neighbor to stop having loud public events in a residential community, by contrast, doesn't undermine his entire interest in enjoying his property. He can still get drunk and play his music with friends. He just can't take over the whole neighborhood and make everyone an inadvertent guest at his event. The court might even give you some money to compensate you for any damages you can prove, or to punish your neighbor if he's been intentionally nasty or malicious.

But are you likely going to be able to get the court to solve the problem, once and for all, by ordering him to sell his house and move? (He's really annoying. All the neighbors hate him. They've even signed a petition!)

Ask your lawyer. But I doubt it.

Can you keep it simple? If not, consider whether court is actually going to address the problem you really want to fix.

What You Should Do:
Take a Beat

A lot of people say *I went to court as a last straw.* "Last straw"? Sometimes they only used one straw.

You know how things can get out of hand. Sometimes things can get off to a bad start because people meet on the wrong side of a bad day. Things escalate quickly. The texting happens. (Those damned texting fingers. You always get service precisely when you probably shouldn't have it.) Then some voicemails. Then some *I'll see you in court, you *&#$#@'s!!!*

While that escalation is happening, people don't always think about losing a day's income if they have to sit for a deposition; or juggling childcare issues in order to make a necessary court appearance; or spending time chasing down and confirming the facts that lay at the heart of the dispute because the judge may not just take their word for it. People can sometimes end up badly reacting to someone else's bad reaction, while the match that lit the flame in the first place gets buried beneath a rapidly growing pile of ire. In court, you'll have to dig up that match and explain why it entitles you to whatever you're seeking.

By the way, I've noticed that communications that light the fuse tend to follow certain patterns.

They are less like this:

> *Hey, I'm noticing that after you fixed my roof, it started to leak. I'm concerned. Could you give me a call?*

And more like this:

> *My roof is leaking two days after you supposedly fixed it. Your total negligence and incompetence has resulted in my having to cancel an excellent party and you're going to pay for that party. You stole my money you *&^^#head. I want it back.*

Accusing someone of ruining your life while you are trying to get them to fix your roof, for example, is not always the best strategy.

Alternatively, there's this:

> *Hey, my roof leaking two days after you fixed it. Can you give me a call please?*
>
> *(No response. Crickets.)*
>
> *Hey, I'm trying you again, having problems with the roof. Can you please call me?*
>
> *(No response. More crickets.)*
>
> *Listen, you charlatan, I'm calling a lawyer.*

Crickets aren't good. Ignoring someone who has paid you to do something that still isn't quite right, isn't good. These are things that typically are taught in Common Sense School, where enrollment has been down for several years.

In other words, there's a certain way of approaching an issue that I'd call "Buying a Front Row Ticket to the Litigation Circus." It's a show that you won't enjoy that much because you'll be exhausted and broke. Plus, you'll be in it.

When people don't know how much that provocation may cost them, or how expensive ignoring that phone call will be, they might be inclined to act in ways that make the march to the courtroom door seem more inevitable than it actually may be.

Who knows if you can settle a dispute simply by being polite, or by being a responsible businessperson, or simply by acting like you have a little decency and good sense? Sometimes you may be able to, sometimes you won't. What I do know, however, is that often people do little to deescalate a situation because their texting fingers got ahead of them.

Focusing on the "why" of your fight can help you ensure that the fight doesn't get bigger than whatever the dispute was about in the first place. Make no mistake, fighting in court is an escalation; a *digging in*; a rigorous exercise not just for your opponent, but for you.

What You Should Do:
"Pitch" Your Lawsuit

When someone wants to sell a TV show or movie, they pitch the idea to someone at a network who they hope will buy it. They explain why the show is likely to be a success; they're prepared to answer the other side's questions about potential weaknesses.

Do the same thing with your lawsuit. Pitch it to yourself. Think about your claim or defense—what evidence do you have to prove it? Is it evidence that someone who isn't in love with you or who didn't give birth to you would believe? Remember, in order to get something from your fight you are going to have to be able to convince a judge or jury who knows and cares much less about the issue than you do. What about your story is convincing?

Your "pitch" is important not just for the purpose of convincing a judge or jury, but also for getting a lawyer in the first place. This is not as easy as it seems on TV. True, your lawyer will be the one to help you understand whether you have a valid basis for a lawsuit, but in order for them to make that determination you need to be as particular and detailed as you can. Why should this person want to take your case? What persuasive facts do you have? Why is it worth their time? Why is it worth the money you'll have to spend for their time? I'll talk more in Chapter 4 about how tough it sometimes can be to find a lawyer willing to take your case.

Sometimes people can get so caught up in a fight, or they've been fighting it for so long, that they don't always take time to explain the different pieces of it; how it became a fight or what it is they're fighting about. They've been living it. The outrage seems obvious to them. They've got a lot of backstory—it inflames them further but it may not be relevant to the current dispute.

Maybe they come to court describing an issue that is just camouflage for the real problem animating the fight. Maybe the real problem is something court can't fix. Then again, maybe court can.

What You Should Do: Gather Your Evidence Early

As part of your pitch, start gathering the documents—copies of contracts, emails, text messages, and the like—that will help explain to someone who doesn't know you and who has no reason to believe you, why they *should* believe you. Are there any witnesses and where are they located? Are they willing to testify or will you have to fight to bring them forward?

Collecting your evidence early will help you get your head around what your case *is,* which will in turn give you a better sense of the path and hurdles that lay ahead. You can use your time to think through your story—how compelling is it? Do you have all the information you need to tell it—and to figure out what may be missing? Thinking through your story can help you better think through your case, and just how it is you're going to make it. Think about your fight the way a very skeptical decision-maker would. Don't give yourself the benefit of the doubt.

Plus, it will help you in your dealings with your lawyer, should you have one. Your lawyer will need a set of facts in order to determine how best to pursue the remedy that you want. Your case can proceed far more efficiently (and at less expense to you) if you have key elements of your story together and arm your lawyer with facts early.

TO SUM UP . . .

- Know *precisely* who you're suing. Is the target of your lawsuit a person or a company? If it's a company, do you know who the registered agent for service of process is? Collecting the necessary information before your case gets going can save you time and fights down the road.
- Make sure you're bringing your lawsuit in the right place. If not, you could end up in a protracted and expensive battle about where the fight should occur.

- Know that dates matter. Just because something happened a long time ago doesn't mean you can't still sue for it, especially if the injury is continuing, but the facts of your case, the legal claims you're bringing, and where you're bringing them will determine that. Also, make sure your case is "ripe"—that you've actually been injured.

- Think hard about why you're fighting. Is court going to scratch that itch? Is your fight being spurred on by the issue over which you *say* you're fighting, or is it something else?

- Think about what you want. Are the potential remedies you'd like in line with what court can or is likely to give you? And is the work you may have to do worth it?

- Be aware of the downsides. There are some delays you just can't control and for which there may be no remedy. There are also some inconvenient, long, expensive tasks associated with litigation from which there may be no escape. In the sometimes angry and determined march to the courtroom, people give short shrift to just how inconvenient and painful court really can be. Many people go to court before they've tried or exhausted other options, sometimes because they don't know just how much of a monster the process sometimes is.

- Keep track of bad behavior. While there may be little you can do about the protraction and delay caused by your opponent's antics as they're happening, you should still keep tabs on it. You may have an opportunity later to make your opponent pay for any outrageous or bad faith behavior.

- Finally, keep in mind that *it's never too late to work it out.*

2

WHEN YOU
ARE SUED

"I can't believe that *&$%# sued me!"

Well, that *&$%# did. If you get sued, now is the time for you to make your own case.

Maybe you did do something you regret. When translated into the language of a legal complaint, however, that "something" may make you sound like Medusa's twisted offspring. *Whatever* you did, you insist it wasn't *that* bad. A minor mistake, maybe, that has been completely blown out of proportion. A little grain of wrong that your opponent wants to cultivate into a rainforest of diabolical behavior. *They're stretching!* you may think. Well, maybe, but now they've filed the lawsuit. They're not just "stretching," they've gone full yoga*, so it's time to deal with it.

Or, maybe you contend you're facing something even worse than

---

* Sorry for that analogy. If there is anything that is the opposite of yoga, it is litigation.

that. Perhaps you insist that the entire situation is completely made up. An accusation can hop a transatlantic flight, set down new roots, and raise two generations of children before anyone has confirmed whether or not it was actually allowed to board the plane. Or even whether it paid for the ticket.

For the moment, let's assume that it's not *that* bad. Let's assume that you fall into the majority of disputes where maybe there was a little wrong on all sides, but you think that whatever the other side is claiming you did isn't really what you did; or at least, you didn't do that much of it. And it *certainly* didn't impact them the way they say it did.

What do you do? You're in court now. You can deny something; you can say that whatever the other side did is worse; you can say that your opponent is taking something out of context; or blowing it out of proportion; or doing any number of things to turn something you contend wasn't really that bad into something really terrible. How do you communicate all this? What do you do?

As painful as it may be to have to endure court process, you can at least take satisfaction in the fact that while there, you'll be able to demand and obtain proof of what someone claims. You can challenge people who you claim are lying. Allegations aren't treated as casually as they may be elsewhere. In court, allegations can be strip searched. You'll have an opportunity to tell your own side of the story but remember—just like a lawsuit is a time where your accuser has to show their goods, so will you.

Your particular response to any lawsuit, of course, will depend on the circumstances of your case. Obviously, I can't advise you about that. I can, however, point out some things about how court works so that you can avoid what might be potentially costly mistakes.

What You Should Know: Responding to a Lawsuit

There are a variety of ways you can respond to a lawsuit when you are sued. You can file an *answer,* in which you generally deny the allegations of the complaint and you can also assert one or more *affirmative defenses.* You can seek to have the complaint dismissed before doing any discovery ("discovery" is the way you collect evidence in your case) or you can try to have it dismissed afterward. Depending on the nature of your case, each of these strategies can result in a substantial investment of time and money, regardless of the merits of your case. I'll discuss these different devices later but first, a note on something you probably *shouldn't* do.

Something You Probably Shouldn't Do

If someone is suing you and if you care about things like your credit; your reputation; your ability to be licensed; or anything along those lines, you probably shouldn't ignore the lawsuit.

This is true even if you think the case is a bunch of trumped-up nonsense aimed at you by a chronically dishonest person. A lawsuit is usually not the type of weapon you can duck forever (unless you manage just to duck service for so long that the case is dismissed—but then the other side may be able to refile, and you may have to start ducking all over again).

Ignoring a lawsuit can have horrible consequences:

Jane kept getting notices from a bill collector regarding her ex's debts. She ignored them. Then the bill collector sued her.

Jane, unable to pay her bills, clearly couldn't pay a lawyer to fight back. So she ignored the lawsuit.

What were they trying to get anyway? Blood from a stone?

When she failed to appear, the court entered a default judgment against her.

A "default judgment" is when one party loses simply because they didn't show up or respond to a claim.

> Because of the default judgment, the bill collector was able to garnish Jane's wages. When she remarried, her new husband's wages were garnished, too.

When you don't show up, you can forfeit your right to fight back and tell your side of the story.

The consequences of a default judgment can include having your wages garnished; being evicted; being held liable for a debt you may not even owe; or losing some other right or privilege that you might have successfully been able to defend. There are a number of reasons you might not show up—you might not have a lawyer; you might have to work that day; you might not really understand what it is you can do to fight back, so you conclude it isn't worth it. In many circumstances, not showing up can make a bad situation worse.

That's not to say that you don't have options if you've been found in default. You can claim you made a mistake; that you missed the response time inadvertently; or that you were in the middle of some emergency that justifies your neglecting to respond.

> You are served with a complaint. The process server puts down the wrong date of service. As a result, you miscalculate the date your response is due, and a default judgment is entered. You ask for relief. Since the court finds that the process server's mistake is the one that led to your miscalculation, you get a break.

But what about this:

> You are served with a complaint. You've been meaning to forward it to your lawyer, but you were so busy actually running your business

that you forgot! You're busy! You ask for relief from the default judgment. *Nope,* says the court.

When you're fighting in court, being "too busy" might be its own type of mistake.

You were in the hospital. You were very sick.

Even this may not be enough. One court held that you have to be so incapacitated that you are "unable to act."[1]

Different courts—even in the same jurisdiction—might interpret a similar set of facts differently. Remember, similar facts are not *identical,* and what may seem to be minor distinctions in different situations could be enough for a judge to exercise her discretion in a different way.

Other Bases for Getting Relief from a Default Judgment

The standards in different jurisdictions vary, so you should be sure to check your own. Some require, for instance, that the party seeking relief from the default have a "meritorious defense"; others do not. Here are some other bases that might justify getting relief:

1. You discovered new evidence;
2. The judgment was based on a fraud, misrepresentation, or misconduct by the opposing party;
3. The judgment is void or has otherwise been satisfied;
4. The judgment was based on an earlier judgment that is no longer effective, or that has been reversed or vacated, or that continuing to apply that judgment is "no longer equitable";

5. And then there's the catch-all—"any other reason that justifies relief."

Again, judges have a lot of discretion in applying these standards, as they do many others that will have an important bearing on how your case plays out. That's why we're supposed to take so much care selecting judges. (We'll talk about judges in a later chapter.)

Don't underestimate how much time and energy (and money) can go into litigating why you should even be given your day (years) in court if you missed a deadline to respond to something. And don't underestimate the potential consequences if something critical is on the line in your lawsuit. Default judgments have led to people being deprived of citizenship; evicted; having their wages garnished and liens put on their homes; among other things.[2] Do everything you can to respond on time so you don't create bigger problems for yourself later.

> Debt Collector knew that it had a bunch of old debts on the books that it couldn't prove. Some of them were probably time-barred by the statute of limitations. Still, Debt Collector thought it had a good likelihood of recovering some amount from alleged debtors if it filed claims against them and they just didn't show up.

Debt Collector may have known it had no basis to bring a time-barred case. But if its targets don't show up to explain that baselessness to the court, Debt Collector will be able to bring life to a claim that should have been dead on arrival.

It is *your* job to defend yourself in court. The process isn't going to naturally unfold in ways that will give you a chance to prove the justice of your position.

What You Should Know:
Fighting a Lie

We'll discuss this more in a later chapter, but for now know this: you will have to prove that what you say is a lie really is one. There is no express lane for challenging lies, unfortunately, even when they're patently obvious or flatly ridiculous.

Plus, keep in mind the difference between an absolute lie, and a story that has *some* truth to it, however exaggerated that story may be. In any event, the important thing to remember is that for purposes of deciding in the very beginning whether a case can go forward, a court will assume that the factual allegations in the complaint are true.

Let's now consider the absolute, worst case scenario. Let's say someone files a completely made-up lawsuit against you—not an exaggeration; not something that is just "taken out of context," but an out-and-out lie. I don't have any basis for suggesting that this constitutes a majority of cases (nor even a "substantial" number—whatever that means—given the millions of cases that are filed each year and all the various ways we have of interfering with and finding ways to be bothered by each other). It does, however, happen—and not just in our *Hot Bench* courtroom, where we have the time to address the impact of false accusations. It happens in non-TV courtrooms too, where judges burdened with heavy dockets may not.

Maybe the accuser has an axe to grind over some other things; maybe they're using the litigation threat to get something from you to which they wouldn't otherwise be entitled. Now you're staring at a pile of lie-riddled documents, surprised that the big forked tongue that spewed them forth has enough room left in its mouth to ingest food.

I'll discuss in Chapter 8 some of the options you may have for being forced to defend against claims that the other side has no reasonable basis for believing to be true, or for having to fight a defense for which there is no good faith basis. What you should know now is 1) as I stated earlier, the court generally will assume the facts in the complaint to be true until you take the time to prove otherwise; and 2) even when rules about moving forward in good faith are broken or violated in the most obvious ways, no one but you may care unless you take the time and spend the money to bring a motion. (Even then, the court still may not care.)

People aren't supposed to commit perjury but they sometimes do, and sometimes it's blatantly obvious. Plus, it's very rarely prosecuted.

IT'S NOT A TOTAL FREE PASS

That's not to say that every litigant can enjoy a complete free-for-all in court. Courts have affirmed perjury convictions arising from civil prosecutions—sometimes someone other than you *will* care about your opponent's brazen disregard for the process and your right to a fair one.

Consider this for instance. One court affirmed a litigant's conviction for perjury which arose from statements he made in a deposition. His deposition transcript might help explain why the court was unsympathetic to his position:

So you just lied to me? the (deposing) lawyer asked.

That's right, the litigant responded.

The lawyer: *How are we going to know when to believe what you say?*

You don't, the litigant responded.[3]

In another case, a court affirmed the conviction of a defendant for "corruptly seeking and accepting $20,000 to be influenced in her testimony as a witness" in favor of a defendant in a sexual harassment suit.[4]

In a case involving a grand dragon of the Ku Klux Klan, the court "categorically reject[ed] any suggestion, implicit or otherwise, that perjury is somehow less serious when made in a civil proceeding." According to that court, "Perjury, regardless of the setting, is a serious offense that results in incalculable harm to the functioning and integrity of the legal system as well as to private individuals."[5]

When you're confronted in court by something you contend is an absolute lie, don't forget that there is no Express Lane for Nonsense. You'll have to grind it out with someone you believe is just making something up and you'll have to use the tools afforded by court process to poke holes in their story.

Almost every lawsuit is going to cost you something regardless of how nonsensical it may be. Plus, ignoring a blatant lie may be the best thing that ever happened to that lie, because if it becomes the basis of a court judgment, its mythology can become your new reality.

At least in court some constraints will be put on the ability to exaggerate (or just out and out lie), the main constraint being that court includes a record of what's been said and done. It's not the type of record you can just ignore, or where you can act like the things it contains didn't really happen. (Or at least, you can't do that without enduring consequences to your credibility and your case.) Court allows you the chance to put some controls on both the out-and-out liar, e.g., the neighbor who says he broke his ankle when he tripped in your driveway when he actually fell down drunk in a bar, and also on what I'll call the "Troubled Exaggerator," e.g., the neighbor who scraped his knee on your driveway and now claims he's semi-permanently disabled. Court allows you to keep track of what's been claimed and to hold people accountable for claiming it, and to prove that the things they say happened actually did happen.

If you end up litigating against someone who you believe to be entirely or mostly untruthful, or a Troubled Exaggerator, you'll have an opportunity to ask them questions; to test the basis of their claims and injuries; and to make them prove that they are damaged or injured to the extent they claim. It will be costly to do but sometimes there is no way around it. For some people, a mistake by you is an opportunity for them, and litigation is their necessary cost of maximizing that opportunity.

Don't underestimate the burden and expense of disproving a lie (or an exaggeration) and don't assume lying won't ever work (if you're even inclined to assume this). Not everyone will share your interest in getting to the bottom of things. A trumped-up claim could be frightening to your insurance company (if you have insurance), for example; the company might settle a claim that you believe has no merit simply because it's cheaper than litigating. You may have little say in whether that settlement happens or not, by the way. You may just have to sit back and wait for your insurer to act like you never paid a dime to protect against precisely this sort of thing, and then watch as it hikes up your premium in a way that makes it seem like you're a complete stranger, and not someone who has turned over to them thousands (or tens of thousands, or hundreds of thousands) of dollars in premiums over the past several years.

Pay attention when someone claims you've injured them but won't give you any evidence. Document their claims as well as your efforts to understand the basis for them. If they don't respond or respond with something that is factually off-base, keep track of it. The fact that someone is trying to hold you hostage to the prospect of litigation without giving you any basis for the pile of money they're demanding you pay could be of use to you later. It might impact their credibility with the judge or jury, for example.

If it turns out the other side just spun a tale out of whole cloth, then you can perhaps get some penalty against them for doing so but as I mentioned, you usually won't have a chance to do that until you're much further down the road. It sounds like a pain and it is.

But, if someone's blanket denials were enough to let them off the hook or if we all could be held liable just because other people said so, we'd rapidly devolve into a finger-pointing, other-person-blaming, acting-with-impunity-and-doing-thing s-just-because-we-could, mess.

So, thank you court.

What You Should Know: "Making It Go Away" Before Trial

First, you should understand that "making it go away" usually requires you to spend *some* amount of time and probably money (if you have a lawyer), and more likely, a lot of both. You'll see, as I describe in some of the examples below, that the strategies and tactics for avoiding trial often rely on presenting evidence and making legal arguments, neither of which happens automatically or is necessarily intuitive.

In other words, doing any of these things—*making the case* to make something go away—will require you to dig in and do a little (maybe a lot of) work. Once you get tagged by court process, it can be a miserably stressful and expensive ride before you find a way out.

What You Can Do (Perhaps): Getting Rid of It Before Trial

Here, however, are some examples of the ways you can avoid a full-blown trial:

Demurrer/Motion to Dismiss

This is a response based on the argument that regardless of the nature of the claim made against you, there is no merit to it. It assumes the allegations in the complaint are true and argues that even if they are, they don't constitute a basis for a lawsuit. This means you need to know what the law is and to explain why the plaintiff's claims don't satisfy the standards for ensnaring you in the process.

WHO KNOWS WHAT THAT BAD SANDWICH CAN COST?

In November 2018, a U.S. District Judge in Fort Lauderdale dismissed a suit by two McDonald's customers who claimed they were charged full price for the Quarter Pounder with Cheese even though they asked for no cheese.[6] The judge called their claim "absurd" and dismissed the suit with prejudice, barring them from relitigating this claim. A "fowl" disappointment (sorry, I couldn't resist) was the subject of a suit in Tennessee where a man sued Popeyes for not having the chicken sandwich he wanted to order.[7] The case was dismissed in February 2020 when the disappointed Popeyes patron was also ordered to pay all litigation costs.

A political humorist *goes to town*[*] on an energy resource operator. The humorist didn't mince words. He took issue with the operator's safety record—in a very unflattering way—and suggested that the operator was less than diligent in his efforts to protect workers. The host mentioned the operator's opposition to a federal rule intended to reduce black lung disease among coal miners; the host also described the mine operator as a "geriatric Dr. Evil." The segment featured a giant squirrel with a novelty check made out to "Eat Shit [energy resource operator]" and on the memo line, it read "Kiss My Ass."

The operator claimed the broadcast was false, injurious, and defamatory. Court papers pointed out that he'd worked underground for the first sixteen years of his life and used his life savings and mortgaged all he owned to get into the business; those filings also emphasized his commitment to safety; pointed out that his employees had received harassing phone calls as a result of the broadcast; and also revealed that his family had received death threats.

Defending his record and his approach toward the safety of mine workers, the operator sued the humorist and his corporate partners, among others. In the complaint, the operator challenged the way in which the humorist characterized his safety record and took issue

---

* "Goes to town" is what my mom says when she means "let them have it." "Rakes over the coals." "Makes them wish they were anywhere else or invisible." That kind of thing.

with the claim that his action or inaction contributed to the mining disaster that the host discussed in the broadcast. He sued for defamation, false light invasion of privacy, and intentional infliction of emotional distress.

The court put the kibosh on the energy resource operator's lawsuit, finding that the defendants' arguments in their motion to dismiss were "well-founded." Among other things, the defendants had argued that there was no basis to dispute the program's fair and accurate description of some of the conduct mentioned in the report (which would entitle them to "the fair report privilege") and also that the satire and jokes included in the broadcast weren't false statements purporting to be factual.

Anti-SLAPP Motion to Dismiss

Some states have special protections for statements that are made in the course of judicial, legislative, and other official proceedings. Participating in these types of activities is an important civic right; lawsuits that are based on statements made during these types of proceedings could discourage people from speaking up when they need or have a right to engage in certain speech.

Some states have special protections against what are known as Strategic Lawsuits Against Public Participation ("SLAPP").

The activities to which anti-SLAPP protections apply are:

- Written or oral statements or writings made before a legislative, executive, or judicial proceeding, or any other official proceeding authorized by law;
- Any written or oral statement or writing made in connection with an issue under consideration or review by a legislative, executive, or judicial body, or any other official proceeding authorized by law;
- Any written or oral statement or writing made in a place

open to the public or a public forum in connection with an issue of public interest;

- Any other conduct in furtherance of the exercise of the constitutional right of petition or the constitutional right of free speech in connection with a public issue or an issue of public interest.

In an era where we can talk to and about each other so constantly, this is a particularly relevant defense. It's easy for people to make accusations—to authorities; to newspaper and online press platforms; and in court pleadings. Sometimes the accusations are true; sometimes not. When they aren't true, they may be based on a mistaken assumption or belief, or they may be inspired by hatred, malice, or a desire to exert leverage when there really isn't any. It's probably never been so easy to say things that will rile someone up and to make sure that multitudes of people hear them almost as quickly as they're said.)

If someone is suing you because of something you said during one of the types of "official proceedings" described above, they have to show a "likelihood of prevailing on the merits" before the case even can go forward.

The protections offered by anti-SLAPP statutes don't depend on whether the statements the lawsuit targets are true or false. Instead, the pertinent question is whether the statements fall within the category of protected speech. In other words, the Constitution gives people some freedom to get under our skin, even when we disagree with their basis for doing it.

A celebrity is caught in a tabloid's crosshairs. This time, the tabloid alleges that the celebrity is transitioning from male to female and includes pictures of him in costume as a woman.

The celebrity denies all of this and is none too happy about it. He sues, alleging libel and false light invasion of privacy.

The company that owns the tabloid files an anti-SLAPP special motion to strike, alleging that the article was protected speech and that the celebrity is not likely to succeed on the merits.

False speech is subject to some First Amendment protection, too, the court concluded. Misidentifying someone as transgender couldn't support a claim for libel or for false light because, according to the judge in that case, that misidentification wouldn't, in itself, have a natural tendency to injure a person's reputation.[*]

Because the tabloid won, they were also entitled to attorneys' fees, which the court awarded. The parties ultimately settled.

True. The defendants in both the tabloid and talk show cases were able to get those matters dismissed before the parties had to undertake the time and expense of going to trial. This is a big deal! Going to trial involves conducting an extensive amount of discovery, with all of the time and expense associated with that, which might also include fighting about the information you will and won't provide to the other side. If you can avoid this, that can be great for you. You'll also avoid the time and expense of subpoenaing witnesses; paying lawyers to prepare; getting your exhibits ready; pre-trial battles about what will and won't come into evidence at trial; and so much more. If you can get out of the case in a way that permits you to avoid these things, you have much to celebrate indeed! Here's to you!

Also true . . . It was not a short or painless process and it still may not be over, but still, here's to you! You deserve it for what you've been through and what still may lay ahead.

What you need in order to dismiss a case can require a significant expenditure of time and resources, even if you don't have a

---

* Illegally putting a tracking device on the celebrity's car as part of one's efforts to investigate him, however, would fall outside of anti-SLAPP protections.

full-blown trial. In the case of the humorist and the energy resource operator, it took approximately 8 months from the time the complaint was filed to the granting of the motion to dismiss. The litigation reportedly contributed to a tripling of insurance premiums and cost hundreds of thousands more in expenses.

(In some instances, certain types of insurance will cover the costs of litigation and any judgment against you, within certain policy limits. Your insurer may be cooperative, or it may end up treating you like a hated stepchild.)

In the case of the celebrity and the tabloid, things took even longer. There, it was four months between the complaint's filing and its dismissal on anti-SLAPP grounds. Since the tabloid was the prevailing party it was entitled to attorneys' fees—still, it had to work for its food by filing a motion for fees (and it didn't get the full amount it requested). It did so a little over a month after the court rendered its decision.

The celebrity filed his opposition to that motion roughly two-and-a-half months after the tabloid filed its request. Then, just under two months after that, the court issued its decision, granting the tabloid's motion for fees but awarding it less than the amount that it requested.

Then, the celebrity appealed. (A final judgment—one that results in the dismissal of a matter, for instance—can be appealed to the appellate court. I'll discuss appeals in a later chapter.) The parties ultimately settled the matter and then the celebrity withdrew the appeal, eight months after the court issued its decision.

As you can see, even the process of getting rid of a case before it "goes all the way" can be long, involved, and perhaps quite expensive.

Motion for Summary Judgment

In this motion, you have to first do discovery so as to determine whether there are any facts to support the plaintiff's complaint. If there aren't, you can move for *summary judgment*. The basis of this motion is that there aren't any facts in dispute and that you must win as a matter of law. This means, of course, that you have to know what the law is, but it also means that you may have to take some time doing and submitting to discovery about the facts. I'll discuss discovery in Chapter 6.

Jorn and Sheila had been romantically and professionally involved for a number of years. Jorn was the primary breadwinner. Then, it ended.

While they never married, they both engaged lawyers to negotiate a settlement that would allow Sheila to live comfortably while not leaving Jorn entirely broke.

They negotiated an agreement in which Sheila would receive over $5 million, which was over half Jorn's net worth at the time.

The agreement they signed expressly superseded—or took precedence over—any agreements between the two of them that may have taken place prior to that time.

Several years later, Sheila brings a lawsuit against Jorn claiming that he obtained the agreement by fraud.

She'd been represented by a lawyer and advised by others who thought she should sign; she claimed, however, that they were all in a conspiracy with Jorn to defraud her. She alleged that the agreements were obtained by fraud and that the parties' relationship was instead governed by an earlier oral agreement. Under the terms of that agreement, Sheila alleged she was entitled to lifetime support and half of Jorn's gross income for life. Jorn argues that the only evidence of any such oral agreement is Sheila's own testimony.

Jorn denied being a part of any conspiracy and argued that the agreement was fair, especially since he and Sheila were never married. Jorn's lawyers argued that, beyond Sheila's speculation and conjecture, there was no evidence of any conspiracy.

To recap: "Jorn" had an agreement with "Sheila." We'll call it **Written Agreement A. Written Agreement A** said, explicitly, that it took precedence over any prior agreement.

Sheila says that **Written Agreement A** was procured by fraud and it should be disregarded. The agreement that should govern the parties' separation, according to Sheila, is **Oral Agreement 1. Oral Agreement 1** took place before **Written Agreement A**. Jorn says that other than Shelia's word for it, there is no evidence that **Oral Agreement 1** ever happened.

In order to support his motion for summary judgment, Jorn submits declarations, or sworn statements by witnesses. He takes depositions. He submits to the court a *Memorandum of Points and Authorities*, laying out his argument as to why Sheila has no case. He attaches evidence in support of the motion—exhibits that include portions of the deposition testimony and other evidence.

Sheila submits her own evidence in opposition to Jorn's motion, as well as her own Memorandum of Points and Authorities. They each file objections to each other's evidence.

The trial court denies Jorn's motion, arguing that there was a triable issue of material fact as to the existence of Oral Agreement 1.

Jorn's case took place in California, where you can't appeal from the denial of a summary judgment motion. The same is true in some other states,[8] although in some jurisdictions you can.[9] What you can do is file a **writ petition,** which is a request for what's known as an "extraordinary remedy."[10]

In Jorn's case, he argued to the court of appeal that the trial court made a huge and obvious mistake and that going to trial would be an unnecessary burden and expense, since any judgment likely would be reversed on appeal anyway.

Jorn argued that the trial court "missed the boat."

The issue wasn't, according to Jorn, whether Oral Agreement 1 existed, but instead whether Sheila presented any evidence that Written Agreement A was procured by fraud. Jorn argued that going to trial on this basis, when there was no evidence to support

Sheila's claims and the trial court was proceeding on a mistaken legal basis, would only require everyone to undergo an expensive and intrusive proceeding that likely would be reversed on appeal. In order to make these arguments, Jorn submitted a brief to the court that summarized his arguments, and hundreds of pages of exhibits.

Without explaining why, the court of appeal agrees with Jorn. The court issued a decision ordering the trial court either to vacate its decision, or in the alternative, to explain why it shouldn't be ordered to do so. The trial court vacated its decision, and Jorn received his summary judgment, thus avoiding trial.

In court, "making it go away" isn't just a matter of deep breathing and visualizing yourself in a brighter, happy place. It's not even just a matter of explaining to your lawyer why it's all nonsense, and then having her briskly and efficiently take what you believe may be that very obvious explanation to the court. In court, there is almost never any "brisk and efficient." In short, "making it go away" can sometimes take *a lot.*

What You Can Do: Fighting Back

What are you going to do?

Are you going to just sit back and let the plaintiff do their thing, tell their story, throw blows at you, and then see what happens?

There may be some circumstances where you should do this. It depends on your case. (Remember, I'm not giving you legal advice.) Maybe they'll file a complaint, serve you, and then not do any discovery or further pursue it and not respond to a dismissal. Who knows what could happen? People do all sorts of strange things. You could get off very easy.

Or you may not. Many people assume that the telling of and responding to a story in court proceeds in a more efficient and intuitive way than it actually does. They don't understand the particular way court works—the way it bounces burdens back and forth and what it takes to carry one.

When someone brings a lawsuit, they carry the burden of proof, which means they have the job of proving that the things they claimed happened actually did, and that they were damaged in the manner they claim.

For instance, if someone claims you owe them money, they have the burden of proving that the money changed hands, that you had an obligation to repay them (unless there is a *stipulation,* or agreement between the parties, regarding the amounts owed), and that you failed to make that repayment as you were obligated to. There are a variety of ways in which they can do this—they can offer their own testimony and/or that of others; they can submit documents such as a loan agreement or emails in which you acknowledge the debt. These would be direct evidence. They can also offer evidence of a pattern of loaning money and a history of repayments on other obligations by you—this would be circumstantial evidence, or evidence from which an inference must be drawn in order to prove the point against you. ("Circumstantial evidence" are facts from which one might reasonably infer the existence of other facts.) The plaintiff may or may not be able to meet their burden.

What if they do? Is all then lost for you? Not yet.

Affirmative Defenses

An "affirmative defense" is a defense that you can bring but for which you carry the burden. It is a defense that is based on facts that the plaintiff doesn't bring up in their complaint—probably because they're such good facts for you! That is, if you can prove them.

Going back to my example regarding loaning money: if you simply deny that you owe the plaintiff money, that's a general denial.

If you claim that you already paid the money back, the fact of and circumstances surrounding that repayment are new facts, and the claim that you repaid the loan would be an affirmative defense.

While the plaintiff carries the burden of proving their case, the defendant carries the burden of proving any affirmative defense.

Here are some examples of affirmative defenses that potentially could be used to avoid or limit liability in my above example. I'll also point out some of what you'd have to prove in order to prevail. I come across a lot of these kinds of claims in our *Hot Bench* courtroom and sometimes people don't seem to have a strong sense about what is required to prove something. Remember, this isn't at all intended to be an exhaustive list and I'm providing you only a very general summary of what may be required. Different jurisdictions will have different requirements for meeting them, and whether and to what extent they apply in your case requires a consideration of your individual circumstances and a more in-depth consideration of the pertinent standards that I am providing here.

I simply want you to have some idea about how what you believe are common sense conclusions about your circumstances can be tested and challenged in court, where common sense doesn't always prevail. There's a method and there are steps to proving things in court—and I want you to have some general sense of the types of things you might have to prove.

Payment. *I may have owed you money, but I already paid you back!* You should be prepared to offer evidence of the repayment. Cancelled checks? A Venmo statement? Your own testimony? That of others who witnessed the repayment? Remember, witnesses who have a clear bias in your favor—your mom or your boyfriend—will be viewed differently than those who don't have a reason to fudge the truth on your behalf (not that I'm saying your mother is dishonest).

(Note that there is a fine line here between meeting your burden on this affirmative defense and what the plaintiff must prove in order to make their case in the first instance. You may undertake the burden of providing you paid, but the plaintiff carries the burden of proving you didn't.)

Release. *I may have owed you money, but you told me I was off the hook.* Do you have evidence of this? A statement from the other person indicating cancellation of the debt? Note that someone telling you that *it's okay* when you can't repay them on time doesn't mean that they don't want you to repay them again *ever,* or that you should ignore the obligation owed. *It's okay* doesn't always have the broad meaning that people would sometimes like to attach to it.

Res Judicata. *You already tried to hold me liable for this debt and a court found that you can't.* Been there and done that. It's over. Here, you have to prove that there previously has been a judicial determination that you have no liability for the debt over which you're being sued. You could prove this by presenting evidence of an earlier judgment or court order.[11]

Statute of Frauds. *The debt has not been put in writing.* Please note that this defense is only available with respect to certain categories of contracts (such as those that involve the sale or transfer of real estate; the leasing of property for a period longer than one year; debts that can't by their nature be satisfied within a year; and certain contracts to loan money, for example).[12] In other words, if someone is claiming that you breached a contract to sell them a house, for instance, but the agreement isn't in writing, you could plead the statute of frauds as an affirmative defense.

Statute of Limitations. *You waited too late to sue me for this debt.* As I mentioned in the first chapter, there is a time by which someone must bring their claim if they want to sue. If you want to rely on this defense, you'll provide evidence that they waited too long to file the claim after you made clear your intention to breach your promise. The pertinent date is not when the debt was incurred but instead when you had the obligation to pay and didn't.[13]

One response to a statute of limitations defense would be that the statute was "tolled" for some reason. This means that the plaintiff should have more time—perhaps because there was a delay in discovering the basis for the claim.

Fraud. *You only were able to secure my agreement to repay you this debt under false pretenses*. You might offer evidence that your opponent promised to do something in order to secure your agreement and that they never had any intention of following through with their promise.[14]

Undue Influence. *You only were able to secure my agreement to repay this debt because you have some power over me and my affairs*. We were on an unlevel playing field when you secured my agreement for this.

The law generally presumes people are capable and competent. In some situations, however, one party may be in a particular position of trust over another, or may be in a position to exert some kind of control over them.[15]

Duress. *You created a situation where I had no choice but to accept the terms of this alleged debt*.

Remember when I said that the law has a different sensibility than might be found in "real life"? Well, depending on the nature of your life, the definition of duress is a good example of that.

Duress is one of those defenses that I hear a lot, usually because litigation often arises after or in response to a situation that is stressful. Chances are, you wouldn't be going to court in the first place if you weren't in a situation involving stress of some sort. In many instances, people suggest that they only agreed to do something—sign a repayment agreement for a loan, for instance—because they were "under duress."

"Stress," however, is very different from the type of "duress" that will serve to create or dissolve some type of legal obligation. Some courts have pointed out that duress is to be evaluated according to the "conduct of the party accused of duress, not the emotions of the purported victim."[16] Often you have to show that the person against whom you're claiming the duress also must have engaged in a wrongful act that resulted in your having no choice but to accede to their terms.

You manufacture picture frames. DanCo is your supplier, based in another jurisdiction.

You've begun to notice that DanCo is sending you a lot of parts that don't conform to your specifications. DanCo representatives disagree and want you to keep paying for them anyway. You and DanCo reach an agreement, of sorts, about the issue, but you don't sign it because you've got some concerns. DanCo files for bankruptcy.

You then happen to be traveling in the jurisdiction where DanCo is located, as you have a number of other business and personal interests there. You're nicely settled into your hotel, looking forward to winding down because you've had quite a rough day. The knock on your door isn't room service, however; it's the local police who have come to arrest you for fraud. The fraud is related to your refusal to pay for what you believe are DanCo's inferior products.

You are held at the police station, where the local authorities tell you to sign the agreement with DanCo or you're going to jail. You're allowed to see a lawyer but not to speak to him privately. The only thing he is allowed to discuss with you is your signing the agreement; when you attempt to speak to him about your arrest and the underlying charges against you, the authorities abruptly escort him out of the room.

Representatives of DanCo, who were able to initiate the criminal proceedings against you, then visit you in jail where you negotiate the final terms of the contract.

You sign the agreement with DanCo. You go home. You perform under the agreement.

A few months later, DanCo contacts you again regarding an amendment to the settlement agreement you signed. You delay. Then, one of the law enforcement officials from the foreign jurisdiction calls you, advising that you will be arrested when you return to the jurisdiction if you don't sign.

You sign.

Later on, you say enough is enough.

Duress?

The court says yes. Even though DanCo wasn't the party keeping you locked up or making further threats to do so, they plainly were aware of your duress and benefited from it. In fact, DanCo even facilitated it by making the criminal complaint—which arose from the same facts at issue in your civil dispute.

BY THE WAY, BE CAREFUL ABOUT THREATS

In most U.S. jurisdictions, it is improper for a lawyer to use a threat to initiate criminal proceedings in order to gain an advantage in civil litigation. Even laypeople can get in trouble for this. In some instances, threatening to initiate criminal prosecution as a means of getting goods and services from the other party can constitute extortion.[17]

Maybe DanCo needed to calm down a little. Still, I'm not suggesting that the only way a duress claim would survive is if things went that far—people have all sorts of ways of trying to get you to do things that may or may not cross the line, and I can't even begin to tell you what those lines are because they depend on the facts and circumstances of your case. I can say, however, that "duress" constitutes more than the type of pressure about which I hear many complain. "Duress" is more than just driving a hard bargain.

You are a consultant for interior designers. The way your business works is that designers send you pictures of their clients' homes, and you collect information from local suppliers about available inventories that will suit the project.

CanCo has developed software that allows you to digitally match fabrics to the intended furniture pieces. Now, you can allow your design clients to preview their choices before buying.

You begin using CanCo's product but notice it has some glitches. Your technical team is prepared to fix them, but you need CanCo to provide you the source code.

CanCo refuses to do so unless you sign an agreement that places strict limits on how you can use the acquired information. You sign it.

The deal goes south. You claim that CanCo was dishonest about the software's capabilities. You never could manage the digital matching of fabrics to furniture. You developed your own way of doing it.

CanCo claims you breached the agreement and misused its source code.

Breach of agreement??!! you think to yourself. The only reason I even signed that agreement was because they put a gun to my head. After all, I couldn't keep using the product unless I fixed it and they wouldn't let me fix it unless I signed that document! I was under duress!

Perhaps not really.

The court finds that being on the other side of a tough negotiator doesn't necessarily constitute duress. Just because someone insists you do something doesn't necessarily mean you were improperly pressured into it.

HOW MUCH STRESS FOR DURESS?

Different courts have described "duress" in different ways. I'll give you a random sampling of some of those descriptions, mostly to show again how court puts a much finer point on commonly held terms than we do outside the courtroom:

In Texas, a plaintiff is required to show: "(1) [Defendant] threatened to do some act that it had no legal right to do; (2) the threat was of such character as to destroy the free agency of [Plaintiff], and that it overcomes [Plaintiff's] will and causes [Plaintiff] to do that which it would not otherwise do, and which it was not legally bound to do; (3) the restraint caused by such threat was imminent; and (4) the threat was such that [Plaintiff] had no present means of protection."

In Wisconsin: The party alleging economic duress must show that they were the victim of a wrongful or unlawful act or threat; that the threat deprived them of their free will; that the threatened person was forced to exchange something for nothing; that the threatened person had no adequate legal remedy.

In Ohio and Massachusetts: A party must show that one side involuntarily accepted the terms of another; that there was no alternative; and that the circumstances were the result of the coercive acts of the opposite party.

In Alabama: "To demonstrate a prima facie case of economic duress, a party must show '(1) wrongful acts or threats; (2) financial distress caused by the wrongful acts or threats; (3) the absence of any reasonable alternative to the terms presented by the wrongdoer.'"

In Delaware, the elements are: "(1) a 'wrongful' act, (2) which overcomes the will of the aggrieved party, (3) who has no adequate legal remedy to protect himself."

In Oklahoma: There must have been a wrongful or unlawful act which (1) was initiated by the coercing party, (2) was committed with knowledge on the part of the coercing party of the impact it would have, (3) was made for the purpose of, and reasonably adequate to secure coercion over the other, and (4) resulted in obtaining undue advantage over the other. Plus, the act or acts complained of must have put the coerced party in a position where they had no reasonable alternative and were deprived of their free will.

> The point of all this is to show that you usually must demonstrate that the person you're accusing of duress participated in a wrongful act that forced your consent to something. The mere fact of your dire circumstances usually is not enough to get you off the hook.[18]

Remember, every case is different. Even if your facts are similar to those described above, a judge still could come to an entirely different conclusion.

When Things Turn Upside Down

As everyone who has lived through any global pandemic or moment of civil unrest knows—which, right now, is all of us—sometimes things come up that no one imagined happening and that change the entire landscape.

You can't avoid news reports about people getting sick and dying as a result of a highly contagious disease. You're shell-shocked as you see governments limit activities in an attempt to limit the spread of the disease.

The shell shock gives way to fear when you have to shut down your small business. You're ordered to stay at home as much as possible. You lose a gut-wrenching amount of money and the government stimulus check you're finally able to get won't make you completely whole. Not only are you unable to fulfill orders from customers, you can't pay for the products you've ordered from your suppliers. You never thought something like this could happen.

This is a problem. Your vendors want to be paid. Given the aforementioned global pandemic, they may be under some of the same pressures you are.

Litigation or the threat of it can follow all kinds of disruptive events that change the landscape or throw you off your game, to put it mildly. While the law sometimes makes allowances for these disruptions, getting relief is more than just a matter of spilling your soul to the court.

Some jurisdictions allow for defenses that either excuse

performance of contractual obligations in whole or in part when the unexpected happens. A defense of *frustration* or *commercial frustration* may be available, in which you allege that something happened that the parties couldn't reasonably foresee, which destroyed the value of the other party's performance.[19]

The defense of *impossibility* is another that may be available to you, provided you can show, for example, that the obligation you are to satisfy cannot by any means be accomplished.

For example, if John's consent is required before you do something, and John dies without making any provision about who should take his place as a decision-maker (and the law doesn't otherwise specify one), then impossibility might be a defense to a claim that you breached your obligation to get consent before you did whatever it was you did. Some jurisdictions have clarified that for the intervening event to relieve someone of their performance obligations, the "non-occurrence" of that event must have been a "basic assumption" of the parties.[20] Not having enough money, or the fact that performance will put you in dire straits, is typically not enough.[21] Some states also provide statutory protection too, providing that a party may be excused from performing their contractual obligations in the event of, for example, "an irresistible, superhuman cause, or by the act of public enemies of this State or the United States, unless the parties agreed to the contrary."[22]

Contracts also may specify circumstances that will relieve parties from their obligations, in whole or in part, by including *force majeure* provisions. A *force majeure* provision may relieve a party of certain obligations when specified types of intervening events take place—such as a labor strike; a war; certain types of governmental action; civil unrest or disturbance; or a riot.

All of these defenses require you to do more than show that things are much tougher for you than you ever imagined they would be. I'm not making light of how tough things can be; I'm simply pointing out that getting the benefit of these protections requires you to arrange the facts of your story in such a way as to convince the decision-maker that you deserve them. You may have to fight for those protections, even if their need seems obvious to you.

> You're in the restaurant business; the governor of your state issues a statewide lockdown order to stem the spread of a contagious virus. The lockdown order prohibits you from offering dine-in services, but you can offer delivery and takeout.
>
> The lockdown order means you lose a lot of your business. Losing a lot of your business means you've lost a lot of the money with which to pay your rent, as well as to pay the other expenses that being alive requires. You believe, however, that your lease agreement with the landlord offers you some protection. The lease has a *force majeure* clause, which provides you are excused from your rental obligations where "governmental action" or "orders of government" prevent you from complying. The force majeure clause specifically makes clear that not having money doesn't count.
>
> Your landlord, lockdown order or no, wants you to pay your rent and claims the force majeure clause doesn't apply. They claim the lockdown order didn't shut down the banks or the post office, so there was nothing to prevent you from going to get the money. They also claim that the only reason you couldn't pay rent was because you had no money, which the contract specifically rejects as a basis for invoking force majeure. Your landlord also maintains that you could have applied for some of the available federal relief programs in order to meet your obligations.
>
> The court rejects all of these arguments and holds that you only have to pay that portion of your rent that applies to your delivery and takeout activities, which were not affected by the lockdown.

So no, the fact that the bank was open does not mean that you were wrong for not going in to withdraw the money that didn't exist because you were legally prohibited from making it. Phew!

Still, the fact that seems like an obvious point to you doesn't mean someone won't try to put you to the trouble of arguing it, or something similarly unpersuasive to common sense ears, in court. Court is a place where the "right" thing can happen, but it doesn't always happen as easily as you might think it should.

Counterclaims

An affirmative defense is a defense you must prove and that can get you off the hook in the event the plaintiff meets their burden. A counterclaim is a claim you make against the plaintiff for some relief of your own, in the same way the plaintiff is seeking relief against you in the complaint.

You should think about your potential counterclaims as soon as possible. If you don't file them when you respond to the complaint, you may have to seek the court's permission to file them later. You'll seek that permission by filing a motion (time and money) and waiting in line. If you weren't planning on suing someone but they come for you first, a counterclaim can provide useful leverage—and you might win even if they don't.

What You Can Do: Reflect

Look, there aren't always a whole lot of external incentives to "owning up to things." While some may accept an apology or concession graciously, others can use it as an opening with which to savage you. You might feel better about having gotten that thing off your chest, but that doesn't mean your admission won't be used against you in some way, maybe even in ways that go far beyond your admission.

It may be this fear of admissions-being-used-against-them that can cause people to deny things reflexively. This can be especially true in court, where serious consequences attach to misconduct. Besides, being sorry you did something doesn't mean that you admit that it falls within the legal category of wrong that the plaintiff is alleging. Or, maybe you didn't do exactly what they're saying you did; or maybe you didn't do as much of it as they say you did. You might be sorry about something, but your apology doesn't mean that you're conceding the legal validity of your opponent's position.

The filing of the lawsuit doesn't mean that you have to let it go the distance. Sometimes a lawsuit is an effort to bring people to the table or stop things before they go even further. Remember the lawsuit I mentioned in the last chapter that Public Counsel and other groups brought on behalf of homeless individuals in Los Angeles? Subsequent to that filing, the governor issued an order ending funding to cities that engaged in the challenged practice (of unilaterally vetoing, in secret, affordable housing projects) and the City of Los Angeles agreed to stop it. No one wanted to spend years litigating that case—those would have been years when even more people would have been relegated to sleeping on the streets. By the same token, certain decision-makers may not have been sufficiently incentivized to solve the problem had they not been facing the prospect of expensive litigation.

In other words, even after someone files a case against you, you shouldn't assume it's too late to come to the table.

Bruce and Lorena were senior employees of Sunrise Corporation. They wanted to start their own business. They quit.

First, however, they wanted to receive severance.

Their severance negotiations were not going as well as they would have liked. They wanted more money.

Sunrise Corporation pushed back. *No more money for you,* Sunrise said.

Dissatisfied with this, Bruce and Lorena decided to create some leverage for themselves. *Let's take some company files! Then they'll have to deal with us on our terms.*

Oh no we won't, said Sunrise.

Sunrise Company sued Bruce and Lorena for misappropriation of trade secrets.

Oh no, said Bruce and Lorena. *We weren't expecting that.*

Bruce and Lorena came back to the table, bringing the misappropriated files with them. Sunrise Company dropped the lawsuit and finished the severance discussions.

Will you always get such a benign response when you try to come to the table after a lawsuit has been filed? Not necessarily. That doesn't mean it's not worth a try. As I will say over and over throughout the course of this book, *it's never too late to try to work it out.*

An Early Note About Working It Out

When you're engaged in settlement discussions, there are some protections you have that will prevent the other side from using against you something that you discussed while you were trying to work it out.[23]

Some jurisdictions go even further—they provide that if the other side rejects your settlement offer and later obtains a judgment or decision that is less favorable to them than the deal you offered, they can be liable for *your* costs.[24]

What does this mean? It means that the court system, however wacky it may sometimes seem and however much it doesn't always ensure this happens, prefers to have disputes resolved rather than litigated. It means that there's a preference that you not spend time fighting about something when you could have obtained appropriate relief in a more efficient way.

I think it would be fair to say that courts generally don't want to be your platform for "working through stuff." In court, it's often better to get in, get to the point, and get out when you can. During the litigation process, there will be various opportunities to resolve things with your opponent long before you go to trial. The judge likely will ask you if you've tried and she even may order you to do so.

Defending against a lawsuit isn't always just a matter of sitting back and waiting to see what happens. You definitely shouldn't ignore it. Even the weakest claims may require your attention, especially since ignoring a weak allegation could give that claim the shot of adrenaline for which your opponent is looking.

And then again, there still may be opportunities to figure things out with your opponent. Sometimes a lawsuit can be the beginning of a resolution, albeit an expensive, uncomfortable, and very frustrating beginning.

TO SUM UP . . .

- Understand that even if the lawsuit is entirely bogus and made up, it will still take time. If you are served with a complaint, the consequences of ignoring it can be serious.
- The advantage of a court fight is that if someone is exaggerating or just being dishonest, you may have the opportunity to use that dishonesty against them later. Court doesn't forget.
- In addition to poking holes in the plaintiff's story as soon as you can, make sure you're paying attention to how you will put your own story together. Even if the plaintiff is able to meet their burden, you still have the opportunity of mounting an affirmative defense, which you can use to avoid or limit your liability.
- Your response to the lawsuit can be the time for you to bring your own claims against the plaintiff. Maybe their first strike is a sign that it is time for you to strike back. Prepare your counter attack. They may have started this fight, but perhaps they need to be on the hook for something too.
- Oh, and did I mention that it's never too late to try to work it out?

3

IT'S ALMOST ALWAYS GOING TO TAKE MORE TIME THAN YOU'D LIKE

It's A Simple Case. It Won't Take *That* Much Time, Right?

Wrong.

"Simple," when you're fighting in court, can have an entirely differently meaning than it does in "real life."

You may have thought through as much as you know to. You may be really prepared.

You may have organized your evidence; considered all your claims and defenses; made preparations to obtain evidence and witnesses or worked with a lawyer to do so; confirmed you're suing the right person in the right place at the right time and for something that seems right. You may have buttoned everything up for a strong defensive case.

That doesn't mean you still won't have to hurry up and wait.

Remember what I said about due process? Well, it applies not just when you're filing and serving your complaint and answer, but it also impacts the timing and manner of other parts of your fight, too.

When you're fighting in court, the way you hash issues out before the judge, generally, is by filing a motion, which is a written request to the judge explaining the legal and factual basis for the relief you're seeking. Was the case filed after the statute of limitations? File a motion. Does the court have jurisdiction? File a motion. Is the other side trying to pull a fast one in discovery? File a motion. These and other issues are the types of things that you may need to settle before you even have the chance to get a decision about the question that brought you to court in the first place.

What You Should Know: There May Be Long Delays No Matter What You Do

When you file your motion, you must submit it to the court within a certain period of time in advance of the hearing. The amount of time varies depending on the motion. The other side must have notice of the motion and a fair opportunity to respond and be heard. This is where due process comes in.

EX PARTES—COURT, I NEED YOU NOW!

The exception is for emergencies that may be heard on shortened time.

All the fights you have before you get to the main event are going to take some time.

Plus, on top of the necessary procedural requirements, you may just have to wait in line to get before a judge who probably already has a pretty crowded schedule. Getting a hearing date, however, can be a real struggle. Why? Because there are a lot of people who also are in the middle of their own fights in that court, and they're having their own fights-within-the-fight just as you are. Plus, the judge in your case may also be presiding over trials (so your matter will be sandwiched in between them), or he may be handling various emergency matters that will take precedence over your case (we'll discuss what an "emergency" might be, later). Get in line.

Courts are crowded. In my home state of California, for instance, nearly 900,000 civil cases alone were filed in 2017—and that's just in state court.[1] Some judges have taken matters into their own hands; one court issued an order advising litigants that there wouldn't be any oral arguments in that court and that trial dates might be vacated with little or no notice. (The judge who issued the order had a docket of roughly 1675 cases—composed of both criminal *and* civil matters.)[2]

FROM BAD TO WORSE

The COVID-19 pandemic and the resultant shutdown and disruption of many public operations has had a severe impact on court functioning. According to a letter from the Judicial Conference of the United States to the U.S. House of Representatives Committee on Appropriations, "[m]ost Judiciary personnel nationwide are teleworking, grand jury proceedings and jury trials have been postponed, civil litigation has significantly slowed, courts are using video and teleconferencing technology for proceedings in criminal cases and for other court matters to the extent practicable[.]"[3]

So what does all this mean?

The Judicial Council of California (JCC), an organization made up of judges from across the state, has observed that the judicial shortage has resulted in a "lack of access to the courts, compromised public safety, an unstable business climate, and backlogs in some courts that inhibit fair, timely and equitable justice." The situation is not good: "Some courts may be unable to provide an adequate level of justice to people who need access to the courts," the JCC noted in its 2018 Fact Sheet. "An insufficient number of judges may result in delays in civil case processing, harming civil litigants including business owners, families, children and victims of domestic violence."[4]

What does this mean? It means the judge may have to reschedule an important motion in the case involving your business dispute because of someone else's bigger emergency. It means that when you want the court to do something about the unfair and incredible things your opponent is doing to break the rules (you might be surprised at some of the things with which people get away, more on those later), it may be months before you can tell the judge about them, and then even more time before she decides whether she's going to do anything. It means you're at the mercy of timing and scheduling dictates over which you have very little control.

WHEN JUDGES NEED HELP

While judges can't fire back when people say snarky things about them in the media, they can bring attention to what some perceive as a crisis arising from their heavy caseloads. As discussed above, one judge had taken to putting a disclaimer on his rulings: citing a "shortage of district judges and staff," the judge advises that the court only will address arguments "necessary to reach the decision in this order." His rulings further advised that "[j]udges in the Eastern District of California carry the heaviest caseloads in the nation," and encouraged parties and counsel to contact the state's senators "to address this court's inability to accommodate the parties and this action."[5] Indeed, that judge presides over a court that one report described as "struggling with extraordinarily high and sustained workloads," where "[t]he severity of conditions . . . require[s] immediate action." (The other courts mentioned in that particular report were in Delaware, Florida, Indiana, and Texas.)[6]

But What If I've Got an Emergency?

Courts don't always see "emergencies" in the same way that you do.

> You are an architect. You hire Adam to make copies of some of your designs for an important meeting with a potential new client.
>
> After making the copies, however, Adam refuses to deliver either the copies or the originals unless you pay him more money. You had a signed contract indicating an agreed-upon fee but now Adam wants more. Your business meeting is in a month and those designs are critical. It will be impossible for you to recreate them.

There are ways of getting some emergency help or relief from the court, like a temporary restraining order or preliminary injunction. (A restraining order is the type of relief that prohibits someone from doing something, while a mandatory injunction may require them to take action of some kind.) The standard for getting emergency relief, however, is extremely high. Among other things, you'll have to show that you'll probably win the underlying case and you'll also have to show that you'll suffer "irreparable harm" if the court doesn't get involved now. "Irreparable harm" generally means some kind of harm that can't be remedied with money damage; or that will undermine or void the effectiveness of any relief that might be obtained when the case is all said and done. Perhaps your upcoming meeting will qualify; perhaps not.

Courts have a much higher standard about what sorts of harms are "irreparable" than do normal, ordinary humans. A court might say that depriving you of critical medication constitutes "irreparable harm."[7] A court might also say that denying you medical treatment while you await the completion and results of arbitration, does not.[8] It's a hard standard to meet and one whose outcome is even harder to predict.

You may simply have to assume the costs of someone else's bad behavior as you prepare for the long journey of obtaining relief.

What You Should Know:
Almost Anything Can Happen

Sometimes people get sick. They or family members may need surgery. Children have events that require you to show up; parents need your attention; people in your care or otherwise dependent on you need something urgent. Or (if you have any money left for vacations while you're fighting in court), maybe a preplanned trip will require you to seek a delay. Stuff happens.

Courts usually require parties to cooperate with one another about scheduling issues. Isn't that nice?

Does it always happen?

Do you work out as often as you should? Regularly stick to your diet? Keep all your New Year's resolutions? In other words, even if your opponent is acting in good faith, the heated atmosphere of a court battle can impute toxicity to even the most basic of matters.

What You Should Know
(and Probably Already Do): People Can Make
Things Harder Than Necessary

Do you think that everyone decides to play by the rules; cooperate with one another; and only bring forth claims and defenses for which there is a good faith basis? Do you think everyone abides by the *I-shouldn't-forge-documents-or-commit-perjury-or-destroy-evidence* principle?

No, they do not.

Sometimes people will use the court process to harass you for no good faith reason; sometimes litigation may be their preferred means of torture; a way of sucking as much out of you as they can, even if that something is just your attention. People like this live for, derive oxygen from, and thrive on conflict—and court gives them plenty of room to maneuver.

It's not a question of using the system to try to obtain things to which they know they aren't entitled; some people also use it to avoid doing things they know they have an obligation to do. Knowing they can hide behind the time it takes for a situation to work its way through the court system, they may seek to string things out for as long as they can. They'll schedule meetings and not show up; they'll say they are sick and you'll highly doubt it; they'll oppose every request you make and force unnecessary court appearances. They will take as much of your time as they can and try to use the process to make you as miserable as humanly possible.

Do you think that with some courts being as busy and understaffed as I just mentioned that judges have the time and resources to police all misconduct? Do you think they'll even have a chance to hear about the misconduct and make a decision about it before several weeks if not a few months have passed? Do you remember what I said about how hard it is to prove that something is an emergency? Plus, do you know how much money you'll have to spend in order to try to prove it?

It's not fair to say that you don't have protection from this sort of thing. I'll discuss some of your potential options in Chapter 8. Taking advantage of those options, however, will cost you time and money, and may further delay resolution of your matter. While there may be circumstances where you need to use those resources in order to deter future bad behavior, you should realize that there's some amount of wasting of your time and money with which someone can almost always get away.

Why?

Because 1) as an initial matter, the court will assume the factual allegations of the complaint are true. If someone asserts something you claim is an outright lie, you may have to undertake the burden of showing there are no facts to support it (which also may require you to wait things out a bit); 2) if and when you finally disprove their claims, you have to prove that they asserted a claim or defense with no good faith basis; 3) even after you do that, you have to show how much you were damaged by their dragging you through the process with no good faith basis; and 4) since court doesn't value your time, energy, or right to be free of injustice as highly as you do, the court may put a lower value on your time or discount the amount you paid to fight the other side's conduct. In other words, don't assume that the court will follow the "a dollar spent is a dollar returned" approach.

You might be thinking that things will go more smoothly if you have a lawyer. After all, lawyers are supposed to keep things in check. They are supposed to play by the rules and impose order. While loyal to their own teams, lawyers are supposed to make sure that the game is played fairly and doesn't get out of hand. They have legal duties to deal honestly with each other and not to engage in conduct designed to protract disputes unreasonably. They are the ones who act as buffers, advancing their clients' interests within the appropriate ethical bounds.

Yes, all those things are true. But sometimes . . .

You and your former business partner Madge had a manufacturing business and when you decided to shut it down and end the partnership, things got ugly. You believe Madge is making things more difficult than necessary. You end up having to go to court on numerous occasions in order to wind down the business.

In the course of your litigation dealings, Madge has had many lawyers, Maud the most recent among them. You and your lawyers contend that the purpose of much of Madge's legal maneuvering has been simply to annoy you and make things difficult, and you believe Maud is continuing that strategy.

Maud ignored her duties to communicate and cooperate with your lawyers, driving up expenses by forcing your counsel to engage in multiple unreturned communications and protracting disputes on simple issues. She also refused to respond to requests to resolve some of Madge's claims, forcing your lawyers to spend time (and you to spend money) preparing them for trial. (Madge later dropped those claims at the beginning of the trial, so spent a lot of money on those issues for nothing.)

There were a number of scheduling changes that resulted in moving the trial date, but the judge eventually set what was supposed to be a firm date. You rearrange your schedule accordingly, cutting short an overseas trip and modifying business and other family plans so as to comply.

However, about a week before trial, Maud claimed she was too ill to move forward on the scheduled date.

Your lawyers suspect that Maud just wanted another delay, but the judge accepts her claim and moves the trial to a date months later. (As it turns out, you changed your plans and upended your schedule for absolutely no reason at all.)

What options did you have in this situation? You could spend a lot more money having your lawyers try to "prove" that Maud was lying. But was that even possible? While you and your lawyers may believe that Maud and her client had an allergy to the truth, perhaps *this* time she was being honest. If she was not, what would you have to invest to prove it? Would pursuing the point have undermined the value of the victory?

As an attorney, Maud had an obligation to try to cooperate with your counsel. Still, remember what I said earlier about how crowded some court dockets are? You may have to live with some uncooperative behavior. Chasing down and proving a violation may be more work than anyone—including the judge—wants to invest in the issue.

As I'll explain later, the court is also accountable to the court of appeal for its decisions. Imagine the consequences if the judge said to Maud, "enough is enough, show up and try this case." Madge could have used that ruling to appeal any adverse judgment against her. *Appellate judges*, Madge might argue, *my attorney, Maud, didn't put on her best case because the judge made us go to court while she was sick.* If the judge had forced the trial to go forward, your successful verdict could have been vulnerable on appeal.

Time is one of the most unpredictable elements of court process and unpredictability can be expensive. There are more reasons than most of can imagine why a case can take more time than it should—or for which you've budgeted. Being aware of that unpredictability—even expecting it—will position you to make necessary changes to your strategy and budget.

What You Can Do: Embrace Time as a "Frenemy"

If you're taking your fight to court, be prepared for it to take more time than you think it will. Expect this. Misplaced faith in court's efficiency is what sometimes causes people to bring fights there that might have been resolved more efficiently elsewhere.

There are ways of using time to your advantage. You can use it to 1) find a lawyer, which may not be easy; 2) confirm you have the evidentiary support you need to prove to someone who isn't just going to take your word for it that you're right; 3) gather that evidence, if you don't already have it; and 4) gather even more, if you think you do.

Another benefit of time is that it gives everyone a chance to see whether or not they really want to go down this road. Many people resolve their cases during the long period during which their fight winds its way through the litigation process. Taking advantage of that delay can end up saving you some time, money, and hassle down the road.

> TO SUM UP . . .
>
> * Even if you think you have a very simple case, there are many ways the process can take far more time than you expect. Plan for and prepare for this.
> * Start thinking early about options you may have for avoiding litigation. I'll go over some of those with you in Chapter 11.

- Use your time (and you'll have a lot of it) to collect facts, examine the outcome you're seeking, and evaluate how well your facts lay the groundwork for that outcome. It will help you better to determine what's most important to prove (as opposed to what's making you the most peeved) and what isn't. You'll be a better navigator of your story through the process. Carefully assess why you're going to court in the first place. How well will court serve your purposes? Are there better options for resolving the issue?
- Don't forget—*it's never too early or too late to try to work things out*.

PART II

The Players

Honesty in dealing with the courts is of paramount importance, and misleading a judge is, regardless of motives, a serious offense.

—*Utz v. State Bar of California*, 21 Cal. 2d 100, 105 (1942), quoting *Paine v. State Bar*, 14 Cal. 2d 150, 154

4

YOU AND
YOUR LAWYER

How Can I Manage Things with My Lawyer?

First, know that it may be difficult to find one.

What You Should Know: Finding a Lawyer Isn't as Easy as It Seems on TV

You may be more likely to see a television commercial for a lawyer than to find one to take your case. There is a shortage of attorneys who are available to serve the clients who need them; in some jurisdictions, the situation is critical. People can't always afford lawyers and lawyers can't always afford to represent every client or cause important to them.

INVESTING IN LIFESAVERS

Many law schools subsidize students who choose to go into the public sector. Yale Law School, for instance, subsidizes public interest work through various programs, including summer fellowships, postgraduate fellowships, loan repayment programs, and student-driven public interest projects during the academic year.

New York University School of Law offers first-year students funds to cover expenses for their summer public interest jobs, as well as discounted housing and loan repayment programs. Boston University provides postgraduate public interest fellowships. Case Western Reserve's Social Justice Law Center offers funding for summer and semester-long public interest work. Stanford Law School's Levin Center for Public Service and Public Interest Law provides public interest fellowships and loan forgiveness programs for students who pursue public interest work.

Some jurisdictions have even considered licensing non-lawyers to provide certain legal services in civil cases.[1] (In some jurisdictions, judges don't even need to be lawyers. Some states even allow non-lawyer judges to sentence defendants to jail time.)[2]

Aside from the general questions of availability and access, there is also the more specific issue of finding a lawyer willing to take your case. Why should a lawyer consider taking it? Why is it worth their time? How are you paying for that time?

What You Should Know: The Money

You may have a great case but unless you're lucky enough to find one of those generous souls willing to take your case for free—lawyers have to eat too, and all we have to sell is our time—you have to think about how you're going to pay for this exercise.

Contingency Fees

A contingency fee agreement is one where the lawyer agrees to take a percentage of your recovery as a fee, instead of charging you an hourly rate. The lawyer may or may not advance the costs associated with your case. Those costs can be substantial.

FEES V. COSTS

Fees are what the lawyer charges for their time. Costs are items that are required to process your case—copying costs; exhibit preparation; court filing fees; and the like.

Costs can be substantial. If you're filing an appellate brief in California, for example, it has to be formatted and bound in a certain way[3]—there are even companies that specialize in doing that work. It can cost you thousands of dollars simply to have your documents prepared, and that's not including the time your lawyer spends writing and reviewing them.

Some lawyers are willing to represent clients who have little or no ability to pay them, and where the dollar recovery might be minimal. Some cases aren't even primarily about the money and little may ever end up changing hands. (One example might be when someone is trying to stop government officials from enforcing rules or statutes that they believe are unconstitutional; another would be the lawsuit that Public Counsel and other lawyers brought on behalf of the homeless in Los Angeles.) Even lawyers who are in for-profit practices can donate a significant amount of their time to *pro bono* activities.

If your lawyer isn't one who is taking your case on that basis, however, you should expect them to give serious consideration to the time it will take to obtain a recovery and what the likely or probable recovery is. There is no hard and fast rule about what makes a case a "good" one—different lawyers will make different judgments based on their own priorities, the dictates of their business, and maybe their relationship to you, if they have one. It can take more time than people realize to put a case together. So, don't be surprised if the economics of your particular problem make it harder for you to find legal representation. As annoying as that dispute with your neighbor may be, it might be difficult to find someone who is willing to take a flyer on it.

Hourly Fees

If you're paying your lawyer by the hour, the expenses can mount quickly. You've already read in earlier chapters about how rapidly things can spin out of control, or about how many disputes you may have en route to a decision about the main dispute that brought you to court in the first place. The price of those fights adds up.

It's for that reason that it sometimes may be difficult to find even an hourly lawyer who is willing to take your case. Even lawyers who work on an hourly basis may be reluctant to take a case where the amount in dispute doesn't warrant the expense.

You and your lawyer will execute a retainer agreement—your lawyer should provide you one—which specifies the scope of the retention: the basis on which the lawyer is being paid (hourly or contingency) as well as the amount or percentage of any hourly or contingency rate. The retention agreement should specify other matters, too, such as the basis for resolving any disputes between you.

What You Should Know: (Some of) Your Rights

Your lawyer has a number of specific duties to you. You should be familiar with them. Here are a few—what they mean in the context of your specific relationship with your lawyer will depend on the nature of your case.

Your Attorney Must Be Loyal

Your lawyer can't represent you and your opponent, obviously. Nor can your lawyer represent anyone else in the case, such as a witness, when there is *or could be* a conflict between the two of you. Even if the witness is a "friendly" one, this type of dual representation still could be problematic—how can a lawyer maintain loyalty to both of you when discrepancies between your accounts, for instance, might emerge?

In some instances, this duty can continue even after the case ends, and the lawyer can be limited in what future representations he can make unless you agree to waive potential conflicts.

Your Attorney Must Communicate with You

Unlike other alliances that come apart at the drop of a hat in our fight-friendly age, the relationship with your lawyer is different.

First of all, your lawyer *must* communicate with you. This is a key part of the relationship. It's impossible for your lawyer to represent you effectively if they aren't communicating with you and if you aren't giving them the information they need to go to battle on your behalf.

AMERICAN BAR ASSOCIATION MODEL RULE FOR COMMUNICATIONS WITH CLIENTS:

Rule 1.4: Communications

Client-Lawyer Relationship

Rule 1.4 Communication

(a) A lawyer shall:

(1) promptly inform the client of any decision or circumstance with respect to which the client's informed consent, as defined in Rule 1.0(e), is required by these Rules;

(2) reasonably consult with the client about the means by which the client's objectives are to be accomplished;

(3) keep the client reasonably informed about the status of the matter;

(4) promptly comply with reasonable requests for information; and

(5) consult with the client about any relevant limitation on the lawyer's conduct when the lawyer knows that the client expects assistance not permitted by the Rules of Professional Conduct or other law.

(b) A lawyer shall explain a matter to the extent reasonably necessary to permit the client to make informed decisions regarding the representation.[4]

Here's an example of the rules for keeping open the channels of communication from my great state of California:

California Rules of Professional Conduct for communications with clients:

Rule 3-500. Communication.

A member shall keep a client reasonably informed about significant developments relating to the employment or representation, including promptly complying with reasonable requests for information and copies of significant documents when necessary to keep the client so informed.

Rule 3-510. Communication of Settlement Offer.

(A) A member shall promptly communicate to the member's client:

(1) All terms and conditions of any offer made to the client in a criminal matter; and

(2) All amounts, terms, and conditions of any written offer of settlement made to the client in all other matters.

(B) As used in this rule, "**client**" includes a person who possesses the authority to accept an offer of settlement or plea, or, in a class action, all the named representatives of the class.

These rules can help provide the foundation for a resolving any number of commonly-experienced problems.[5]

Not communicating with you can land your lawyer in serious trouble.

You meet with Lawyer Smith in late February in order to obtain advice about your legal separation from your spouse, which took place the month before.

You sign a retainer agreement shortly thereafter. Lawyer Smith agrees to represent you and to perform all necessary services in connection with your separation and divorce.

Your spouse files for divorce the next month. Lawyer Smith responds to the complaint and represents you in your successful attempt to seek a protective order.

In May, two months later, you meet with Lawyer Smith to discuss next steps in the case.

Your spouse sends some discovery to which Lawyer Smith responds. Other than that, Lawyer Smith does nothing in your case until January of the following year. That's when you meet with her again and let her know that you want to get this divorce train out of the station.

You email her in March and May, asking for the status. Lawyer Smith doesn't respond.

In June, you call Lawyer Smith. No response.

The papers Lawyer Smith filed in answer to your soon-but-not-soon-enough-to-be ex-spouse didn't include some of the documents and information that were required.

In July, you call her again. You tell her you're disappointed with the progress of the case and her lack of activity on it. She calls you back and says she'll give you an update after the July 4th holiday. She never calls you back.

Between July and August, you call her at least eight times and leave four messages. Lawyer Smith responds to none of your messages. In one instance, Lawyer Smith actually takes your call, but says she's on her way to court and will have to call you back. She doesn't.

During all this time, Lawyer Smith was busy! She was working on a political campaign; handling an issue related to the administration of client funds; and training a new secretary who needed around-the-clock supervision. Her hands were pretty full—and the court found that when it came to you, she dropped the ball.

Lawyer Smith had previously been reprimanded for a violation of her duties, and the court found that the facts of your case warranted an indefinite suspension of her right to practice (she had the right to reapply after six months).

Your lawyer is not supposed to make you feel like a stalker. They are supposed to call you back, answer your questions, and proceed diligently to move forward with your case. "Diligently" doesn't mean "as fast as you want" because, as I've already explained, there are a number of factors that might result in your case taking longer than you'd like. Many of those factors won't necessarily have anything to do with your lawyer.

"Diligence" doesn't require your lawyer to drop all their other matters so as to be at your beck and call on a 24/7 basis; that wouldn't be fair to their other clients. (Still, I do know lawyers who do make themselves available to a number of clients on this basis.) By the same token, a lawyer isn't supposed to take on more cases than they can reasonably handle and in order to reasonably handle a case, the lawyer obviously should be communicating with their clients.

In short, if a lawyer signs up to take your case, they're obligated to execute their duties in a way that's consistent with their professional obligations. They took you on, so they can't *always* be too busy to call you back.

Your Lawyer Must Keep Your Secrets
The exception is if the lawyer knows you are going to participate in a crime or fraud, or if you are going to engage in some activity that will bring imminent harm to someone.[6]

What You Should Know:
It Won't Always Be Easy

Don't expect your relationship with your lawyer to be smooth sailing.

If people always could be trusted to be honest, moral, and upright with one another at all crucial moments; if they could be trusted always to treat each other as they would wish to be treated; if we all loved one another during our toughest moments in precisely the ways wise people from every corner of the earth have urged us; if all those things were true . . . we'd be in some scary times indeed. What kind of lobotomized automatons would we be?

Humans being humans, it's inevitable we'll have conflicts with one another. Lawyers being humans, it's inevitable that should you end up in a situation where you need one, there may be occasions when the relationship feels . . . bad.

Some of this is to be expected. Regardless of the merits of your position, because of the various twists and turns of litigation there's a very high likelihood that at some point you'll feel assaulted by something that feels unfair. It's hard to be thankful for the opportunity to pay a lot of money to fix something that shouldn't have happened in the first place, or to address a situation that may even be a frivolous waste of time. Problems may arise. As with all situations, you should look for opportunities to resolve it—the time your lawyer has invested working on and preparing a case may represent a significant investment of your money.

That's not to say, however, that you're at your lawyer's mercy when things get strained, and your lawyer should be open to working things out too. It's in everyone's interest to not let a lawyer-client dispute take on a life of its own. You're already in the middle of one fight—try not to add another to the mix.

If things get really bad, you should know that a lawyer can't just dump you as a client without considering a few things first.

UNDER THE ABA MODEL RULES OF PROFESSIONAL RESPONSIBILITY, A LAWYER *MUST* WITHDRAW IF:

1. the representation will result in violation of the rules of professional conduct or other law;
2. the lawyer's physical or mental condition materially impairs the lawyer's ability to represent the client; or
3. the lawyer is discharged.˙

The lawyer *can* withdraw if:

1. withdrawal can be accomplished without material adverse effect on the interests of the client;
2. the client persists in a course of action involving the lawyer's services that the lawyer reasonably believes is criminal or fraudulent;
3. the client has used the lawyer's services to perpetrate a crime or fraud;
4. the client insists upon taking action that the lawyer considers repugnant or with which the lawyer has a fundamental disagreement;
5. the client fails substantially to fulfill an obligation to the lawyer regarding the lawyer's services and has been given reasonable warning that the lawyer will withdraw unless the obligation is fulfilled;
6. the representation will result in an unreasonable financial burden on the lawyer or has been rendered unreasonably difficult by the client; or
7. other good cause for withdrawal exists.

---

* Model Rules of Prof'l Conduct r. 1.16 (Am. Bar Ass'n 1983), https://www.american-bar.org/groups/professional_responsibility/publications/model_rules_of_profes-sional_conduct/rule_1_16_declining_or_terminating_representation/

Texas and West Virginia have similarly worded regulations.[*]

In California, a lawyer *must* withdraw if:

1. the lawyer knows or reasonably should know that the client is bringing an action, conducting a defense, asserting a position in litigation, or taking an appeal, without probable cause and for the purpose of harassing or maliciously injuring any person;

2. the lawyer knows or reasonably should know that the representation will result in violation of these rules or of the State Bar Act;

3. the lawyer's mental or physical condition renders it unreasonably difficult to carry out the representation effectively; or

4. the client discharges the lawyer.

A lawyer *can* withdraw if:

1. the client insists upon presenting a claim or defense in litigation, or asserting a position or making a demand in a non-litigation matter, that is not warranted under existing law and cannot be supported by good faith argument for an extension, modification, or reversal of existing law;

2. the client either seeks to pursue a criminal or fraudulent course of conduct or has used the lawyer's services to advance a course of conduct that the lawyer reasonably believes was a crime or fraud;

3. the client insists that the lawyer pursue a course of conduct that is criminal or fraudulent;

4. the client by other conduct renders it unreasonably

---

[*] Tex. Disciplinary R. Prof. Conduct r. 1.15 (1989), https://www.legalethicstexas.com/Ethics-Resources/Rules/Texas-Disciplinary-Rules-of-Professional-Conduct/I–CLIENT-LAWYER-RELATIONSHIP/1-15-Declining-or-Terminating-Representation; W. Va. R. Prof. Conduct r. 1.16, http://www.courtswv.gov/legal-community/court-rules/professional-conduct/rule1.html#rule1.16

difficult for the lawyer to carry out the representation effectively;

5. the client breaches a material term of an agreement with, or obligation, to the lawyer relating to the representation, and the lawyer has given the client a reasonable warning after the breach that the lawyer will withdraw unless the client fulfills the agreement or performs the obligation;

6. the client knowingly and freely assents to termination of the representation;

7. the inability to work with co-counsel indicates that the best interests of the client likely will be served by withdrawal;

8. the lawyer's mental or physical condition renders it difficult for the lawyer to carry out the representation effectively;

9. a continuation of the representation is likely to result in a violation of these rules or the State Bar Act; or

10. the lawyer believes in good faith, in a proceeding pending before a tribunal, that the tribunal will find the existence of other good cause for withdrawal.*

In Florida, a lawyer *must* withdraw if:

1. the representation will result in violation of the Rules of Professional Conduct or law;

2. the lawyer's physical or mental condition materially impairs the lawyer's ability to represent the client;

3. the lawyer is discharged;

4. the client persists in a course of action involving the lawyer's services that the lawyer reasonably believes is criminal or fraudulent, unless the client agrees to disclose and rectify the crime or fraud; or

---

* Cal. R. Prof. Conduct r. 1. 16.

5. the client has used the lawyer's services to perpetrate a crime or fraud, unless the client agrees to disclose and rectify the crime or fraud.

A lawyer *can* withdraw if:

1. withdrawal can be accomplished without material adverse effect on the interests of the client;
2. the client insists upon taking action that the lawyer considers repugnant, imprudent, or with which the lawyer has a fundamental disagreement;
3. the client fails substantially to fulfill an obligation to the lawyer regarding the lawyer's services and has been given reasonable warning that the lawyer will withdraw unless the obligation is fulfilled;
4. the representation will result in an unreasonable financial burden on the lawyer or has been rendered unreasonably difficult by the client; or
5. other good cause for withdrawal exists.*

In New York, a lawyer *must* withdraw if:

1. the lawyer knows or reasonably should know that the representation will result in a violation of these Rules or of law;
2. the lawyer's physical or mental condition materially impairs the lawyer's ability to represent the client;
3. the lawyer is discharged; or
4. the lawyer knows or reasonably should know that the client is bringing the legal action, conducting the defense, or asserting a position in the matter, or is otherwise having steps taken, merely for the purpose of harassing or maliciously injuring any person.

---

* FL R. Prof. Res. r 4-1.6.

A lawyer *can* withdraw if:

1. withdrawal can be accomplished without material adverse effect on the interests of the client;

2. the client persists in a course of action involving the lawyer's services that the lawyer reasonably believes is criminal or fraudulent;

3. the client has used the lawyer's services to perpetrate a crime or fraud;

4. the client insists upon taking action with which the lawyer has a fundamental disagreement;

5. the client deliberately disregards an agreement or obligation to the lawyer as to expenses or fees;

6. the client insists upon presenting a claim or defense that is not warranted under existing law and cannot be supported by good faith argument for an extension, modification, or reversal of existing law;

7. the client fails to cooperate in the representation or otherwise renders the representation unreasonably difficult for the lawyer to carry out employment effectively;

8. the lawyer's inability to work with co-counsel indicates that the best interest of the client likely will be served by withdrawal;

9. the lawyer's mental or physical condition renders it difficult for the lawyer to carry out the representation effectively;

10. the client knowingly and freely assents to termination of the employment;

11. withdrawal is permitted under Rule 1.13(c) or other law;

12. the lawyer believes in good faith, in a matter pending before a tribunal, that the tribunal will find the existence of other good cause for withdrawal; or

13. the client insists that the lawyer pursue a course of conduct which is illegal or prohibited under these Rules.*

---

* NY R. Prof. Conduct r. 1. 16.

What You Should Know:
Solving Problems

Your relationship with your lawyer is governed by a set of rules that should make it easier, as opposed to more difficult, to resolve conflicts.

Just like it is far beyond the scope of this book to attempt to address all the things that could happen in a lawsuit, it would be similarly unavailing for me to try to dissect all the things that can go wrong or cause trouble in an attorney-client situation. It is a list as long as the one detailing all human faults.

Many problems in the attorney-client relationship arise from a failure to communicate. When you're already in a stressful situation, which a lawsuit is, you may not be at your best when it comes to your people skills. Plus, your lawyer is someone you have to pay for conversation, usually. It makes you want to talk to them less, but sometimes it's really unavoidable. Be clear about what it is you want from the conversation before you go into it, and be clear about whatever response you're getting, even if you don't like it.

Your agreement with your lawyer should specify how disputes will be resolved. Don't be surprised if your lawyer wants to avoid trial and instead tries to direct you to arbitration; don't be further surprised if that arbitration first takes place before a panel of lawyers from a local bar association, with whom your lawyer may be professionally acquainted. That doesn't mean they don't still have an obligation to be fair. I'll discuss more about arbitration generally in Chapter 11. Further, if your lawyer works with a law firm, there may be opportunities to resolve it through their colleagues' intervention as the management of a firm has every incentive to see things work out. You can also file a bar complaint—a severe measure but one you may want to consider if you believe the situation is beyond repair. Disputes with your lawyer can feel particularly debilitating because your lawyer is supposed to be on your side. Look for opportunities to resolve things if you can. If you're involved in a lawsuit, you already have enough fighting going on.

There are some problems that seem to arise pretty commonly in the relationship—so here are a few suggestions I can offer that might help smooth the rough patches so you can stay focused on the problem you're both there to solve.

You think the bill is too high. First, let me throw this out there: unlike others who may provide you valuable services that you can readily appreciate, lawyers don't watch your kids; cook your food; clean your house; build bridges; fix roads; or sell bright and shiny things to distract you from the drudgeries of life. Lawyers have but one thing to sell: their time and expertise. To put it simply, most cases take more time than clients would like, for some of the reasons I've already mentioned. I've represented and advised clients in situations with their lawyers and have at times stood in the position of having to negotiate and interact with their lawyers on their behalves, so I'd include myself in that. The process is almost always more involved and requires more maneuvering than any client would like. And it gets expensive.

But you, the client, have the right to ask questions about your bill or anything else, and your lawyer has a duty to answer them. You also can establish a budget up front and ask your lawyer to advise when you're about to exceed it. Your lawyer's duty to communicate with you is key to their ethical obligations. Communication is key. It's what makes this particular alliance more effective than others in our conflict-prone era.

Your lawyer won't return your calls. We've talked about this. Your lawyer has a duty to communicate with you. If they aren't, then you need to remind them of this. Send them emails. You deserve and are entitled to a response. It is their duty.

If your lawyer isn't responding, you should point this out. In the worst case scenario, again, you can also file a bar or professional complaint. An uncommunicative lawyer can seriously compromise your case. You deserve better than that.

Your lawyer is rude. People are strange, sometimes, and everyone can have a bad day. I know that sometimes people are inclined to believe otherwise, but lawyers are actually human (!). Being human, we can be subject to the same personality quirks, annoying traits, bad habits, and biases as the rest of humanity. The difference with your lawyer is that they can't just get mad at you in a critical part of your case and drop the matter without the judge's permission. As an officer of the court and a fiduciary to you, your lawyer can't let their bad mood, or *your* reaction to their bad mood, or even *your* bad mood determine what happens in your case. They can't just drop you because they're mad (although they probably will be able to drop you if you're not paying them).

That said, you, too, have to provide some cooperation, and you can't let your irritation over what may sometimes be a strained personal dynamic interfere with your duty to provide your lawyer accurate and complete information about your case. Your lawyer doesn't have an obligation to make you feel good or keep you happy (although some are much better than others at managing client sensitivities). Your lawyer's job is to represent you—and if that representation is going to be effective, you're going to have to cooperate with each other.

Your lawyer lets stuff slip through the cracks. Your lawyer owes you a duty of care. If you find that they aren't paying attention to you, ask them if there is a reason they are ignoring critical details. Since you're the one providing the information about the facts of the case to your lawyer in the first place, ask to review important filings before they are filed with the court, so that you can determine whether and to what extent your lawyer is assimilating the information you're providing. If you find a lot is missing, ask why.

Your lawyer won't always do what you say. You and your lawyer are a team, not a Wild West posse or a lawless gang. Your lawyer's job is not to blindly parrot your outrage—it is to determine whether there is any good faith basis for it and to obtain for you, within the bounds of the law and their legal obligations, any potential remedies to which you may be entitled. Sometimes that will mean that they won't play tit for the tat your opponent is dishing out, and sometimes they won't fight back in the way you want them to. Sometimes it would be inappropriate, but if you want to know why they aren't following your direction on strategy, ask. You're entitled to an answer.

Certain decisions are *yours* – such as whether to settle a case. Your lawyer may provide recommendations, even strong ones, but the final decision is yours, as I'll discuss next.

Your lawyer is pressuring you to do things you don't want to. This really depends on what it is you don't want to do. If the "thing" you don't want to do is to show up and take the deposition, then your lawyer *should* pressure you since there can be consequences for refusing to cooperate in discovery. What if your lawyer is pressuring you to settle? The decision is yours—you are the client—but it is your lawyer's job to explain to you the pros and cons of settling as well as of moving forward. Still, you can't be made to do something you don't want to do. You may later regret having agreed to whatever it is, whether it's settling or pressing forward, but remember that the decision is yours in the first instance. Your lawyer has an obligation to present any settlement offer to you and the decision whether to take it is *yours*.

(Also, remember that if you end up agreeing to a settlement—and you've indicated in that document that you read and discussed it with your lawyer, as many settlement agreements do, you'll be held to those words. Sometimes people will later regret their agreements—*my lawyers rushed me through it; my lawyer didn't explain; I thought that it would still let me pursue some other claims; it was a bunch of legalese and I didn't read it carefully*—but deep regret is not a basis for unwinding the deal. You will be assumed to have read and reviewed the documents just as the agreement says you did, and proving otherwise may be an uphill battle.)

Your lawyer keeps losing. What is your case about? Have they advised you of risks that you're ignoring? Have you provided them everything that they need to respond to the issues before the court? Look, sometimes great lawyers with great cases lose. The judge could decide the other side's witnesses were more believable; could refuse to admit evidence because they think it's too prejudicial; or could otherwise exercise the broad discretion that judges have to make a ruling or decision unfavorable to you. It's not necessarily your attorney's fault.

What if your lawyer really is incompetent? If you find that your lawyer is missing critical details, you need to write things down; detail what you believe your lawyer is missing, and insist on a response. Confirm that they've got everything they need from you and that you've answered all questions.

Of course, you always have the option of firing your lawyer and hiring another before they do too much damage. Your lawyer has an obligation to turn over their files to your new counsel; they can't simply hold your case hostage if you're in the middle of a dispute.

YOUR LAWYER CAN'T
JUST LEAVE YOU HANGING

ABA Model Rules of Professional Conduct 1.16(d) provides:

Upon termination of representation, a lawyer shall take steps to the extent reasonably practicable to protect a client's interests, such as giving reasonable notice to the client, allowing time for employment of other counsel, surrendering papers and property to which the client is entitled and refunding any advance payment of fee or expense that has not been earned or incurred. The lawyer may retain papers relating to the client to the extent permitted by other law. However, in the event you still owe your lawyer money, they may in some circumstances be able to assert a lien for unpaid fees and retain your file if doing so won't prejudice your case.[7]

If you feel you need to go further and take legal action against your lawyer, you should know that the standard for suing them is really high. You have to show not only that they made a mistake, but that the particular mistake was a material factor in your loss.[8] You'll have to spend time ruling out other factors that may have contributed to your defeat.[9] When there are a lot of factual questions before the judge that allow her to exercise her discretion as to what she'll do, or who she'll believe, there can end up being many bases for why your loss happened. Do everything you can on the front end to make sure you're giving your lawyer all the necessary facts; make sure your lawyer has in fact received and digested those facts; and understand and confirm whether and how those facts will be used in the various pleadings you'll be filing with the court.

The case is taking much longer than your lawyer told you it would, and in turn costing much more money than you expected. Hi. Welcome to my book. That is why I wrote it.

They're letting the other side get away with everything! They're not fighting hard enough! During the course of your case, there will be a lot of strategic decisions made about what claims to pursue; what to do about obstructive and harassing conduct; how to respond to the other side's evasive and, perhaps according to you, untrue discovery answers; and the like. One of the things I want to point out in this book is that the court system, for all of its beauty in attempting to protect us from each other's arbitrary and unfair behavior, is a system where people get away with all kinds of nonsense because the system just isn't equipped to deal with it all.

Chasing all the bad antics in which your opponent may engage can protract matters. Whether it serves your ends is something only your lawyer can tell you but, as I'll explain in the chapter on sanctions, do not expect to be reimbursed all the money you spent seeking justice for bad behavior.

Know also that your lawyer may have been down this road before. They may have a strategy for getting you what you want which, while perhaps not emotionally satisfying to you, might be effective in meeting your objectives. Some lawyers find that taking things down a notch and keeping things civil can be far more beneficial to their clients, as a lawyer friend of mine once pointed out in a social media post:

> I received a call today from opposing counsel, agreeing to accept our insurance policy-limits settlement demand for a considerable amount of money. Before he accepted the offer, he said, I want to thank you for being civil and helpful moving this case along— It made it easier for me to want to go to bat for you with the Insurance company to get you your full demand.
>
> I really appreciated that feedback and affirmation of my style. I've long believed that humanizing my clients, and treating opposing counsel as partners in solving a problem, even when they are hellbent against that and doubled down on oppositional positioning, is the best way to resolve disputes. I can be your adversary, and at the same

time work with you to tee up the fight. Humanity in the practice of law is possible. Being kind, polite, and cooperative can go hand in hand with being a fierce advocate and champion for your client.

It was just nice to hear that feedback from an adversary (and to make a bunch of money, and get a great result for my client during some pretty shaky times).

Humanize the practice of law!

There can be an upside to being nice and playing fairly. Still, everyone doesn't always do that. Make sure your lawyer explains the upsides and downsides to various strategies and why he is or isn't doing something. Remember, this is *your* case.

In short, you and your lawyer are a team and is as true of any team, you will need to rely on each other. Know the boundaries of the relationship and the rules by which you both are governed. Most importantly, keep your eye on your case and don't let anything distract you from that. If you have to move on from the relationship you should, but make sure your case is protected.

What You Can Do: Some Tips for Working with Your Lawyer

- Get your evidence together—or at least, as much as you can—before your first meeting or consultation with your lawyer. It will help them better evaluate your case and give you a better sense about what it will require going forward.
- Be realistic. I know you saw that television ad; or read that article; or saw the social media post about the lawyer who received that through-the-roof-gravity-defying verdict; or the lawyer who "got someone off" of what seemed to be an airtight set of claims; but don't assume that same magic will happen for you. Every case is

different. Pay attention to the cautions about your case that your lawyer provides.

- On that note, thicken up your skin. Your lawyer may tell you some things about your case that you don't want to hear. Listen to them anyway. And remember, it's usually in your best interest to be candid with your lawyer so you don't have to deal with any (potentially expensive and time consuming) problems later. The duty of communication, which I'll discuss in more detail below, goes both ways.

TO SUM UP . . .

- Don't assume that it will be easy to get a lawyer, even if you've got what you think is a very good case. Your "good" case might end up being a "long" case, for which recovery is uncertain and into which a lawyer may not want to invest their time, which is the only commodity they have to sell.
- Remember that your lawyer has a duty to communicate with you. There is almost no chain of communication more important during your case than the one between you and your lawyer. Your lawyer is a soldier going into the field to do battle for you. The information you provide is her weapon. Don't send her out unarmed.
- Be prepared to deal with conflicts with your lawyer as they come up. You may shy away from talking to them too much since it's conversation for which you normally have to pay. Still, those expensive chats can reduce the likelihood of misunderstandings later and can also minimize the chance of things slipping through the cracks.
- Make sure your lawyer is exploring options for getting you out of this mess, in a satisfactory way, as you go forward.
- And in the middle of all this, don't forget that it's never too late to try to work it out.

THE DECIDERS: JUDGE AND JURY

Can the Judge and Jury Just Do Whatever They Want?

No.

This is one of the reasons why, for all of its shortcomings and imperfections, we should appreciate our court system. It is one of the few institutions where there is (usually) some dispassionate mechanism for holding people accountable. Their court decisions (usually and ideally) are not based on whether they'll generate a lot of "likes."

You understand how important this is. Some problems—whether large or small—will fester or persist because there aren't enough people to do anything about them. Whether it's a longstanding problem involving a national policy or a longstanding problem involving a neighborhood conflict, some things go on as long as they do because not enough people are willing to take a stand against them.

Perhaps your lawsuit, or your response to someone else's, is an effort to take a stand for something. If nothing else, perhaps it's a stand for your right not to be subject to someone's unfair treatment—whether it be their attempt to dodge some obligation you believe they owe you, or to impose upon you one you don't.

What do you want when you're in the middle of such a conflict? Someone who holds up their finger to the wind and decides your fate based on what would be pleasing to the most? Someone who simply passively observes a no-holds-barred conflict and announces the winner as the last person standing? Would you mind if the decision-maker was indebted to or in partnership in some way with your antagonist? If you're in a dispute with your neighbor, would you trust someone on his payroll to resolve the thorny issues between you two? What about his mom?

A system for resolving our many fights with one another will only have credibility to the extent it is perceived as objective and fair. Otherwise, what's the point?

When you're fighting in court, the judge is one of the two most important decision-makers you'll have. (The other one is the jury—but as I'll discuss later, it's the judge who controls what information ultimately gets to them.)

You may think that she is nice, or mean, or warmly empathetic, or callously brutal, but there is something you are supposed to be able to expect from your judge regardless of their personality or mood: fairness and objectivity. How judges decide the matters before them have a significant impact on how you should think about and present your case.

What You Should Know: Judges

Civil cases, as I've explained before, may be heard in state or federal court. Federal judges are nominated by the president and confirmed by the Senate.

PICKING JUDGES

When the president submits a candidate to fill a federal court vacancy, the Senate Judiciary Committee must first consider and approve the candidate, after which the nomination goes to the full Senate for a vote.

As part of the Senate's role to provide "advice and consent" on judicial appointments, the Judiciary Committee has sometimes relied on a "blue slip" procedure. In that process, the chair of the committee sends a "blue slip" to the senators from the nominee's home state; those senators then can return the slip with either a positive or a negative response about the nominee. (Alternatively, the senators can withhold the slip, which is understood to reflect an objection to the candidate.) In some instances, the chair of the Judiciary Committee has refused to give a judicial nominee a hearing if the nominee's home state senators either don't return the blue slip or return it with a negative response: Senator Pat Leahy, for example, who chaired the Judiciary Committee during President Obama's tenure, would not advance nominees who did not have two positive blue slips. During his two presidential terms, President Obama made 334 judicial appointments.

Blue slips have not, however, always been so dispositive, nor does the Senate always adhere to the practice. Under Senator Mitch McConnell, majority leader during President Trump's tenure and majority leader as of the time of this writing, return of the blue slip is not required in order to advance a judicial nominee. At the time of this writing, President Trump has made 200 judicial appointments before completing one presidential term.

The Senate also has had different rules for how many votes are required to confirm judges. At one point, 60 votes (out of 100) were required to end debate on a nominee and proceed to a vote. (Nominations could be held up by use of the "filibuster," in which senators debate as long as they can so as to avoid voting.) In 2013, then-Senate Majority Leader Harry Reid spearheaded a change in the rules in which a simple majority vote of 51 votes could end a fili-buster on most federal judicial nominations, although that did not apply to nominations to the Supreme Court. For those nominations, 60 votes were still required to end a filibuster and proceed to a vote on confirmation.

In 2017, under Senator McConnell's leadership, the rules were changed so that 51 votes could break a filibuster of a Supreme Court nomination, allowing a nominee to proceed to a confirmation vote with the support of a simple majority of senators.[1]

Federal judges are never elected—they are always appointed—and their status as symbols of the "Big Government" can some-times make them the subject of ire by those with big platforms: the "Unelected Judge As Enemy of the People," as it were. Still, it's important to remember that these judges have the job of standing up for the Constitution—which protects We, the Peo-ple—even when that puts them at odds with the executive who appointed them. In *United States v. Nixon*,[2] for instance, a unani-mous Supreme Court held that President Nixon could not with-hold secret recordings made in the Oval Office when those tapes were pertinent to a criminal investigation; in that case, the Court made clear that the president of the United States is not above the law.[3] Three of the Justices who joined in that unanimous opinion, including then-Chief Justice Warren Burger, were Nixon appointees. (Justice Rehnquist, who had served in the Nixon ad-ministration as Assistant Attorney General, recused himself from the case.)

Sometimes, however, court decisions can ring with tones of the same partisanship that sounds so loudly elsewhere. We won't all agree about what constitutes "justice" and what constitutes "parti-sanship," but at least we can take some solace in our government's system of checks and balances, which can help keep everyone's ex-cesses at bay.

NO FIRE FOR FIRE

Judges can't really talk back and fight fire with fire. That's why it's so easy to pick on them in public. Someone can blame a sitting judge for just about anything and the rules of judicial conduct require that judge, for the most part, not to respond or to tell them anything that they may or may not need to hear.

ABA Model Code of Judicial Conduct 2.10 (A) generally prohibits extrajudicial statements. "A judge shall not make any public statement that might reasonably be expected to affect the outcome or impair the fairness of a matter pending or impending in any court, or make any nonpublic statement that might substantially interfere with a fair trial or hearing."

However, "a judge may respond directly or through a third party to allegations in the media or elsewhere concerning the judge's conduct in a matter." (Rule 2.10 (E)). Any such response preferably should come from a third party. "Depending upon the circumstances, the judge should consider whether it may be preferable for a third party, rather than the judge, to respond or issue statements in connection with allegations concerning the judge's conduct in a matter." (Comment 3) So far, about half the states have adopted this exception.[4]

Here's the thing—regardless of who you are or what side of whatever aisle you may or may not sit, there has been a moment in history where you're probably glad some "unelected judges" kept the "majority" (or whoever was counted as such) at bay. I focus on the "unelected" judges because their status makes them easy targets for disdain, as if their lifetime appointment means they can simply make up new rules as they go along. They cannot. They are pretty tightly constrained, among the primary constraints being the directive to avoid "arbitrariness," a horrible thing about which I've already said quite a bit. Their lifetime appointment makes sure they aren't overly vulnerable to popular will, which has sometimes sought to run roughshod over people.

Have a small business and find it difficult to turn a profit? Be happy that those unelected judges told FDR during the Great Depression, when nearly one-quarter of Americans were out of work and desperate to make ends meet, that the government couldn't force you to charge certain below-market prices in order to help stabilize the economy.[5] Live in public housing? You might appreciate the fact that those unelected judges said police couldn't just burst into your home whenever they felt like it.[6] Feeling like giving a prayer of thanks in the mall? Then also give thanks to the unelected judges who said that you must be allowed to pray in public places if you choose.[7] Feel like watching porn? Before you do that (and whatever else it is you're going to do), perhaps you should be thankful that some unelected judges told the government that it can't block channels against your wishes just because it doesn't want you to see things it finds offensive.[8]

Those "unelected judges" have been sticking their noses into all kinds of business. There have been any number of moments when a whole bunch of people could be counted upon to do something terrible and it was only the unelected judges who kept them at bay. We don't even have to fight about what those "terrible" things were because majorities on all sides of every aisle have been inclined to do "terrible" things ever since, well, forever. Some of them have been particularly terrible—more terrible than others.

(This is why it's important to pay attention to the decision-making process and priorities of the elected officials who nominate judges— and why it's important to cast your vote and make yourself heard when those elected officials stand for office.)

Anyway, thank you, unelected judges, for doing what you can to protect civilization.

State Court Judges

State court judges may be either appointed or elected. Either the governor, the legislature, or a nominating commission of the state in which the court sits is responsible for appointing state judges. State court judges who are appointed may have to stand for subsequent election in order to keep their seats. And just so we're clear, state court judges have played their own role in protecting civilization—both in terms of addressing "big picture" issues and in resolving the micro-conflicts that are so common to many. Micro-conflicts can go macro fast. Where would we be if we didn't have some unbiased referees?

READING IS FUNDAMENTAL— TO DEMOCRACY (AND CIVILIZATION!)

Some state courts have gone further than the U.S. Supreme Court and have held there is, for instance, a fundamental right to an education. California, Texas, Kentucky, New Jersey, Tennessee, and Pennsylvania are among them.[9] It does seem like a literate population is a pretty basic requirement for a democratic republic like ours. Otherwise we'd just have to take our leaders' word for things and that's not always an approach that works out very well for us.

All judges are subject to rules regarding impartiality and objectivity that are more stringent than those governing almost any other institution with decision-making power over your life.

Judges who run for office are under stricter rules than are others who campaign. They can't take money from contributors with cases pending in the court to which they're seeking election. Judges running for judicial office "shall not engage in political or campaign activity that is inconsistent with the independence, integrity, or impartiality of the judiciary." That means that unlike other office seekers, judges can't promise that they're going to do certain things, or deliver particular results, which could indicate that they had a predisposition or a bias toward a position in a particular case (although judges can make promises regarding increasing judicial efficiency and improving administrative functions).

Judges can't lead political organizations, publicly endorse or oppose political candidates, buy tickets to campaign events or attend them.[10] A judge is prohibited from "abus[ing] the prestige of judicial office to advance the personal or economic interests of the judge or others, or allow others to do so."[11] They can't fundraise or donate to political campaigns;[12] use endorsements from political organizations; or personally solicit money or accept campaign contributions (except through what's known as a Rule 4 Committee[13]), or use court resources for judicial election campaign.[14]

Judges can't financially benefit—even indirectly—from the disposition of their cases; in one instance, a court struck down a practice in Louisiana in which bail amounts were used to pay staff salaries and expenses; the practice constituted a conflict of interest, according to the court, creating incentives to set high bail bonds.[15]

BAD JUDGES, NO JUSTICE

When judges violate their duty of impartiality, the consequences can be appropriately harsh. They are held to a high standard because they are our last, best hope of rule enforcement and fair treatment. When they violate that duty, they should be held to task.

In what became known as the "kids-for-cash" scandal, two Pennsylvania judges were alleged to have imposed unduly harsh sentences on juveniles to increase occupancy in for-profit prisons in which they had a financial interest. One of the judges was charged with using his authority to have a county facility closed, and both were accused of sentencing juveniles to these for-profit facilities, even against the recommendation of Juvenile Probation officers. The two were alleged to have been paid millions of dollars. One of the defendants, Judge Michael Conahan, pled guilty to one count of racketeering conspiracy and was sentenced to seventeen-and-a-half years in prison. The second defendant, Judge Mark Ciavarella, went to trial, was convicted on twelve of thirty-nine different counts, and sentenced to twenty-eight years in federal prison.[16] His conviction on charges of racketeering, racketeering conspiracy, and conspiracy to commit money laundering were overturned in 2018 and federal prosecutors decided not to retry Ciavarella on those charges. His fraud-related convictions remained. As of the time of this writing, his lawyers were seeking to reduce his prison sentence while federal prosecutors argued it should stand. Michael Conahan was released in June 2020 on a 30-day furlough that could lead to permanent home confinement for the remainder of his term due to COVID-19 concerns. [17]

Judges can be as fallible as other office-holding humans, and they can engage in the same sorts of abuses that may be found elsewhere.

But you *do* have some protection from their making decisions arbitrarily—perhaps even more than you might have when you're subject to other arbitrary decision-makers. That protection comes in the form of the record that you make in your case. Your record consists of the facts and evidence you and your opponent introduce into it, as well as the legal arguments that you make in court. If there's no justification in the record for what was decided, that can possibly subject the decision to reversal by the appellate court.

Judges have the most discretion when they are evaluating factual questions. Does the court find your story credible? Are your witnesses likely to convince anyone (other than your mother) that they're telling the truth? The judge's decisions about these kinds of things are given a lot of latitude and deference—if you want to successfully challenge them, you'll have to demonstrate to an appellate court that the judge *abused her discretion.* What this means is that the trial judge has a lot of latitude in making certain decisions—about the credibility of witnesses and the admissibility of evidence, for instance—since that judge was closer to the facts and witnessed everything firsthand.

The judge, however, doesn't always have such wide latitude. When it comes to legal questions—such as what law applies to your case or whether you've complied with the applicable statute of limitations—the court of appeal will give the judge's decisions a fresh look. This is called *de novo* review.

There is some discretion, however, that you just can't measure; some decisions that are hard to understand or justify, except by viewing them as examples of some of our worst tendencies and biases. Baffling and troubling things happen in virtually every institution peopled by humans. In court, you maximize your prospects for success by laying a pathway for the judge that will allow her to justify a decision in your favor and by giving her a strong basis for doing what it is you want done.

All of the rules for judges—regarding impartiality; objectivity; having a factual and legal basis for their decisions—impact how you should make your case. Judges aren't supposed to rule in your favor because they like you; or they can't stand your opponent. Instead, you increase your prospects for a favorable ruling when you are prepared to give the court a legal and evidentiary roadmap to precisely where you want to go.

What You Should Know: The Jury

If your case makes it through all the twists and turns of pre-trial process, you may finally end up before a jury. A right to trial by jury does not exist in every civil case[18] and if the parties agree, they can waive a jury trial and instead have a judge decide the matter.

If your case is heard before a jury, you should know that both sides—plaintiff and defendant—play a role in jury selection in a process called *voir dire*. Each party (through their lawyers, if they have them) asks the panel of prospective jurors questions so as to determine whether they judge the case fairly. Both, of course, want to choose people strategically, hoping to select those jurors who they believe will favor their position. They ask questions intended to discover the existence of any actual or potential bias.

Each side is also allowed a certain number of *peremptory challenges*, which are when one side "excuses" a juror for any reason they want. In fact, they don't even have to explain why.

. . . BUT YOU CAN'T TROLL JURORS

The exception, however, is that peremptory challenges may not be exercised so as to exclude jurors because of their race or gender.[19]

The parties are allowed an unlimited number of *challenges for cause*, which are challenges based on something in a juror's response or background that indicate that they won't be able to judge the case fairly. The judge will then do her own inquiry and make a finding as to whether the potential juror should be excused from the case.

The judge will instruct the jury to follow the law and to consider only the evidence that is presented at trial. If you or your lawyer think that a juror's experience or background suggests they won't be fair and want to challenge them for cause, the judge may dig deeper. The judge may ask the juror if they believe they can follow the judge's instructions in the case (including the instructions to follow the law as the judge explains it), and whether the juror will consider only the evidence that is presented in court. If the juror says they will, don't be surprised if the judge takes their word for it. The judge may not share your views about who will and won't be fair.

All that pre-trial maneuvering has a purpose: each side wants to narrow the issues that end up going before the jury. If there is evidence that is unduly prejudicial to one party, they may seek to exclude it by filing a *motion in limine,* in which they may ask the judge to limit or exclude any mention of the prejudicial evidence at trial.

Importantly, each side also wants the judge to give the jury instructions that will help frame the jurors' thinking about the case in the way that's as advantageous to their position as possible. Sometimes disputes about instructions can give rise to yet another front in what may already feel like a perpetual war.

When arguing for the instructions each side wants, the lawyers will reference the record that the parties have established in the case so as to justify their preferred position. Where a plaintiff has presented no evidence of a defendant's malicious, outrageous, or grossly negligent conduct (elements necessary to justify an award for punitive damages), for instance, a defendant may argue that the jury instructions for calculating damages shouldn't take the defendant's net worth into account (because net worth may be relevant only where there is a basis for a punitive damage claim).[20] Similarly, if a defendant has produced no evidence that the plaintiff caused his own injuries, the plaintiff may argue against instructions that ask the jury to consider whether and to what extent the plaintiff was responsible for his own harm.[21]

You and your lawyer aren't allowed to talk to the jury or otherwise communicate with them directly during the trial. Your job simply is to make your case. Your ammunition with the jury is the same as that with the judge: presenting a story, supported by facts, that leads the jurors in the direction of where you want them to go. *Of course* you want them to "like" you; of course you want to get the non-verbal cues that may indicate people are listening to and believe you (e.g., eye contact) but you can't rely on any of those things. The best weapon you have in your case is the evidence and your ability to explain clearly why it shows you should win.

What You Can Do:
Be Prepared and Be Flexible

Every trial, like every case that gives rise to it, is different. All of the discovery and pre-trial maneuvering you endured was intended to put you in the best situation possible for this, the main event.

That said, don't be surprised if the trial is subject to some of the same uncertainties and delays that factor into so many other parts of your case. Witness testimony may be longer or shorter than expected. You may have to interrupt the proceedings so the judge can deal with an urgent matter in another case. Or, you may have to interrupt the proceedings so that the judge can resolve some dispute about the evidence or testimony that came up in trial, and the dispute will need to be resolved outside the presence of the jury. Any variety of things can happen. Court is uncertain.

By the way, just because the trial has started, that doesn't mean it's too late to work it out.

TO SUM UP . . .

- Judges aren't perfect, but they are held to stricter rules than are many decision-makers. You also have a means, the record, for keeping track of judicial decisions and holding judges accountable for them.

- Judges have a lot of discretion, although not absolute discretion, in deciding factual questions. What this means is that *you* have to give a lot of thought to the factual path you are laying in order to lead them to your win. You have to give the judge reasons to rule in your favor and do all you can to make it hard for them not to. There may be matters within the judge's discretion over which you have little control, such as who the judge ultimately determines is more credible in the case—but if you want to make your case, you have to give the court compelling, non-arbitrary reasons to rule in your favor.

- The judge very likely will, at some point, ask if you've tried to work it out. In fact, she'll probably order you to give it another shot even if you've already tried. Try.

- You will have the chance to participate in jury selection with your lawyers. Do so. Let the jury see you and you, too, should have a sense of who the people are who will be evaluating and judging your case.

- Remember, the point of all that (expensive) pre-trial maneuvering you did was to whittle the issues down so that the jury can get the most favorable version of the story from which to decide as possible. That doesn't mean, however, that new things won't come up and that the trial won't take twists, turns, and time you hadn't previously expected.

- One of the best strategies with decision-makers like these—who are held accountable for adhering to the law and basing their judgments on facts—is to make sure you've buttoned up your case as much as you can. Pay close attention to the twists and turns at trial so you'll know on what you'll need to focus their attention. Holding judges and juries accountable for their decisions can best be done if you've provided them a roadmap which leads to the result you want.

- *No, it's not too late to work it out.*

PART III

The Laws and Lawlessness of Uncovering the "Truth"

There are some hard things that crossed Isabella's life while in slavery, that she has no desire to publish, for various reasons. First, because the parties from whose hands she suffered them have rendered up their account to a higher tribunal, and their innocent friends alone are living, to have their feelings injured by the recital; secondly, because they are not all for the public ear, from their very nature; thirdly, and not least, because, she says, were she to tell all that happened to her as a slave—all that she knows is 'God's truth'—it would seem to others, especially the uninitiated, so unaccountable, so unreasonable, and what is usually called so unnatural, (though it may be questioned whether people do not always act naturally,) they would not easily believe it. 'Why, no!' she says, 'they'd call me a liar! they would, indeed! and I do not wish to say anything to destroy my own character for veracity, though what I say is strictly true.'"

—*The Narrative of Sojourner Truth,* by Sojourner Truth

6

COLLECTING EVIDENCE

Pulling the Pieces of Your Story Together in Discovery

When you go to court, you're going to have to pull apart that Heaping Mass of Problem and explain how the troubles that comprise it relate to your claims and defenses. You have to dissect your story and give the factfinder a basis for believing you.

Discovery is where you get the evidence to make your case. It's also where your opponent seeks to get evidence that will undermine *your* case and make *theirs*. There are probably some things you'd probably like to keep to yourself but when you're fighting in court, they may become your opponent's business, too.

What You Should Know: Discovery

There are different types of discovery:

Form Interrogatories. These are preprinted form questions approved by the judicial council of the jurisdiction in which your litigation is taking place. They collect basic information about you and your case.

Special Interrogatories. These are questions that are specifically tailored to get more detailed information about a party's claims and defenses. For instance, if you are suing someone claiming that they damaged your kitchen counters while they were installing new cabinets, you could propound special interrogatories to ask them about what, specifically, they were doing that day; had they consumed any liquor; how many other projects did they have scheduled that day; and how much time they spent on your project.

Requests for Admission. These are propounded as statements that the recipient must either admit or deny. For instance, if you were trying to establish that your wedding dress designer breached an agreement to provide your dress on time, you could propound an RFA asking that they "[a]dmit that [they] agreed to provide a dress to [you] on x date." Where a recipient denies the statement, they have to provide some information about that denial.

Request for Production of Documents. These are exactly as they sound—itemized requests that you produce documents related to the topic specified in the request. You'll need to review emails and other correspondence, and make sure that you're not turning over privileged communications or other confidential communications.

(An example of documents that might be "privileged" are communications between you and your lawyer, which would be subject to the attorney-client privilege, or your lawyer's notes and/or analysis of the case, which would be protected by the attorney work product doctrine.) You usually are required to turn over all documents within your "possession, custody or control," which means that just doing a cursory production of the things you have handy is not enough. If the request is unduly burdensome—if someone is seeking documents from time immemorial relating to everything but the name of your first puppy—you can file a motion seeking to limit the request.

Requests for Inspection. This type of discovery allows you to examine and analyze physical evidence that is in the other party's control.

Depositions. This is when the other side's lawyer gets to ask you a variety of questions, usually in a law office conference room. Your lawyer is present, as is a court reporter who will transcribe the questions, your answers, and any other conversation that takes place unless the parties go "off the record."

Your lawyer may object to the question, but that's just for purposes of making a record about the question and the issues it raises, so the lawyers can fight about it later, if and when it comes up in the proceeding. You still have to answer the question, unless your attorney instructs you not to answer.

Subpoenas. When you want someone who isn't a party to the case to show up and testify about something, you have to subpoena them. The subpoena has to be served within a specific period of time before you want the person to show up, so you'll have to do some advance planning.

You should recognize that even people sympathetic to your position, or who say they are, still may be hesitant to show up and testify on your behalf or to provide you the crucial evidence you need. You can't always rely on voluntary compliance. Spending time and money on subpoenas may at some point be unavoidable.

What You Should Do: Buckle Up

"Discovery" involves examining documents; asking and being asked questions that will annoy you and your opponent; cancellations; delays; attempts to get on your nerves so as to discourage you from continuing with the case; attempts to show the other side just how nasty your arsenal is so as to discourage their efforts to get on with the case—and that's just its way of saying "hello." You may be provoked into fights that may make you feel better (for a bit, at least until you get your lawyer's bill) but that don't do much to advance the aims of your case. On the other hand, sometimes in order to advance your aims you have to draw some boundaries for your opponent—who may have less regard for the rules than you do—and rein them in. Perhaps if you don't, they'll simply thumb their noses at you and at the process and make things even more convoluted than they already may be. The process may do nothing to protect you and you'll be left wading through a mess. I can't tell you where those boundaries are since it depends on the nature of your case and your opponent, but it's something you should keep in mind as you plot your way to a resolution that doesn't feel like a loss even if you win.

You May Lose Some Privacy

Privacy is an endangered species. The little we do have is something that most of us try to guard pretty carefully. Our information is everywhere and it's more accessible than many of us would like.

Understand this: a lawsuit is a pass for someone—a person you may seriously dislike—to dig into your life to some extent. In that sense, court is like many other places where people fight—a venue where an opponent can use information about their adversary to hurt the other side or to otherwise gain an advantage over them. In fact, court can be even worse than some other places in this sense, because you *have* to give them some of that information. The reality of a lawsuit—whether you're making a claim against someone or defending against a claim someone is making against you—is that certain personal details of yours, including some potentially embarrassing ones, may become part of the story. You and your opponent can spend an enormous amount of time and obscene sums of money fighting over just which ones. Fortunately, there are limits on obtaining that information and rules for providing it. Also, some states have explicit protections for privacy, which can increase the hurdles over which you have to jump when you want to obtain information.

PRIVACY IS FUNDAMENTAL

The California Constitution expressly guarantees the right of privacy. (Cal. Const. Art. I §1.) While state constitutional privacy protections aren't absolute, they do provide a bulwark against discovery requests that may be too intrusive. In California, for instance, those protections require the person asserting the privacy right to establish the extent of the prospective invasion, which the court will weigh against the need to obtain the requested information. Alaska, Arizona, Florida, Hawaii, Illinois, Louisiana, Montana, New Hampshire, South Carolina, and Washington have explicit privacy protections.[1]

Big fights may happen. The other side will want you to turn over information and you won't want to. Or vice versa. And in order to resolve the issue, you or the other side will need to file motions, wait for a hearing date, and meander down what may be a black hole of time and expense before all is said and done. Yes, you can also file your discovery motions on an emergency or "ex parte" basis, but hopefully you remember what I said earlier about how stingy courts are about granting emergency relief.

It is easy to get drawn into a discovery battle, especially when you feel like the other side is just digging around for information to antagonize or embarrass you. Here's the thing to remember: You are in a lawsuit. Proving that you're entitled to something requires that you show more of your cards than you'd like. While people are entitled to information, they aren't allowed to annoy and harass you. But remember: people have a lot of leeway when they're trying to prove things or defend against them. Just because you think something is embarrassing, too personal, or too intrusive doesn't mean it isn't relevant to your case.

PUTTING IT ALL OUT THERE

You think those emails of yours are embarrassing? In a case where the plaintiff sued a hospital, claiming that a negligently performed hernia operation resulted in his being sterile, the court held that the defendants were entitled to test his semen—again—even though he'd already submitted his own specimen: "While it is true that the manner in which a semen analysis is taken may be embarrassing and may even be humiliating, the defendants cannot be precluded from such an objective and decisive test in the face of this serious claim, which is allegedly permanent in nature."[2]

You May Have to Fight It Out

Obviously, discovery isn't as simple as just sending out questions and then getting answers. Sometimes the other side refuses to answer.

Perhaps they don't produce documents that they are required to turn over.

In some jurisdictions, there is a requirement that the parties "meet and confer" before taking discovery disputes to the judge. This is another example of how courts seek to encourage people to work things out—although if you're represented by a lawyer you should recognize that "working it out" can mean paying your attorney to write long letters detailing the basis of your objection and explaining why your opponent should accept a compromise, perhaps, or just back off entirely. These letters, however, can come in handy if you want to demonstrate to the judge that you made a good faith effort to resolve things. They also might provide a good defense to a claim by the other side that you were improperly withholding information, or improperly demanding it. Communications between the lawyers all can become a part of "the record" in the case, and they can be used to either support or undermine the arguments that you end up having before the judge. Making an effort to ensure they are effective can increase your prospect of getting some sanction or fine against the other side for engaging in bad faith tactics, or defending against a claim that you were acting in bad faith.

Sometimes the meet-and-confer requirement can help the parties narrow the issue or even resolve it. The meet-and-confer can take place in writing, with each party explaining to the other the bases of their positions as they try to work it out amongst themselves.

Painful as they can be, these fights are sometimes necessary. If you let the other side get away with not turning over evidence, for example, you may lose access to material that could be really good for your case, and your opponent might not even have a good reason for not giving it to you. (Or they might. That's why you meet and confer first and try to work it out.) In other words, don't assume that your opponent will play fair and comply with their obligations as the rules require.

If the parties are unable to work it out, one side or the other might file what is known as a "motion to compel." We've already discussed motions; in this instance, it's a motion where you explain the nature of the discovery dispute before the judge and ask for a resolution—and you'll usually have to explain to the judge that you tried to resolve it before bringing the motion to court.

You can also ask for sanctions—payment of your fees and expenses—which the judge may order if she finds that one side brought the motion for no reason, or that the other side had no good reason for refusing to provide the information sought. I'll discuss sanctions in more detail later, when I discuss bad faith conduct. Remember, however, that you shouldn't rely on being made completely whole, even if you do manage to get some relief.

When will the depositions happen? Are you going to provide another extension because the other side says they have pressing business matters? Court rules require lawyers and parties to cooperate with each other in a reasonable way and not to make things more expensive and difficult than they should be. They are supposed to meet and confer, be reasonable, and avoid escalating things for no reason.

Good luck with that.

When you're fighting in court, the burden of rule-breaking usually falls harder on the victim than the rule breaker. While there are supposed to be penalties for bad conduct, as I've said repeatedly, don't expect those penalties to compensate you fully for the hassle and inconvenience of having your schedule put through a paper shredder.

Discovery is a part of your lawsuit where all sorts of gamesmanship (or more accurately, *nonsensica*) can happen. Yes, there are rules against that. Yes, you are supposed to "meet and confer" when there are disputes. You may even narrow the matters in dispute or you might actually resolve it.

Sometimes that just won't be possible. Some litigants are as committed to their discovery abuse as other people are committed to chocolate. The difference is that chocolate isn't always bad. Discovery abuse, by contrast, *is*—it's when one party misuses the process or ignores their obligations, resulting in their opponent spending time and money unnecessarily.

> Your lawyer sends a letter to the other side, requesting dates for depositions of key people.
>
> Nearly a month goes by with no response. So, your lawyer sets the dates unilaterally.
>
> You ask your opponent, a company, to identify its corporate representatives who are most knowledgeable on a variety of subjects.

Sometimes, when you're suing a company, you may not know which employee or officer is the person with the most information about the specific topics you're addressing in discovery. When that is the case, you can serve a deposition notice for the "Person Most Knowledgeable" on a particular topic.

> The company still doesn't identify those officers.
>
> You have scheduled a deposition for one of the company's employees, Witness 1. Less than 24 hours before the deposition is scheduled to begin, the company cancels, claiming that Witness 1 is too sick. You agree to move the deposition to a date three weeks later.
>
> You've also noticed a deposition for Witness 2, another company employee. The company files a Motion to Quash the deposition. However, the company missed the deadline for filing the motion to quash, so the court denies the motion as untimely. The company agrees to produce Witness 2.

When you want to challenge something the other side is trying to force you to do in discovery, like show up for a deposition, you can file what is known as a Motion to Quash or a Motion for a Protective Order. These are motions asking the court to limit or excuse your obligation to respond.

In order to do this, however, you have to file your motion within a certain period of time after the request is made. The dates may vary by jurisdiction. (In California, for example, a party must serve the Motion to Quash on the opposing side at least five days before the scheduled date for producing documents. In Florida, on the other hand, a party seeking to quash a subpoena must file their motion within fourteen days of the subpoena request.[3] Once again, you should always be careful to check the rules in the jurisdiction where your case is or may be pending.)

> Having lost the Motion to Quash, the company says it will produce Witness 2 for deposition in January. You agree.

So now, finally, you're going to get this discovery train going! Finally! Yes, well, not exactly . . .

> You've also served a deposition notice for Witness 3. The company's lawyer is going on vacation. You agree to postpone Witness 3's deposition for a week and a half to accommodate opposing counsel's holiday travel.

By the way, you may not want to be so accommodating—you might be thinking that the other side has been playing too many games as it is, so *%$#! opposing counsel's vacation. Your lawyer, however, may suggest to you that you'll look bad to the judge if you refuse the extension and force your opponent to file a motion on the issue. Remember, the parties are *supposed* to cooperate with each other when it comes to these types of scheduling matters.

> Less than 24 hours before Witness 3's deposition is to happen—now that the lawyer is back from vacation—the company cancels, claiming a work emergency. The deposition is then rescheduled a month and a half later.
>
> Less than 24 hours before Witness 3's rescheduled deposition is to

happen, the company cancels again, claiming yet another work emergency. The deposition is rescheduled for over a month later.

Now it's January. Less than 24 hours before Witness 2's deposition is to occur—remember, this is the witness whose deposition was the subject of the untimely Motion to Quash and who the company said it would produce to testify. The company cancels again, claiming . . . yet another work emergency.

It's now less than 24 hours before Witness 3 is to testify yet again. Guess what? The company cancels, claiming—you guessed it—a work emergency. The company says it will produce him a month later. You serve another deposition notice for the agreed-upon date, but the company cancels again.

These shenanigans didn't go over well with the court. The judge sanctioned the company for the reasonable and necessary attorneys' fees you incurred and orders the company to present the difficult-to-obtain witnesses within thirty days.

Again, you never know what will happen in your case or what a specific judge may (or may not) do, but there can be serious penalties for discovery misconduct.

You operate a clothing boutique. To keep better track of your clients, you maintain customized profiles of your clients' purchasing habits and style preferences. (Not only does this make the shopping experience fun and efficient for your clients but it also allows you to focus your purchasing on items most likely to sell.) Your team developed algorithms that will help predict your client's future purchasing habits. A big part of your employee training program involves showing your key employees how to use these algorithms.

Your business is going through the roof! One of your competitors, Rose, wants in. *Why reinvent the wheel?* Rose thinks. Instead, she hires away two of your key employees—the ones with primary responsibility for updating the algorithms that make your client profiles so successful. Not only that, Rose also wants your client profiles and your algorithms, so your two former employees upload key information onto external drives and deliver the information to Rose.

One of your clients tells you that Rose has offered that client a customized styling service similar to yours. You're suspicious. You're also not stupid. Putting two and two together, you sue Rose and your former employees for stealing your trade secrets.

During discovery, both Rose and your former employees deny accessing any of your confidential and proprietary information. *Of course we didn't take your confidential files! Upload them and remove them from your business computer? What nonsense! Poppycock!* they insist.

In this situation, "poppycock" might be loosely translated as "yes we did it but you can't prove it."

As it turned out, however, only half that sentence was true.

Fortunately for you, you have the funds to hire a computer forensic expert. Not only did your former employees upload your proprietary client information, but they also destroyed the transmittal documents that verified the time and date of the upload.

Sometimes the penalty for discovery abuse goes beyond a monetary remedy.

Your lawyers are on it. They bring the issue before the judge, and she awards you *issue sanctions*. This means that instead of having to pay you money as a sanction, the judge makes an adverse finding against the other side which results in a benefit to you.

Think of it as a yardage penalty, if you're into football. (I'm not, really, and am pretty proud of myself for coming up with that analogy. Anyway...)

The issue sanctions included a finding that Rose and her colleagues had, in fact, improperly destroyed evidence. The jury was allowed to consider this fact in determining the credibility of Rose's position. It didn't help. Not only did the jury find against Rose, but it also awarded you punitive damages.

So what happens if you mess up, and don't provide something that you're required to turn over? You may get in trouble, or you may catch a break.

The Artist created a special line of wine bottles. He entered into a deal with the Dancer to base one of the bottles on a pose that was one of her more dazzling onstage contortions.

As sometimes happens with deals, this one didn't work out. The Dancer's representatives didn't like it anymore. The Artist shrugged it off—one difficult dancer wasn't going to kill his entire project. So the Artist went forward with his new line of bottles.

The Dancer was incensed. One of those bottles looked just like her! She sued the Artist for violation of her right of publicity, claiming he was improperly seeking to monetize her image without her consent.

Discovery battles ensued as the Dancer requested that the Artist produce information regarding every design he had ever made. His lawyers thought the request was absurd and objected. The Dancer moved to compel, and she won. The Artist still didn't comply. It was just too much. The judge awarded sanctions against the Artist for his non-compliance.

Enter Artist's new lawyer, who explains why the discovery questions was overreaching. He argues to the court that it has been more focused on whether the trains were running on time than on what was inside the compartments.

The court agrees with him, and reverses its sanctions order and limits the scope of allowable discovery.

The trial court has a lot of leeway when it comes to managing and resolving these kinds of issues. You usually have to give it a good reason to change its mind over something like this, and in this instance, the Artist's new lawyer convinced the court that complying with the request would handicap his ability to get any other work done.

Discovery battles can take up an extraordinary amount of your time and can force you to spend amounts of money that might break your bank. Their outcomes can be uncertain. It may seem obvious to you that your opponent should comply with a request, but the judge may think the request too burdensome, or that there are easier, less intrusive ways of getting the information. You never know what's going to happen. There are so many ways in which this part of the process can add to the time and expense of your case that it would be impossible for me to consider even half of them here.

Special Masters

In some situations, a "special master" might be appointed in order to resolve discovery issues. The parties may have to pay the special master's fees (who in their right mind would want to get in the middle of your discovery fight for free?) but having one on board can help expedite troublesome discovery issues.

You'll Spend More Money Than You Want

You probably don't want to be in court at all, so *any* money you spend is more than you want to. But as you can see from some of the examples above, discovery is where every kind of fight can and probably will happen.

What happens if the court orders you to turn over a collection of documents, some of which you contend are private and irrelevant to the lawsuit? Maybe there's a page containing information that tells the other side more than (you think) they need to know or is otherwise too private. Sure, you can redact it—but be prepared to justify the redaction or fight over that, too.

Need to change a deposition date because you're traveling? Was that a preplanned/prepaid trip or did you make travel arrangements on the assumption that your annoying lawsuit could take a backseat to the rest of your life? (You may end up fighting over that, too.)

Those fights cost money, usually money that comes out of your pocket.

Usually, but not always.

You have more money than you can spend. So does Wyatt, whose company is your opponent in litigation. You hate Wyatt, Wyatt hates you, and your lawyers—each of whom realizes that you and Wyatt love it when they parrot your outrage—hate each other.

In an unfortunate geographic coincidence, your lawyers and Wyatt's company have offices in the same building.

It's time for Wyatt's company to produce documents. Wyatt's lawyers tell yours to come up in the elevator, look at their documents in their office, and decide what they want to copy.

Your lawyers tell Wyatt's lawyers no, and that they should instead just put them in the elevator and deliver them. Since both you and Wyatt have so much money, you don't mind paying your lawyers to fight about this—each side refusing to give an inch—both of you insistent on making a point. Your lawyers, happy to be paid tons of money to be your proxies in a paper duel, are as vicious with each other as you and Wyatt are hoping they'll be.

Since you can't reach agreement on the issue, you and Wyatt decide to take the issue to the judge.

She's not happy about having to spend time on an issue that she thinks is silly. A bad use of court time, she thinks.

Still, you've brought the fight to her door so she has to let you in and fix things. She holds that Wyatt has to deliver the documents, and she orders that he pay the fees you incurred as a result of bringing her what she believes is a ridiculous problem.

She also knows that you and Wyatt don't care about money the way most humans do, and she decides she needs to fashion an order that is going to discourage the parties, and their lawyers, from wasting her time with silly disputes. She issues an order that, in the future, the lawyers themselves would be liable for any fees.

Things settled down then.

It Can Seriously Interfere with the Living of Your Life

Maybe your opponent conjures (or actually has) reasons why they can't accommodate your work schedule. Maybe the judge says the trial has to happen within a certain window, in which case if you plan to go forward with your case (as opposed to settling, for example), you may just have to rearrange your whole life so as to accommodate the judge's very crowded calendar.

Or, maybe you've already done that rearranging so as to accommodate other complicated scheduling demands—your lawyer's; your opponent's; their lawyer's. Maybe you postponed a trip or cut one short so that you could manage the litigation schedule. Perhaps you delayed something important so the case didn't interfere. Maybe the other side previously refused to accommodate your scheduling requests, causing you to miss out on something great. Maybe you had to forego an exciting opportunity in order to accommodate the calendaring demands of your jealous lawsuit. (Yes, jealous—your lawsuit will sometimes get in the way of everything else you want to do, and insist that you make it a priority. Discovery is a vehicle for that jealousy—it's like a big pile of *You Must Pay Attention to Me Now or Else.*)

So anyway, let's say you've done all that rescheduling and postponing—and you're ready to show up and play ball—and then, the day before your deposition, the opposing lawyer has to cancel. There's an ex parte hearing in another matter. Or his kid is sick. Or . . . anything.

You're probably thinking—*well, if I'm prepared to show up and be where I'm supposed to be and they aren't, then the case is over, right?* (Wrong.) *I definitely don't have to show up again, do I?* (Also wrong.) *Someone will necessarily compensate me for my wasted time and the inconvenience I've endured as a consequence of having to move something around; or miss something important; or change plane tickets* (or whatever), *right?* (So very, very wrong.)

You'll Let Some Stuff Slide

In addition to withholding witnesses, sometimes the discovery abuse happens when one party withholds documents that the other has specifically requested or that may be pertinent to the claims and defenses at issue in the case. Sometimes parties are inappropriately evasive.

Sometimes parties simply lie. Many discovery responses are made under penalty of perjury; but again, don't expect the police to come barreling through the door, prepared to arrest those who commit the crime of providing false testimony under oath. Perjury is a very hard crime to prove and prosecutions for it are rare.

Making your case sometimes can mean *not* fighting every battle. You don't want to be too depleted to fight to the end, and you want to make sure that when you get there, you're celebrating over more than just a bomb-charred wasteland. I can't tell you where your boundaries are or where they should be—because they will depend on you, your case, and your resources. But you should be prepared for a lot of really frustrating situations to arise.

Let's say you're scheduled to depose your slippery opponent, finally. Your lawyer spent hours ($$$) preparing. You missed a meeting; or an afternoon with your kid; or just some better part of your life, so you could discuss this important deposition with your lawyer.

Then, the day before, your adversary cancels. They claim their kid has an important recital. Or that their roof is caving in. Or whatever.

You're sure they're lying. They have a doctor's note claiming illness, but isn't that doctor their family friend? It's a lie. You're sure it's a stall.

Maybe so, but do you know what it will take to prove it? Are you going to subpoena that doctor and challenge the diagnosis? File an emergency motion with the court? What's the emergency anyway? Do you remember what I said earlier about how courts define "emergencies"? Remember how busy the judge is? Don't be surprised if she's just annoyed that you didn't suck it up and reschedule the deposition at a mutually convenient time. Besides, at some point the other side *must* show up—you can file a motion to compel that does precisely that, compel them to show up. (Plus you can ask the court to award you the attorneys' fees you paid as a result of having to file the motion.)

What difference will another week or so make? the judge might conclude, completely unconcerned about the other side's brutal abuse of your schedule and your time. Rather than punish the other side for lying—or taking the time to dig deeply into whether they really are—don't be surprised if the judge is instead irritated with you for further crowding her docket with a matter that she thinks you should have been able to resolve with your opponent.

There are things worth fighting over and things you should let go. It would be impossible for me to give you any suggestions about which fall into either category because that depends on the nature of your case. Maybe you *do* need to go to court when your opponent cancels a deposition the day before—especially when they don't commit to new dates and/or when they have a pattern of blowing things off or telling transparent and obvious lies. I couldn't tell you. Just know that fighting over every broken rule or bad faith antic will have you feeling very broke, financially and otherwise. Plus, you won't always win those fights. You may be bitterly disappointed when the judge lets the other side get away with really bad conduct, whatever the judge's reasons may be for doing that.

If you know you're in a dispute or likely to be in one, get your materials together sooner rather than later. Don't forget to pay attention to what you *don't* have—are you missing evidence that you believe you may need to prove an important fact?

Recognizing where your evidence is lacking, and doing so sooner rather than later, can help you accommodate and mitigate these deficiencies.

Most importantly, when you're preparing for discovery, keep in mind specifically what you're trying to prove and make sure you have a plan for obtaining that proof. If you have a lawyer, make sure you understand the strategy that they are developing and do your part to give them what they need to respond to the other side. To the extent you can, do your own examination of the facts. Don't just be reactive. Unstrategic reactivity can lead to your going down a brutally expensive and time-consuming hole.

But on the Upside—You'll Pin Some Things Down

In the fights that take place outside of court, people accuse others of things all the time. It's a veritable free-for-all of accusations. The claims that are repeated most loudly and most frequently are often the claims that stick, regardless of whether there are any facts to support them.

Court is supposed to be different. Court is where you prove things, and the way you do that is by conducting discovery—where words matter. The facts are recorded—to be used later and especially at trial—and it's not like it is in other places where someone can pretend they didn't say things they obviously said and then ignore the consequences. In court, words stay alive. They can come back and haunt you. In court, it's much more difficult to gaslight people than it is in other places.

If someone is untruthful in their discovery responses, at least you'll have the chance to pin them down. You'll know which lies to corral and debunk. While some liars keep growing new lies just when the other ones are starting to fall off the vine, in court you'll have a record of that, too, and it may prove useful to you. You can't stop a liar from lying, but you can demonstrate that there are good reasons not to believe them.

What You Should Do—Start Early

You'll have a head start in discovery if you start organizing your case sooner rather than later.

If you're suing someone because they owe you money, for instance, you should compile as much evidence of that debt as you can even before you file your lawsuit—it will better guide you and your lawyers as you determine how you'll make your case. True, discovery is an opportunity to flush out fully the basis of your claims, but if you've started pulling your information together early you'll have a good head start and a better idea of where to go next.

Don't wait until you get the other side's discovery requests to start gathering the information that is pertinent to your claim—you should assume that if you're going to court making a claim or defense of some sort, you're going to have to prove it at some point.

Do you have any evidence of that loan, if that's the matter over which you're suing, for example? And if you're being sued over money you say *never* was a loan, do you have any evidence that it was intended as a gift? (While the plaintiff carries the burden of proof, you should be prepared to defend yourself.) Have you reviewed the emails and correspondence between you and your opponent? You may have to turn some of them over—refreshing yourself about some of the background in your dispute can help you better respond to the other side's inquiries, so take advantage of the chance to do some homework. Don't just look at the favorable stuff—know your weaknesses too because you may have to show some of them.

The information you turn over, what you decide to withhold, and the things about which you decide to fight all will depend on the particular facts and details of your case. Expect the process to take more twists and turns than you'd like. I hope it doesn't, but then again . . . you're going to court, so almost anything can happen.

TO SUM UP . . .

- If you're fighting in court, the other side is entitled to some information about you and your position. It will feel intrusive and you may need to take steps to protect your privacy. Still, being in the lawsuit trenches means you may need to reveal more than you'd like.

- Discovery can make or unmake your case. Withholding documents can result in losing opportunities to present crucial evidence. So can letting your opponent get away with being obstructive without seeking to hold their feet to the fire.

- Pay attention to the other side's responses and pay attention to yours. The facts that you're sharing and receiving in discovery will become key parts of the record in your case. Things may come up that you'll want to explain and/or make use of later. You are the one who has lived the facts of your case, so make sure you are clear on the key admissions and concessions that come out during this part of the process.

- Remember that it won't be productive to fight every battle, even though really annoying, really bad things may happen. Filing discovery motions is sometimes necessary—even critical—but doing so will add time and expense to your case. Make sure you're clear about what you're fighting and what you're not, and why.

- A taste of discovery is sometimes exactly what people need to bring them to the negotiating table.

- You know what I'm going to say next. (It's never too late to try to work it out.)

7

PROVING
YOUR CASE

Why Proving Things Keeps Us Civilized

If you want a court to force someone to do something, or to believe or embrace your position, you should be prepared to present some reasonable justification for why it should. You can't just make stuff up or ask the court to guess. If you could do that—if you could just contrive any old reason why you should get your way without providing any legal or factual basis for why—then court judgments would be based on nothing stronger or more solid than whether the judge woke up on the wrong side of the bed that day, or whether they liked you more than they like your opponent. If those were the rules, we'd be subject to *rule by number of Facebook "likes"* instead of *rule of law*.

Rule of law means that people can't use the machinery of the state—which is what court is—to force others to do things *just because they say so*. Don't take this for granted. "Because I said so" frequently has been used as a basis for controlling others' behavior.

For my part, however, I don't think it's a sustainable basis for decision making on a long-term basis. I'm not alone in that.

Think about how much more difficult it would be to live together if "just because I said so" was a legitimate basis for commanding people to do things. We would have a harder time planning our lives. We wouldn't be able to rely on existing rules and standards as we made our choices. In fact, those rules and standards would essentially be irrelevant. If someone could have their way for no reason other than *just because they said so*, then there'd be little purpose in having any rules at all. We're not supposed to be a *rule-by-whim-or-mood* society. We're supposed to be a *abide-by-rule-of-law society.*

Guarding against arbitrary behavior is a commonsense principle, one that applies in all manner of circumstances. The government can take some of your income, for example, but it can't just make up a number about what your income is.[1] (Arbitrary!) It can award contracts, but it can't favor those who don't comply with the rules for a bid while rejecting those who do.[2] (Arbitrary!) Any number of judicial decisions have made clear that arbitrary decision making is just about the worst kind of decision making there is.

In fact, one of the reasons for going to court in the first place is to get some relief from someone's arbitrary behavior. You loan someone money and there is an understanding they will pay you back—they decide they won't pay you back just because it doesn't suit them. They'd rather use the money for something else. (Arbitrary!)

You pay someone good money to re-tile your bathroom; they decide, in spite of the specific time constraints laid out from the beginning, to use your money for a vacation instead. (Arbitrary!) People often end up in disputes because one side or the other decided to upend the agreed-upon rules and understandings between them for no reason other than it suited them to do so.

Challenging this kind of behavior in court, however, requires you to take a higher road. You have to do more than simply show up and implore the decision-maker to believe you. *Why should I believe you?*

I sometimes ask litigants in our *Hot Bench* courtroom. Sometimes they don't have an answer.

Give the court reasons why a decision in your favor *isn't* arbitrary. The way you do that is by basing your position on as many provable facts as you can. This may seem obvious, but you would be surprised at the number of people who show up in court unprepared to do this. They think that opinions they share really persuasively somehow can substitute for facts. Court, however, doesn't work the way some of our cable news fights do. In court you have to do more.

Remember, the purpose of court is to solve a problem. If you aren't offering facts to support the outcome you're seeking, you'll have no way of knowing whether that outcome will solve the problem at all. You'll just be pulling things out of thin air and wasting your time.

COURT—A REFUGE FROM THE WORLD OF MAKE-BELIEVE (SOMETIMES)

It appears the Flat Earth Movement may be gaining ground.

The "Flat Earth Movement" is not the name of a band. It's a movement organized around the idea that Christopher Columbus would have sailed off the edge of the world if he'd kept going because its followers believe the. Earth. is. flat. At the time of this writing, the Twitter feed for the Flat Earth Society, for instance, has more than 90,000 followers. "Trust your eyes," the Flat Earthers urge us.[3] (I, for one, trust my eyes. I don't trust them to see the "edge" of Earth.)

In other words, different people have different bases and standards for proving and believing things. Whether it's a belief in a flat Earth; in vaccines causing autism; in women not being good at math; or in a global pandemic being a grand hoax—people always can find a way to justify the ideas that appeal to them, regardless of the facts on which those ideas are based.

Sometimes, when people think they're offering "proof" of something, what they really are offering is little more than a thinly disguised version of "because I say so" or "because I choose to believe this." (Sometimes it's not so thinly disguised.) Whether we're brawling on social media forums or being drawn into angry "punditizing" by pundits,* we can sometimes be fairly loose when it comes to drawing connections between our firmly held positions and the factual bases on which to support them.

For some, the musings of people they love and respect are "proof." For others, "proof" might be the occurrence of two seemingly unrelated events which happened close in time to one another. Still others might consider "proof" to be the result of cherry-picking different events occurring over a long period of time, and constructing a narrative that ties them together in ways that help make your point. Our views and standards about what "proof" is can vary wildly. At times it seems possible for people to "prove" just about anything, which means they really might be proving nothing at all.

Presenting facts, and justifying our desired outcomes on those facts, is what ensures our fights aren't arbitrary. It's what keeps the dispute from being decided on the basis of someone's bias, or whim, or their various predilections and preferences. When you're trying to make your case in court, "because I say so" or "because I believe this" usually aren't good enough. Court attempts to level the playing field: *believe what you want*, the Court Genie says, *but we're not going to make anyone do any of that unless you present more than your hopes, dreams, and the passions of your heart to justify it.*

Thank you, Court Genie.

---

* No judgment. I myself have "punditized," and sometimes had a lot of fun doing it.

What You Should Know:
What "Proof" Means in Court

The way you justify your demands in court is by presenting competent evidence that the person from whom you are seeking relief has
created or is contributing to your problem. "Competent evidence"
is evidence that the court finds is sufficiently trustworthy to be considered in the case; there are rules for how to get your evidence in
the record and about what sort of evidence the court may consider.
The "word on the street" may be that the Earth is flat, for instance,
but if you want to prove a flat Earth in court, you have to do more
than offer unsupported hypotheses.

You also have to demonstrate that the relief you're seeking actually bears some relationship to solving the problem. If the thing
you're asking for isn't likely to solve your problem, or if the solution
you're seeking goes further than necessary, then it's really no different than seeking to make someone do something *just because you say
so*. This may work in some parent-child situations, but from what I
understand, it doesn't always work even then.

Types of Evidence

Your testimony and that of your other witnesses can constitute evidence. Documents, emails, social media posts, and other items that
have been reduced to image or writing, can be evidence.

Evidence can be either direct or circumstantial.

Direct evidence is something that is observed or witnessed firsthand.
Eyewitness testimony, for instance, is an example of direct evidence. An
admission that someone did something, is direct evidence.

Circumstantial evidence are facts that require a judge or jury to
make an inference about what happened. Your neighbor was seen
lurking around your driveway, and then later you discovered that
your prize roses were trampled. You didn't see him trample the roses,
but he was there and you infer he did it. Plus, he's always seemed to
have it in for you. That is circumstantial evidence.

Factfinders don't have to credit all evidence equally. Maybe your witness's testimony about the circumstances of an agreement are less compelling than the testimony offered by the other side. Maybe the judge believes one party and finds the other less credible. Maybe your unsigned draft agreements, for example, will be admitted into evidence for one purpose—to show the parties were negotiating—but not for the purpose of showing that an agreement had been reached. Just because you submit evidence doesn't mean that the court will give it the same credit you do or that the other side won't do everything they can to question its legitimacy. You have to try to sell—the judge need not necessarily buy.

What You Should Do: Making "the Record" in Your Case

When you're fighting in the comments on someone's social media page, for example, the "record" can consist of just about anything anyone feels like saying. There are no rules about who you must say it to or even whether it must be true. There are no real consequences for lying; in fact, if you're predisposed to like the person spouting the falsehood, the falsehood becomes less important. *Everybody lies*, you might say. *So what?*

(So what??!!)

In court, by contrast, the "record" is a defined, contained account of the proceedings in your case. It includes the documents you submit—the complaint, answer, motions, and other court pleadings; the testimony of parties and witnesses; arguments by counsel and the decisions of the judge. It becomes a reference point and a way of holding people accountable for things so they can't just make it all up as they go along.

That doesn't mean they don't try. It's just that in court it's easier to hold them accountable, since the record doesn't shapeshift according to the tastes and opinions of the one who is using it. If a decision-maker sides with a position that has no or little evidence on its side, you have a good basis for claiming that their decision was based not on the facts, but instead on "passion and prejudice," and you'll use the record to demonstrate the lack of any justifiable basis for the outcome. Because you're fighting in court, you'll have something specific and definable at which to point. In court, decision-makers are charged with considering all the relevant facts in the record. They're not supposed to make judgments based on their personal predilections and bias and when they do, the record gives you a basis for holding them accountable for it.

Your job is to make sure the facts you need in order to make your case get into the record. If the facts aren't in the record, then it's almost as if they don't exist. During the course of your case, you may have many costly disputes with your opponent about just what will and won't be a part of the record. You may file motions to exclude things you think unfavorable to your position, and your opponent may do the same.

Be prepared to do the work necessary to get the facts you need before the court. Don't plan on the judge doing any factfinding for you: it's not the judge's job to stop the proceedings to call your boss so as to verify you were too sick to go to work; or to call a health inspector to confirm your claim that your home was a breeding ground for toxins, for example. *You* have to do the work—and it's not as easy as simply showing up in court and recounting to the judge all the things you'd like to say.

How Much Evidence Do You Need?

How much evidence do you need? What level of convincing do you have to do? There are standards, and as you put your case together you should have a sense of them.

In criminal cases, the pertinent standard is proof beyond a reasonable doubt.

My focus here is civil disputes. There are different standards of proof applicable in those cases. Let's start with the most stringent:

Clear and Convincing Evidence

The U.S. Supreme Court has described "clear and convincing evidence" as an "intermediate standard" that is less stringent than "beyond a reasonable doubt" but stricter than "preponderance of the evidence." It generally applies when important rights are involved and more than just simple negligence is at issue. Cases involving interests whose loss involve a "stigma,"[4] such as civil commitment or deportation, might apply this standard. (It is also the burden you must meet to justify a claim for punitive damages.)[5] Its use "expresses a preference for one side's interests,"[6] such as a preference for keeping families intact (it's the standard required in cases involving termination of parental rights) or allowing people to freely enjoy the benefits of their citizenship or immigration status.[7]

The "clear and convincing" burden requires you to present enough evidence to convince the decision-maker that your position is "highly and substantially more probable to be true than not."[8] The judge or jury needs to have a "firm belief or conviction that the allegations are true."[9]

Preponderance of the Evidence

This is the standard applied in many civil cases. The burden of proof isn't as heavy as that for "clear and convincing" evidence. To meet it, you have to present evidence sufficient enough to demonstrate that your position is more likely to be true than not true. It's not a standard that requires the factfinder to be perfectly and absolutely certain. It's a bit more like a *probably, yes* standard.

PUTTING YOUR STORY IN THE "EVIDENTIARY BURDEN BOX"

To meet your evidentiary burden, you have to dissect your story and make sure you can match its respective components to the elements of a claim for legal liability. Sometimes that dissection and pairing up is easy to do. Sometimes it's more challenging.

The preponderance of the evidence standard is the one that is applicable in many race discrimination claims.[10] Conversations about racial inequality in the criminal justice system have given rise to a larger conversation about the inequality with which African-Americans contend more generally; racial discrimination is, indeed, something that many of us know and have experienced very personally. It is not always explicit. It is not always the N-word; or a noose in the office; or any of the obvious badges of hatred or *I think less of you because you are Black* or *I think I am better than you because I'm not* that overt bigots and their more quiet sympathizers wear.* True, it sometimes *is* those things, but sometimes it's far more subtle. That subtlety deserves its own discussion—there is no way I could do justice in these pages to the experience of racism, whether subtle or very, very obvious—by African-Americans generally. I couldn't even do justice to my own.

There are different ways of pursuing justice for civil rights violations. Some claims require that you show that the conduct or action you're challenging would not have happened "but for" your race.[11] Others require that you show race was a "motivating factor."[12]

In short, the manner in which the law processes and adjudicates questions of race is a topic worth of study on its own.[13] You may have to study it, or you may have to live it, or you may have to do some combination of both. Whatever the case, don't let racism steal you. (More on "stealing" in Chapter 8.)

People can end up seeing the same set of facts in very different ways. Different experiences inform our perspectives about what may or may not be true.

That, again, is where the rule of law comes in—to impose some order on the chaos so that we're not each held hostage to one

* *See, e.g.,* Deborah N. Archer, *There is no Santa Claus: The Challenge of Teaching the Next Generation of Civil Rights Lawyers in a "Post-Racial" Society,* 4 Columbia Journal of Race and Law 55 (2013).

another's bad experiences and biases. When you're trying to meet the burden of demonstrating that a certain fact is "more likely true than not," it's not enough simply to cross your fingers and hope that the factfinder has had the sort of life experiences that might incline them to your position—you have to provide some legal and factual basis for that position. In fact, if you get a favorable decision that has little or no factual basis in the record, an appellate court might conclude that the decision resulted from nothing more than the factfinder's "passion or prejudice."

Does that mean that lawyers and litigants don't try to appeal to the "passions and prejudices" of the decision-makers? Of course they do. Sometimes very blatantly. Sometimes they succeed. If those successes don't have other relevant facts to support them, however, they rest on pretty flimsy ground and might be reversed. (We'll discuss this in more detail in the chapter on appeals.)

As you are assessing and collecting your facts, are you relying on those that can give the court a pathway to the outcome you're seeking to achieve, a path that relies on more than simply your whims and preferences? Is the result for which you're advocating one that would be consistent if the tables were turned? Are you seeking something that has a justification or basis beyond simply the fact that it's what you want?

What You Should Know:
The Rollercoaster Ride of Making Your Record

Your record is the basis of the court's decision and it will be what any appellate court reviews so as to determine whether the trial court made a mistake. After all of those fights you had in discovery you may need to get ready for some new ones—these about how to make the evidence you so painstakingly gathered a part of the record in your case.

Don't Assume You'll Get to Tell the Whole Story

Lots of things happen. There are many "facts" in the world.

All facts, however, aren't created equal. Everything you want to include as evidence won't necessarily end up being a part of your case.

Your evidence must comply with the rules laid down for getting it introduced into the record. Whether it does or not is an issue over which the court has a lot of discretion.

(That discretion, however, isn't limitless; if you think the judge admitted or excluded something she shouldn't have, you can appeal, although usually not until the end of your case. Be mindful of the fact that the appellate court usually gives a lot of deference to the trial court's decisions in this regard. We'll discuss this in Chapter 9.)

One of the things you'll discover if you end up fighting in court is that what may appear relevant to you may not be relevant to the judge. Court is supposed to be a place to step back and put the whole story in context; it's not supposed to be a place where one bad mistake can serve as a predicate for making you responsible for all of life's ills. By the same token, not all of those "ills" will make it into the record. You may not even have a chance to confirm your suspicions as to how bad they are or not.

When you shutter the now-defunct manufacturing business you had with your former business partner, Madge, the court orders you and Madge to sell a commercial building—a manufacturing plant—that was among the partnership's assets. Pending the sale, the court decided that Madge could use it as her own independent manufacturing facility.

There was an instance where you secured an offer on the property, after which Madge produced an allegedly higher offer and your proposed buyer left the deal. You never were able to confirm that Madge's alleged buyer was legitimate and you are suspicious. (Madge wanted to retain the property for her new manufacturing venture and had resisted seeking new premises.)

Madge now wants to raise the price of the building and files a motion in court to do so. You oppose raising the price because you think it will make a sale even more difficult. You want to demonstrate that Madge was improperly interfering with your previous sales attempts, and believe you have evidence that the financial documentation she presented on behalf of the now-disappeared buyer was printed on fake letterhead, and inauthentic.

Madge's lawyers object to the evidence. They claim it's too second-hand and that your witnesses are too biased to be heard on the issue.

Just to recap: you and Madge are in a dispute over the sale of property. You have evidence you believe will demonstrate that Madge is improperly interfering with the sale. You are in court to determine whether the price of the building should be increased, which Madge wants to do. You don't want to—it's been hard enough to sell this thing—and now you think you can demonstrate that Madge has engaged in wrongful efforts to make it even more difficult.

The judge does not admit the evidence. He grants Madge's motion and allows her to raise the price of the plant. It takes you more than another year and many motions and court proceedings before you are able to get Madge to move her operations off the premises.

Might you have appealed the judge's decision to raise the price, given that you believe it resulted from the court's lopsided consideration of the issues? Maybe—but you don't. You conclude it isn't worth the time and expense. Plus, since your lawyers have advised you about how much discretion judges have in deciding what evidence will and won't be a part of the case, you recognize your appeal might be quite the uphill battle.

When you're seeking to offer evidence, the court will consider whether its "probative" value is outweighed by the "prejudice" to the party against whom it is introduced. In other words, is it more likely to incite negative views about the opposing party than it is to provide insight about what happened in the current dispute? If so, the judge may not allow you to introduce it.

You claim that your boss is a racist and that he is discriminating against you because of your ethnicity. You seek to introduce evidence of other discriminatory actions by your boss against people in ethnic groups other than yours. The court finds this evidence too prejudicial.

Or:

You're a part of a group of employees who claim that your employer wrongly labeled you as exempt from overtime and other labor protections. As support for this, you seek to offer evidence of administrative mistakes by the employer that involve unrelated issues, such as eligibility for family and medical leave. The court admits the evidence on the ground that it demonstrates a pattern or practice by the employer of mishandling employee administrative matters.

Demonstrating that the evidence you want to include is a part of a "pattern or practice" of wrongdoing by your opponent is one way of introducing into the record other acts by your opponent that you think will help prove your case. Still, you never know what a specific judge will do or how she will interpret facts of your case. It's always helpful to have a backup plan and to collect as much evidence as you can, since you never know whether the judge is really going to let you fire your silver bullets.

What You Should Know: You May Have to Jump Through Some Hoops to Make Your Evidence Matter

There are other things you have to think about, too, when you're trying to make sure all the evidence you want actually gets before the court.

The "Word on the Street" Won't Carry the Day

The "word on the street." Whose word? Whose street?

You've likely heard the term "hearsay." Maybe you use it in the sense of referring to gossip or those tidbits that "everybody's" talking about, but of whose source you're unsure.

The term has a similar definition when you're fighting in court. Hearsay evidence is any out-of-court statement that is used to prove that whatever is being asserted in that statement is true. The problem with hearsay is that you can't challenge or test its reliability in court. Since court is where we go to have our fights on terms that allow everyone to have a fair chance to challenge accusations, hearsay evidence is generally disfavored.[14]

> You're in a dispute with your former partner and you claim that they are an alcoholic. As support for this, you want to submit into evidence an email to your former partner from a third party, in which the third party claims that your partner's "drinking bouts are getting worse." Not only is the author of the email unavailable to testify in court, but you can't even verify who the author of the email is!
>
> This could constitute impermissible hearsay.

HEARSAY EXCEPTIONS

There are a number of exceptions to the hearsay rule. They include "present sense impressions"; "excited utterances"; statements regarding a "then-existing mental or physical condition"; and statements in certain business or public records, to name just a few.[15]

Also, if you want to admit documents, for instance, you have to be prepared to prove that the documents you want to use are what they say they are. You do that by "laying a foundation," which often requires you to demonstrate how the document came into existence and how you became aware of it. It can be more work than it seems.

> Your former business partner claims that they discovered some designs for a new product that you allegedly created while your business was still operating. Their support for the claim that you wrote the designs while the partnership was still in effect was the fact that the cover page of the design included the words "created by [YOU!]." Your former business partner claimed that the designs became the basis of a product that your new business partner, Betty, invented, and that you helped launch.
>
> You deny creating the designs that your former partner allegedly found. You claim your now-alienated partner simply concocted the entire thing in order to get a piece of your new business. Plus, you argue that Betty's product had nothing to do with these newly-discovered designs and that Betty came up with the idea independently. (There are, in fact, differences between the design of Betty's product and the one based on the allegedly newly discovered designs your former business partner has presented.)
>
> Your former business partner also sues Betty and others who have profited from her new product. In the lawsuit, your former partner claims an entitlement to some of the profits from that new product.
>
> The issue of any potential profit to which your former partner may have been entitled, however, was not before the court. The judge had *bifurcated* the proceedings; the first issue the court would decide was whether you actually created the designs while you and your former partner were still in business.

Bifurcation is what happens when the court decides to hear different parts of a claim separately because it's more efficient to do so. In this case, the issue of whether you used the designs your former partner allegedly found in your new business with Betty was bifurcated from the issue of whether you created the allegedly newly discovered designs in the first place. If your former partner is able to prove that you did, then you will have a second trial on the separate issue of whether and to what extent those designs influenced your new venture with Betty. If your former partner can't prove that, then the inquiry ends there.

Your former-partner–now-nemesis submitted the metadata for the computer disc on which they claimed the designs were stored when they found them. (According to your former partner, they found the disc and then printed the designs from it.) The metadata on the disc, however, showed that the document containing the design had been written on your former partner's computer! Plus, when your former partner submitted copies of the design as an attachment to their court pleadings, they had inadvertently submitted two versions of the design, even though at the time they claimed they'd only discovered one.

Your legal team also discovered an article in a trade journal that contained the same—and in some instances, identical—specifications as the designs that your former partner claimed to have discovered. The article was written years after you dissolved the partnership. Your lawyers want to use the article to undermine your former partner's claim that you created the allegedly newly-discovered designs. You and your lawyers believe that your former partner copied the designs from the trade journal, using the information from the article to create a basis for a fraudulent claim against you.

Fantastic that you found that article! Great for you!

Not so great for you yet. The judge holds that you can't submit the article into evidence without first proving when it was written. The article has a date printed on it, but so what?

It is the twenty-first century. People create fake websites all the time.

You serve a subpoena on the trade journal, which was located across the country. You then incur the substantial expense of flying a witness who works for the trade journal to court. The witness shows up, testifying only about the limited issue of whether the article had in fact been published at the time that the printed publication date indicated it was. His testimony probably didn't even last as long as his wait in the airport security line.

You spent a lot of time and money just to prove that an article printed from the internet was written and published on the date its cover page indicated it was. The judge wasn't just going to take that at face value. (While there are some kinds of evidence that the court might take at face value, such as certain official and certified records or the transcript of court proceedings, the list of things falling into this category is pretty limited.)

Proving things are what you say they are often takes some work. Was that email, for instance, really exchanged between the two parties indicated on the "To" and "From" lines? Is there evidence it actually was sent? Is there evidence it was received? Is the person who sent it available to testify about the circumstances that led them to send it? If they aren't willing to do so voluntarily, are you prepared to subpoena them? Do you know where they are?

Putting your record together means having a plan for how you will get important parts of your story before the court. It isn't automatic that they'll come in. You may have to fight to make them a part of your case and the fight may be neither easy nor cheap.

What evidence do you have? Try to gather as much as possible to support your claim. Sure, you may have your own testimony, but that testimony will be stronger and more persuasive if you've got more than just your own word to support your version of things.

Emails; bank statements; documents that prove things are as you say—these can be critical elements in helping you persuade a decision-maker. Do all you can to make it more than a contest between two competing stories. Sometimes a case turns merely on the credibility of testifying witnesses; sometimes the court will need to see more. "Credibility" can sometimes be easier to ascertain when there is something else to support what you're saying.

What You Should Know— Meeting Your Burden of Proof

Determining whether you've met your burden of proof depends in part on what it is you're trying to prove.

In addition to all the other activities in which you're engaged in this book, you're also a landlord.

Good grief, you're busy!

You watch *Hot Bench* regularly so you *never* rent to tenants without strong references. (You love our show but have no interest in appearing on it, nor have you ever.)

I'm glad about this. Not that I don't want to meet you, it's just that I don't wish litigation on anyone.

Lozzio and Forkie were looking for a new place and really liked the apartment you've showed them. Their rental history, however, was pretty checkered; they'd been evicted from their previous apartment for non-payment of rent and didn't have very good credit.

But they really wanted that apartment. They asked their coworker, Conspirato, if he could help out by posing as their current landlord and providing them a good reference.

Conspirato was happy to do so. Conspirato calls you and gives Lozzio and Forkie a glowing reference. *Phew*, you say to yourself. *No litigation!* You rent the apartment to Lozzio and Forkie.

It's a disaster. Lozzio and Forkie don't pay rent. You are furious. *Who in the hell thinks they get to live for free?* (By the way, it should be noted that at the time of this transaction, there was no global pandemic and the country wasn't shut down. Jobs were open. Businesses were open. Lozzio and Forkie just decided that you weren't that much of a priority.)

You reach out to Conspirato—he'd said they were such good people!—but he doesn't return your calls.

You then learn that Conspirato was not in fact Lozzio and Forkie's landlord, but instead their friend and coworker. (He lied!)

You sue Conspirato for fraud. You argue that he participated in a scheme to dupe you into a rental agreement with tenants to whom you never would have leased an apartment in the absence of the false information he provided.

In order to prevail on a claim for fraud, which must be proven by clear and convincing evidence, you have to show that the defendant 1) made a false representation of a statement of fact; 2) that they knew the statement was false when they made it; 3) that they made it so as to induce you to act on it; and 4) that you did act on it, to your injury.

You present evidence that Conspirato had falsely represented himself as Lozzio and Forkie's landlord; that he knew, of course, that he wasn't their landlord; that the whole reason for the lie was to induce you to rent the apartment to them; that you relied on the false reference in renting to Lozzio and Forkie; and that you suffered losses because these tenants, to whom you would not have rented the apartment but for the good reference, did not pay their rent. The court finds you have met your burden.

But then, things could go differently.

Poinsettia and Rose are in a tumultuous relationship, one that has included alcohol-fueled fights and explosive incidents with third parties. As a result of one of those altercations, Poinsettia and Rose each sue the other for damages. Poinsettia claims Rose physically abused her, and is liable for damages for assault, battery, domestic violence, false imprisonment, sexual battery, and intentional infliction of emotional distress. Rose claims Poinsettia is liable for battery.

Considering their competing stories, the court finds, among other things, that parts of Poinsettia's narrative are inconsistent with other evidence in the case. For example, she claims Rose struck her violently in the face, but photographs taken at the time of the incident show no injuries. The court finds Poinsettia isn't credible.

While judges can't act arbitrarily when making their decisions, they have a lot of discretion in deciding who to believe. Some of the factors they can consider are body language, facial expression, and tone of voice, among other things. Is a witness evasive—attempting to avoid giving direct answers or any at all? Is their demeanor different on direct and cross-examination? There are a variety of factors a court may consider in deciding whether or not to believe someone. Court may not always be a place where common sense carries the day, but judges don't have to leave theirs at the door when deciding which party is more credible.

Rose's claim doesn't meet its burden, either.

It was a messy relationship and a messy altercation. Neither party succeeded in proving to the court that the mess that gave rise to the various claims and counterclaims between them was one for which either should have any liability.

I'm not reciting these examples so as to imply that you may or may not have a good case, or to suggest that one type of claim rather than another is necessarily more credible. I'm simply letting you know that virtually every court battle is a competition between different stories, and if you want yours to win you should give the court as many reasons possible why your version, rather than your opponent's, is a correct one. There is a real uncertainty in all this, and your best insurance is to try to button up your story as best you can.

What inconsistencies may be introduced to defeat your version of events? How will you be able to explain them? Will the judge even let you make that explanation?

When you are bringing or defending a claim against someone, know precisely what it is you need to prove. That's the only way you'll know what sorts of facts you'll need to obtain and how heavy your burden will be. Don't take anything for granted—it's your job to present evidence of every element required.

Every case is different—hence the uncertainties of litigation. The best you can do is assemble as much evidence as you can and try to have a plan for making sure the court will hear it. The only hope you have of winning is to lay out the pathway to your desired outcome in a way that makes it easy for the decision-maker to follow it—and sorting and arranging the stones while you build that pathway won't always be as simple as you might think.

TO SUM UP . . .

- If you're going to end up in court, think about what a skeptical decision-maker would think of your story. Do you have what it takes to convince them?
- Understand that even if you have the *most compelling story* and evidence of horrible wrongdoing by your opponent, the court may not hear your entire story. The judge may determine that parts of it aren't relevant to the matters before the court.
- Know that you may have to work very hard to get important facts into the record in your case. The court won't

automatically include evidence just because you believe it is key or critical to some point.

- Make sure you are very clear on what it is you need to prove in order to meet the particular elements of the cause of action you're claiming.
- Surprise! It's never too late to try to work it out!

8

CONFRONTING
BAD BEHAVIOR

Some People Just Don't Play Fairly

Everyone won't take the process as seriously as you do. Nor will they necessarily respect your right to a fair fight.

There may be things that take place during the course of the process that will frustrate you or make you angry; things that will depress or outrage you. They may be things that deprive you of any sense that justice or fairness can prevail because perhaps you'll see so much unfairness that no one but you will care about. Maybe you'll start to believe that that's the best that you can hope for—some sort of process where you aren't completely eviscerated by what you see as someone else's brazen disregard for truth or what you perceive as the process's lack of concern with fairness to you.

The last words my Grandma Mae said to me in person, the last time I saw her alive, were "don't let anyone steal you." At the time, I had no idea what she was talking about, but afterward, it seemed to apply to everything. Dissatisfying professional situations; bad personal relationships; you name it—a "stealing" could happen almost anywhere.

For you, it applies too. It means if you're fighting in court, you may have stand up for yourself because no one else will—but it also means that you'll have to do it in a way where you don't give your attacker more of your time and energy than they deserve.

Court is our referee. It's the way to make sure the rules are enforced and that we can live together without devolving into, let's just say, a purge. That's why judges and juries aren't supposed to be arbitrary or capricious when making their decisions. That's why we have rules.

So, what does it mean when someone pursues you in court just because they want to cause you as much inconvenience as possible—just because they have an axe to grind against you that has nothing to do with the merits of their case? It means you'll have the "opportunity" to spend a lot of your time and money to show just how heavily invested they are in that axe. You can seek compensation for having to deal with their expensive bitterness, but you likely never will be made whole even if you do get some penalty. In other words, it's *very easy to get away with blatant lies in court, and no one will really be taken to task.* I don't mean "get away with" in Biblical, karmic, or other spiritual senses, because lies catch up with people. When you're fighting in court, however, you can end up engaging with those lies for a really long time—a really, really, expensive, long time. This is why court can be so effective a weapon for your adversary and why it can devastate you even if you win.

Court is supposed to be our mechanism for getting at truth, but if you have the misfortune of fighting someone who views court as a bludgeon to wield against you, then you're in for quite a ride. It's hard to get used to it; hard to assume it's "par for the course" and "just what people do," when that weapon is aimed squarely at you.

Like our other "grown up" institutions, courts are supposed to be a respite from all that. Courts are even supposed to be a respite when the other grown-up institutions can't get it together. When your court fight doesn't seem fair, things can really seem hopeless.

What You Should Know: Frivolous Lawsuits

What is a frivolous lawsuit?

Sometimes people think just because they disagree with what's being said about them in the complaint, that the case against them is "frivolous."

Not necessarily. "Frivolous," for purposes of this discussion, is when someone brings a lawsuit that has no factual or legal basis. While most cases don't fall into this category, some do, and it is costly and difficult for people who have to deal with them. If you want to get some measure of justice for someone for bringing a lawsuit against you that you claim has no basis, you may first have to assume the burden of proving that their case doesn't, in fact, have any basis.

What You Should Know: Bad Faith Conduct

Even if a lawsuit isn't completely contrived, there are innumerable ways in which someone can ignore or flout the rules so as to maximize your inconvenience and expense. Maybe someone knows they did something but is simply concocting a defense because they know you don't have the resources to fight them, or to fight them as long as you'll need to in order to obtain the result to which you're entitled. Sometimes this can be risky; if someone is suing under a contract or statute that provides for the payment of legal fees to the prevailing party, protracting a matter can increase their exposure significantly.[1] Other times, however, there is neither enough risk nor enough disincentive to discourage bad faith behavior.

What You Should Know—Confronting Bad Behavior

There are some things that make it easier than you'd like for someone to get away with advancing brazen lies in court.

There are also, however, some things you can do about those brazen lies. But first . . .

You May Have to Live with It— The Litigation Privilege

As an initial matter, you should know that there is an extremely broad protection that the law gives to statements that are made as a part of court proceedings. This is known as the "litigation privilege."

You generally can't sue someone for statements and communications they make in the course of judicial proceedings. (The exception, however, is that you still can bring a claim against them for malicious prosecution. I'll discuss malicious prosecution shortly.)

THE PRIVILEGE

Every state has a litigation privilege. It's not just statements made in the course of litigation that are protected, however; statements made in other types of official proceedings are privileged, too.

California describes the privilege this way:

A privileged publication or broadcast is one made:

(a) In the proper discharge of an official duty.

(b) In any (1) legislative proceeding, (2) judicial proceeding, (3) in any other official proceeding authorized by law, or (4) in the initiation or course of any other proceeding authorized by law and reviewable in court.[2]

The privilege also applies to those who, *without malice*, provide job references, as well as to those who make sexual harassment complaints (as long as those complaints are made without malice).[3]

There are some exceptions to the privilege. For instance, if in the middle of divorce proceedings one of the litigants says something nasty and untrue about the soon-to-be-ex's new girlfriend, those statements aren't privileged unless they are made "without malice"; the person making them has a reasonable and probable cause for believing them to be true; *and* the statement is relevant to the issues in the action. In other words, you're not supposed to just go around making up stories about your ex's new partner when you don't really have a basis for believing them to be true and they don't really have anything to do with anything.

Communications made in the furtherance of attempts to intentionally alter or destroy evidence so as to deprive a party of the opportunity to use it also aren't subject to the privilege—i.e., you can't shield your efforts to destroy evidence.

Nor does the privilege apply to communications that are made so as to conceal the existence of insurance policies.

In other words, the litigation privilege protects even false statements from liability (except it doesn't protect those statements from liability for malicious prosecution).

Why does this virtual "get-out-of-jail-free" (or rather, this "you'll-never-even-go-to-jail-because-no-one-may-care-about-what-you-did") card exist? It's there to ensure that people with a good faith belief and basis for their claims—even if that belief is mistaken and even if those claims are ultimately unsuccessful—aren't dissuaded from seeking relief in court. Court process is intended to give people an opportunity, through discovery, to develop evidence for their positions. They are allowed to make mistakes or to be wrong.

Also, courts don't want every case to result in the multiple births of new litigation. As one court put it (in the context of explaining the heightened standard for civil perjury cases): the "law ab-hors fraud and perjury, it also abhors interminable litigation."[4]

That doesn't mean that liars get a free pass. Not only does the litigation privilege still allow for actions for malicious prosecution, but it also doesn't prohibit a party from seeking sanctions for bad conduct. (We'll discuss sanctions later, too.) Some statutes also al-low for the prevailing party to recover costs and fees.

Still, you should know that doing the work of getting that redress may, in many cases, be all. on. you. You should also know that the judge may not be as offended by bad conduct as you are. Judges are busy. They see a lot of bad stuff.

You May Be the Only Enforcer You'll Have

What happens when your opponent in court is someone who will lie and/or contrive things out of whole cloth? When they lie to police in order to avoid a court order; forge documents so as to concoct a basis for suing you over an allegedly unpaid debt; don't just ignore court rules, but actually *break the law* in their quest to weaponize court against you?

Sometimes You Have to Just Keep Going

(By the way, I'm sorry that you're having all these problems with everyone: your former business partners; the guy copying your de-signs; the guy redoing your kitchen; your tenants Lozzio and Forkie. I guess you've gone through a pretty rough patch. Hopefully, by the end of this book, these troubles will be behind you.)

> You obtain a court order requiring that your former business partner vacate a commercial building that was held in the name of the now-defunct manufacturing business the two of you used to have. Don't expect much help, though. The judge doesn't send anyone to the building to require them to shut down their new operations (which they're conducting on the property as you're trying to sell it) and leave. You have to do it yourself.

You show up with the sheriff, but your former business partner tells him there is no court order requiring them to leave. Your former partner claims you are trespassing. (Meanwhile, at around the same time this is happening, your former partner's lawyer tells the judge that they've removed their operations from the premises.)

The sheriff tells you to leave and to take the issue back to court. You comply, and then dig back into your wallet for more money to spend on your lawyers in order to get your former partner to comply with the court order.

In the meantime, your former partner tells the police that you called them and threatened to kill them. They claim that you made the call from your own phone number. You deny making the call and believe that your former partner created a call detail showing your number by generating a "spoofed" phone call.[*]

Your former partner also files a restraining order against you; under the terms of the protection they requested, you would be in violation of the order simply by traveling between home and your office. Your former partner then dismisses the order before the judge hears any evidence on the issue, but not before you've spent time and money putting together evidence that they filed the restraining order simply to delay the proceedings and harass you.

You are interviewed by the police. A search warrant is executed on your phone. It doesn't turn up any evidence that you're making death threats from your own phone number. You and your lawyers believe that these were simply attempts by your former partner to avoid moving their new operation off the premises—which, after several court appearances and discussions with law enforcement, you were ultimately able to force them to do.

Were the police outraged at what may have been (and certainly seems to you to have been) a transparent attempt by your former

---

[*] "[W]hen placing phone calls, to 'spoof' [is to] disguise [a] caller ID by selecting the number [the "spoofer"] would like to appear on recipients' caller ID screens." Walsh v. TelTech Sys., 821 F.3d 155, 158 (1st Cir. 2016).

partner to misuse their law-enforcement resources in order to gain an advantage in the litigation? Who knows?

> You ask the officers to submit a declaration regarding their findings to the court, but they decline. You're concerned because you think the court won't get the whole story. You seek sanctions for your former partner's conduct, but the judge denies the motion. The judge ruled that on the facts before him, he would not award sanctions.

The judge may not care about your story the way you do. Plus, everyone won't help you tell your story. Your attorney may even edit out parts of it—perhaps she thinks they are distracting or unlikely to advance the goals of your case. Even if you manage to get introduced into the record all of the horrible things that happened to you, the things that bother you may not trouble the judge as much. Maybe your drama seems like just another Heaping Mass of Problem.

Not everything that happens in court will be something you can understand, or explain, or that will comport with common sense notions of fairness. Common sense fairness doesn't always carry the day when you enter the courthouse door.

What You Can Do: Options for Dealing with Bad Behavior

There are options for fighting back, but you should know that they can be time-consuming and expensive.

In other words, the same general caution I gave before—about deciding whether court is worth your time—definitely applies to this more specific situation. In the event you are in litigation with someone who is inclined simply to lie, you need to weigh the value of your time and decide how much of the nightmare you want to relive.

I work in the law business. I'm used to having to piece together someone else's nightmares.

You, who may or may not be in that business, might not be interested in reliving nightmares. You may want nothing more than simply to move on. You may be looking at the most disgusting injustice right in the face—the most crass and gross abuse of the court system—and you may decide that it is time to move on. You just have to think very carefully about how you want to spend your time, because fighting for your right to be free from litigation abuse definitely will take some time.

Sanctions

If someone brings a lawsuit or makes a claim against you for no good reason, you can try to get sanctions against them. Different standards apply in different types of cases, but the general rule is that sanctions are supposed to impose a consequence for bad faith behavior. Make no mistake—it's not just plaintiffs seeking recovery who can find themselves in trouble for protracting a matter for no reason. Defendants, too, can raise defenses that have no merit. They might do this for any number of reasons: maybe they want to deplete their opponent's resources, or maybe they think that fighting a battle seems cheaper and easier than owning up to the likely penalty. Attorneys and parties filing papers in court should have a good faith basis for what they file. Putting forward a defense that doesn't can get a party into trouble.[5]

Be warned: the thing that outrages you may be something to which the judge, having seen so much of it, has developed a thick skin. You'll need to be able to explain in detail why the conduct in which the other person engaged was so outrageous. It's not enough simply to show that your opponent vigorously prosecuted or defended against accusations—you have to show that they had almost no reasonable basis for doing so. It's a very high standard.

> Your former business partner claimed that you failed to disclose some
> designs for a new product before the two of you dissolved your business.
>   You denied creating the designs. There was evidence they were
> created on your former partner's computer. There was also evidence
> that they'd been copied, in some instances almost exactly, from a set

of product specifications that were published in a trade journal after you dissolved the partnership. Still, your disgruntled former colleague continued with the lawsuit.

They lost. The judge found that they didn't carry their burden of demonstrating that you created the document while your partnership was still in effect. As a consequence, they couldn't pursue their claim for any of the proceeds from your new business (remember, this is an issue that was bifurcated from the question of whether you created the designs in the first place).

You ask the court for sanctions.

The court finds that your former partner had no good faith basis for continuing the case once your lawyers presented them with evidence of the trade journal, which was published after the close of your now-defunct business. Remember, that article contained specifications that appeared to have been incorporated (in some instances, almost word-for-word) into the document your former partner claimed they had discovered. You spend more than a million dollars defending against their claims. But during the *oral argument* (glossary) on your request for sanctions, the judge makes clear he isn't going to give you back all the money you spent. Your lawyer then reduces the request by more than half, and the judge awards you just a bit over half of that (discounted) amount.

On the one hand, something is better than nothing. You now have the benefit of another set of court findings regarding your former partner's bad faith conduct (they had been sanctioned before), and perhaps those findings might be useful later.

On the other hand, their antics cost you a ton of money and the sanctions award doesn't come close to making you whole. You're also aware that your former partner has had some issues paying creditors in the past, so you're not even sure if or when you'll get your money.

By the way, getting the money you're owed from a court battle can often be a challenge, period. I'll discuss more about collection in Chapter 10.

Sometimes a party's conduct can be so bad, however, that the sanctions imposed can compromise their entire case.

The heirs to the creator of a popular cartoon character were suing Big Company over rights and royalties to the character. Hundreds of millions were at stake.

During the course of discovery, Big Company's lawyers noticed something strange: some of their own privileged documents were being turned over by the other side.

Here's what happens when hundreds of millions are at stake—parties invest in turning over every stone so as to debunk the other side's position.

One of Big Company's lawyers followed up on a lead which led him to someone who was then incarcerated—Key Witness. Key Witness confirmed that he and others had obtained certain confidential documents by breaking into Big Company's buildings. Key Witness signed a declaration while in jail, and his declaration resulted in other people admitting that they participated in the illegal acts.

The judge was not happy about this.

He dismissed the plaintiffs' entire case.

Most litigants, however, don't have the resources to track down misconduct in this way—and the fact that their claims may involve far smaller amounts doesn't make the violation of their right to a fair process any less important. They just may have a lot less help and fewer resources in protecting it.

Abuse of Process

As with so many other rules, the standards for proving abuse of process vary across jurisdictions. Speaking very generally, in order to prevail you must show that your opponent used court process for improper purposes, and that you were damaged by it. Unlike a claim for malicious prosecution, which I'll discuss next, you don't always have to win the underlying action in order to bring a claim for abuse of process.

> You have emerged from a successful but hard-fought battle with your employer for workers' compensation benefits. You win, but instead of complying with the judgment, your employer's insurer continues to serve you with legal papers that ultimately are found to be meritless. The only purpose of the filings seems to be to increase your expenses.

This might support an abuse of process claim. Once a party has instituted a case, they are only supposed to use the procedures available for good faith purposes.

STANDARDS FOR PROVING ABUSE OF PROCESS

In New York, an "[a]buse of process [claim] has three essential elements: (1) regularly issued process, either civil or criminal, (2) an intent to do harm without excuse or justification, and (3) use of the process in a perverted manner to obtain a collateral objective." The allegedly abused "process used must involve 'an unlawful interference with one's person or property.'"

In California, the test for abuse of process is two-pronged: "first, an ulterior purpose, and second, a willful act in the use of the process not proper in the regular conduct of the proceeding."

The standards in Texas are similar:

1) that the defendant made an illegal, improper, or perverted use of the process, a use neither warranted nor authorized by the process; 2) that the defendant had an ulterior motive or purpose in exercising such illegal, perverted or improper use of the process; and 3) that damage resulted to the plaintiff as a result of such irregular act.

Florida requires that a party seeking to bring an abuse of process claim show that: (1) the defendant made an illegal, improper, or perverted use of process; (2) the defendant had an ulterior motive or purpose in exercising the illegal, improper or perverted process; and (3) the plaintiff was injured as a result of defendant's action.

West Virginia has similar requirements, as an abuse of process claim in that jurisdiction requires "proof of a willful [sic] and intentional abuse or misuse of the process for the accomplishment of some wrongful object—an intentional and willful [sic] perversion of it to the unlawful injury to another." West Virginia also requires that a plaintiff seeking to recover for abuse of process prove malice.[6]

If the basis of your abuse of process claim is the filing of some pleading or other court document, your claim may run into some difficulty. California's litigation privilege, for instance, bars such abuse of process claims where they are based on pleadings or court papers that are filed in the course of seeking a judicial resolution. The litigation privilege protects even false statements from liability for abuse of process.

Malicious Prosecution

The litigation privilege does not shield false statements from an action for *malicious prosecution.*

If someone brought a lawsuit against you for what you contend was no good reason—if, for instance, they just made something up—you also have the option of suing them for malicious prosecution.

This course of action is much harder and requires much more work than seeking sanctions, and I have to offer you this caution: if your legal battle—however successful—has left you with chills, dry mouth, or any combination of symptoms that are described as the side effects to any of the countless medicines advertised during the evening news, then bringing a malicious prosecution action probably is not for you. (You may not, however, always have the option of bringing a malicious prosecution case. In California, for instance, an action brought in family court cannot later be the subject of a malicious prosecution claim, no matter how baseless that action may have been.)[7]

STANDARDS FOR PROVING MALICIOUS PROSECUTION

California, for instance, requires that a plaintiff "plead and prove that the prior action (1) was commenced by or at the direction of the defendant and was pursued to a legal termination in his, plaintiff's, favor; (2) was brought without probable cause; and (3) was initiated with malice." West Virginia's standard is similar.

In Texas, to "prevail in a suit alleging malicious prosecution of a civil claim, the plaintiff must establish: (1) the institution or continuation of civil proceedings against the plaintiff; (2) by or at the insistence of the defendant; (3) malice in the commencement of the proceeding; (4) lack of probable cause for the proceeding; (5) termination of the proceeding in plaintiff's favor; and (6) special damages." The "special damages" requirement means that a plaintiff must plead and prove damages beyond those normally incurred during litigation, such as attorney's fees and discovery costs.[8]

If you're suing someone for malicious prosecution in a state where anti-SLAPP protections exist, your lawsuit may run into some difficulty. Remember, anti-SLAPP protections apply to statements that are made in the course of legislative, judicial, and other official proceedings; accordingly, you'll need to show that you have a likelihood of prevailing on the merits of your claim before your case can go forward.

What Does "Malice" Mean?

"Malice" for these purposes means more than *you didn't do your homework before you filed that nonsense case against me* or, if suing a lawyer, *your client has had it in for me and you should have known better because your client has made clear that they are out to get me.* You have to show more than that.

Nethen sues Darcy for slander, intentional infliction of emotional distress, and intentional interference with an economic relationship. His claims are based on statements he alleges Darcy made, statements that he contends are false. Among the alleged statements was a claim that Nethen forced Darcy's son into a sexual relationship and that Nethen was a con man.

Nethen then ignores his obligation to participate in discovery— refusing to appear for deposition and providing no substantive response to the ten sets of written discovery that Darcy propounded. Darcy moved to compel Nethen's compliance and the judge granted her motion. Still, Nethen refused to comply.

Darcy then moved for terminating sanctions, seeking an order from the court dismissing Nethen's case because of his non-compliance with discovery. The court granted the motion.

The sanctions in Darcy's case constituted a favorable termination that would support a malicious prosecution action, if she chose to pursue one. The record was lacking any evidence to support Nethen's complaint.

Just because a case ends in a dismissal does not mean that it was terminated in the defendant's favor on the merits. The "on the merits" element is important: it's not enough that the case simply is dismissed, but the dismissal must be one that addresses the merits of the underlying claim. (A settlement, for example, usually wouldn't constitute a "favorable termination" because most settlement agreements include provisions in which both parties insist their claims and defenses had merit, but that they're settling just to avoid litigation costs.)

Darcy claims that Nethen's lawyers proceeded with malice because they prosecuted and maintained the case against her even though there was no evidence to support Nethen's claims. She relies on the fact that they did no factual investigation, and that they had a client who may have harbored ill will against her. (Among other things,

Darcy's son testified in declaration that Nethen told him that Nethen wouldn't rest until he bled Darcy dry.)

Nethen's lawyer brought an anti-SLAPP motion.

The court granted the motion. The court held that Darcy's list of opposing counsel's alleged bad acts was not enough to prove malice. Because of that, Darcy did not have a likelihood of prevailing on the merits of her case.

Attorneys are normally allowed to rely on their client's representations and they are allowed time to build support for those allegations through the discovery process. The fact that a client's claims are meritless isn't enough to support a finding that the attorney knew there was no probable cause for the action. Plus, a lack of probable cause is generally not enough in itself to prove malice.

Bringing an action that one *knows* (or should know) has no probable cause at the outset, or continuing to prosecute a claim that one knows has no basis in law or fact, might have a different outcome:

Peck represented Davina in a foreclosure action. The action concluded with Davina releasing all claims to her house in exchange for a payment for emotional distress damages. The damages were paid by some, but not all, of the defendants.

Davina then sued Peck for fraud, claiming he broke his promise to 1) continue representing her against the non-settling defendants; 2) to represent her in a malpractice action she filed against her former attorneys; and 3) to get her house back. She also claimed he said he'd stop representing her if she refused to settle.

Here's the thing: there were transcripts of the hearings in the foreclosure action that completely contradicted Davina's claims. The transcripts revealed that Davina knew she was releasing her claims to the house and that Peck was not going to represent her in that proceeding. Peck had filed the necessary paperwork to enter a default judgment against the defendants who didn't settle with Davina, and the trial judge explained that Peck would be relieved as counsel. The judge also explained to Davina that she would be responsible for proceeding with the default judgment against the non-settling defendants, herself.

The judge even asked Davina if she had a problem with Peck being relieved as counsel. She replied that she didn't. She also implied that he'd never really been her lawyer.

Still, this didn't stop Davina from bringing a lawsuit that was based on a set of facts that were precisely the opposite of those set forth in case records.

Peck sent Davina's new lawyers copies of the transcript to prove there was no basis for Davina's claims. Her lawyers proceeded nonetheless. Peck defeated Davina's lawsuit, and then brought a claim for malicious prosecution against her and her lawyers. Davina's lawyers sought dismissal of Peck's claims based on the anti-SLAPP statute. The trial judge granted the motion.

The court of appeal, however, reversed. The court held that continuing to maintain a lawsuit based on claims that are expressly contradicted by the facts can support a claim for malicious prosecution.

Darcy's case against Nethen's lawyers failed because she couldn't prove malice. Not doing one's homework is not the same as being malicious.

In Peck's case, by contrast, Davina's claims were expressly contradicted by previous court transcripts. In other words, it's one thing to lack evidence in support of a claim; it's another to openly disregard evidence demonstrating that the claim has no basis.

Malicious prosecution is what courts describe as a "disfavored tort." Courts don't like the "litigation spawn," as I'll describe it, of earlier litigation, so the standard for obtaining relief is high. There are other ways of getting relief for troubling conduct that are more efficient than bringing new litigation (such as sanctions or a motion for relief from a judgment that was obtained by fraud, for instance), and courts tend to discourage brand new rounds of fresh litigation.

The bottom line is that if you want to sue someone for malicious prosecution, *think about your time.* You first have to litigate the original matter to a favorable conclusion, and then you basically have to do it all over again to prove that the other side had no reasonable basis for bringing the lawsuit.

Perhaps taking this action is necessary. If someone has asserted an entirely baseless claim against you, bringing a case just to harass and annoy you and to force you to spend money, it may be in your best interest to hold them accountable for that. Still, as is true with respect to the other points I make in this book, I'm definitely not providing you advice on that (or on anything else here. Remember, you should talk to a lawyer and get advice about what is appropriate for you in your specific situation). Your decision depends entirely on the details of your case, and your resources and bandwidth for a brand new battle.

Remember, suing someone because they brought a frivolous lawsuit against you also requires you to show you've been harmed. You would think that the "harm" would be obvious, but courts don't always see it that way.

In our small claims courtroom, litigants will sometimes show up asking for damages for what they'll call "inconvenience"—not a small thing, since court certainly can be that. Still, as unfair as it seems, wasted time is often not a compensable injury.

Vexatious Litigants

An option you may have for dealing with someone who repeatedly files meritless lawsuits against you is to have them declared a *vexatious litigant.*

This doesn't mean that they won't be able to continue suing you, but it does mean they may have to get permission from the court first.

THE VEXATIOUS LITIGANT

In California, the definition of a vexatious litigant includes, among other things, someone who, "[i]n the immediately preceding seven-year period had commenced, prosecuted, or maintained in propria persona at least five litigations other than in a small claims court that have been (i) finally determined adversely to the person or (ii) unjustifiably permitted to remain pending at least two years without having been brought to trial or hearing or any litigation while acting in propria persona, repeatedly files unmeritorious motions, pleadings, or other papers, conducts unnecessary discovery, or engages in other tactics that are frivolous or solely intended to cause unnecessary delay."

In Florida, Fla. Stat. §68.093(2)(d), defines a vexatious litigant as:

A person as defined in s. 1.01(3) who, in the immediately preceding five-year period, has commenced, prosecuted, or maintained, pro se, five or more civil actions in any court in this state, except an action governed by the Florida Small Claims Rules, which actions have been finally and adversely determined against such person or entity;

or

Any person or entity previously found to be a vexatious litigant pursuant to this section.

In New York, a vexatious litigant is deemed to have engaged in "frivolous conduct."[9] A conduct is frivolous if it is (1) "completely without merit in law"; (2) "undertaken primarily to . . . harass or maliciously injure another"; or (3) "assert[ing] material factual statements that are false."[10] New York courts also "consider, among other issues the circumstances under which the conduct took place, including the time available for investigating the legal or factual basis of the conduct, and whether or not the conduct was continued when its lack of legal or factual basis was apparent, should have been apparent, or was brought to the attention of counsel or the party."[11]

In Texas, a plaintiff is a vexatious litigant:

as defined by Section 11 054 of the Texas Civil Practice and Remedies Code because there is not a reasonable probability that he will prevail in this action and because Plaintiff repeatedly relitigates, or attempts to relitigate, pro se either. (A) the validity of the determination against the same defendant as to whom the litigation was finally determined; or (B) the cause of action, claim, controversy, or any of the issues of fact or law determined or concluded by the final determination against the same defendant as to whom the litigation was finally determined.[12]

As I said, I don't know if it's worth your time to engage in these sorts of strategies, but you should know they are there. Often people think they have no recourse when the other side doesn't play fairly in court. They do. It can just take a lot of work to obtain the justice you deserve.

TO SUM UP . . .

- Court can be a playground for really bad behavior and sometimes there is very little you can do about it. If you want to get any kind of justice for being subjected to these antics, you're very likely going to have to shoulder the burden and expense of seeking it on your own. It may be necessary to do so, however, especially if you feel the need to signal that you won't be an easy target for bad faith antics.

- Recognize that just because you proved that claims were wrong doesn't mean you'll be able to prove that they were brought without probable cause or with malice. All litigation is an effort to shape events to conform to a certain narrative; almost everyone is trying to produce their own version of reality, cutting and pasting bits as they choose. Still, vigorous advocacy is not the same thing as bald-faced lying, and you *are* entitled to a fair process, no matter how things may seem.

- In almost every other chapter, I've said you should try to work it out. "Working it out" usually implies some level of decency and good faith by your opponent, regardless of the nature of the dispute that brought you to court. Certain types of bad faith conduct may suggest that decency is but a distant dream, so you may think there's little hope for a pre-trial resolution. Remember, however, that even the worst of the bad faith players may not have the strength for a full fight. Besides, you never know if and when a dynamic (or a person) may change, so don't lose hope. If you can, you should try to work it out.

- Most importantly, don't let anyone steal you.

PART IV

The End May Be
Just the Beginning

Soon after the war of Revolution had closed and the settlers had returned to their homes, flattering themselves that now they might enjoy their possessions, what little they had left; and which they had so dearly bought, in peace and safety, they were annoyed by a set of land claimants, almost as destructive of the peace and happiness of the settlers as were the Indians and Tories in the time of the war. Ejectments were served upon the people without much discrimination. For many years they were kept in a state of agitation, embarrassment and suspense.—Spending their time and money (of which they had very little to spare) looking up their titles, collecting witnesses, feeing lawyers, attending courts, paying costs, making possession fences, buying new titles, etc., etc.

* * *

MAKE YOUR CASE

The foregoing named troubles should be told to the present generation that they may know how to prize their privileges.

—For the Herald, "Hubbardton, No. 2—
Something relating to original proprietors of the town;
Early surveys, and the troubles of the settlers occasioned by land claimants and their agents," *Rutland County Herald*, January 5, 1855

9

AFTER THE JUDGMENT

The Case Is Over. Are We Done Yet?

Maybe not.

If you won, you may be able to take only a brief sigh of relief.

When you're fighting in court, "over" doesn't necessarily mean *over*.

Or maybe you didn't win. Maybe you're bitterly disappointed in the outcome. Perhaps it's very clear to *you* that the process wasn't fair. In fact, your lawyer walked in on a juror talking on her cellphone in the courthouse bathroom, clearly discussing your case. The judge had told them *not* to do that.

Maybe there are documents that prove that the other side committed out-and-out perjury. Or perhaps the judge wouldn't let you admit certain documents at trial because their source was questionable, but since then, a crucial witness has come forward to verify their authenticity.

Maybe you believe the verdict is based on a total fraud and you believe you have evidence that will prove it.

You may get another shot at it. But first, you'll have some work to do.

What You Should Know: After the Trial

There are circumstances where a case—after all the twists and turns of pre-trial motions, all the grueling discovery battles, and all the fights over the other side's refusal to play by the rules—can end up getting another look.

"Getting your case another look," however, is not always the same as getting a fresh bite at the apple. Plus, demonstrating that you're entitled to that next round will take some work. It might mean throwing more money into the litigation furnace without knowing precisely what you'll get in return.

Or, if you win your case and aren't prepared to defend your victory, your hard-fought success may be short-lived.

"Defending your victory" is often an additional investment of your time and/or money. Don't assume that your losing opponent won't try to give it a shot even if they know they don't meet the standards; court process gives people an opportunity to keep pursuing you even when they know they don't have a good basis for it.

Alternatively, maybe your verdict just isn't built on as strong a foundation as you might like. Or maybe you lost, and you just want to know what you can do.

What You Should Know: Motion for Reconsideration

You can ask the trial judge to reconsider the judgment.

"Reconsideration" requires you to do more than tell the judge *I think you messed up!* Think about it—if there weren't specific standards, you'd be getting a fresh bite at the apple *just because* and the first trial would have no more weight than a crapshoot. Trial courts can't just change their minds without having a basis for doing so. If they could, their decisions would have no force or integrity.

What You Can Do

In California, for example, a motion for reconsideration requires that you show new or different facts or circumstances, or a change in the law, that have arisen since the trial. You normally have only a short time in which to file it (in California, it's ten days) and you must be prepared to demonstrate why the new facts or circumstances you allege couldn't have been presented earlier.

In other words, it's not enough simply to show that you've discovered something new; you also must show that you couldn't have discovered it in time for the trial of your case, or that it is a new fact or change in circumstances that has arisen since the original decision.

In a continuation of the various tumultuous things that have happened to you in the course of this book, you're now seeking to divorce Jine.

During your marriage, you and Jine borrowed money from a family trust ("Family Trust") controlled by other family members. Family Trust now claims you and Jine defaulted on a loan. Family Trust wants to foreclose on your home, which was community property held by both Jine and you.

The house was one of the assets at issue in the divorce. The divorce is pending in family court.

The Trustee—the person who controls Family Trust (which loaned Jine and you the money)—brings the foreclosure action in civil court.

Remember how I previously explained how courts may be divided into different divisions, depending on the subject matter of the case? Sometimes related cases involving some or all of the same litigants can be pending in two different courts at once.

You want the family court to make Family Trust a party in the divorce action. Family Trust is, in fact, trying to control what happens to one of the assets—the house—about which you and Jine are fighting in family court.

You want to *stay*, or put a hold on, the foreclosure proceedings that Family Trust brought in civil court. The family law judge grants your request for a stay and joins Family Trust as a party in the divorce action.

At around the same time, Family Trust was seeking a summary judgment on its foreclosure action.

As we discussed in Chapter 2, if the other side moves for summary judgment, they're claiming that you have produced no evidence that could defeat their claim or defense, and that as a consequence, they *must* win as a matter of law.

The civil court orders the parties to appear in court on Family Trust's summary judgment motion. This happens two days after the family court put a hold on the foreclosure proceedings.

Your lawyer showed up to court five minutes late. (Construction! He couldn't see the courthouse behind the scaffolding!)

When he arrived, the judge was almost finished with the case.

The judge wouldn't let him speak.

And people claim that my colleagues and I on *Hot Bench* sometimes cut off litigants! They should see what might happen in other courtrooms!

Consequently, the court was not advised about the stay order the family court had granted.

The civil court judge granted the Trustee's motion for summary judgment.

But . . . but . . . you had a stay!

You ask the court to reconsider its decision. There was, after all, the new fact of the stay, or temporary hold, on the foreclosure that the family court issued. The civil court didn't even know about it.

The judge sticks with his original ruling.

You appeal.

Fortunately for you, the court of appeal held that the trial judge was wrong, and that it should have acknowledged and deferred to the family court's stay.

According to the court of appeal, the trial court had abused its discretion in denying the motion for reconsideration. The stay was a new circumstance that required reconsideration. The judge made a mistake by not considering it.

We'll discuss later what it means for a court to "abuse its discretion."

By the way, the "stay" was the new circumstance, but don't underestimate the work that it often takes to get a court to employ this procedural device. You may have to explain why you're entitled to a stay—which requires filing a motion and responding to any opposition by the other side. (Also, if you want to join a third party in your action as happened in the example above, you may have to explain why they should be joined and respond to any opposition to that, too.) The necessity may seem obvious to you. But in court matters like these are often bitterly and expensively litigated.

New information doesn't necessarily guarantee you another shot. There could be a situation where you just have to sit on it and it doesn't make any difference at all.

Lolo Corp. was involved in a nasty dispute with SoSo Corp. They each claimed to have invented the same new beauty device and were suing each other over rights to the product.

SoSo Corp. claimed that Lolo had fraudulently obtained a patent in the product. In support of this claim, SoSo submitted evidence that none of the reported tests that Lolo used to support its patent ever worked, which would undermine the truth of its patent application.

At trial, SoSo's expert confirmed SoSo's position, testifying that there was no scenario in which any tests could support LoLo's patent. No scenario at all. The expert held firm, even under blistering cross-examination.

SoSo won the case and was awarded just under $200,000,000 in damages.

This was in Jurisdiction 1. A related case between the parties was pending in Jurisdiction 2. In Jurisdiction 2, SoSo brought a motion seeking to recover fees in that separate but related action.

LoLo was entitled to discovery in the fee and cost proceeding in Jurisdiction 2. In the course of that discovery, LoLo discovered that SoSo had concealed evidence of a test that supported Lolo's patent. This evidence flatly contradicted SoSo's position in Jurisdiction 1.

LoLo Corp. and its lawyers were outraged. They asked the court in Jurisdiction 2 for permission to use the new information in order to reverse the results in the trial at Jurisdiction 1.

You might think that this new information warranted immediate reversal.

It didn't.

In court, very few things are immediate. You have to ask the court to do something. To be even more precise, you have to pay to ask the court to do something. In this situation, Lolo had to pay to ask the Jurisdiction 2 court for permission to ask the Jurisdiction 1 court to use the newly acquired information in its motion to reconsider.

Why did LoLo ask instead of just doing it? Why didn't LoLo just get an automatic reversal? There was clear evidence that SoSo had lied. The rules in Jurisdiction 2, however, state that information obtained in discovery in a cost proceeding can *only* be used in that proceeding. LoLo wanted to be careful.

Lolo's lawyers asked the Jurisdiction 2 judge for permission to use the information about SoSo's obvious perjury and fraud on the court in the proceeding in Jurisdiction 1. The Jurisdiction 2 judge said no. Rules are rules. The information only could be used in the cost proceeding.

Jurisdiction 2 technically didn't have authority to control what happened in Jurisdiction 1. Sometimes, however, parties involved in litigation must bend to other concerns: LoLo did a lot of business in Jurisdiction 2, and couldn't run the risk of running afoul of a court order in that jurisdiction.

Despite uncovering this new information, LoLo never was able to use it to prove SoSo's perjury and fraud on the court.

All wasn't lost, however. LoLo moved for a new trial on the grounds of excessive damages. The new trial motion was granted, and the damages award was reduced from just under $200,000,000 to . . .

Wait for it, wait for it . . .

$1,000,0000.

On top of that, LoLo also prevailed on its counterclaims against SoSo and won more than $20,000,000.

In other words, as a result of a new trial motion, a party went from winning nearly $200,000,000 to owing its opponent more than $20,000,000.

Court battles can have all kinds of twists and turns.

What You Should Know: Motion for Judgment Notwithstanding the Verdict

In court, arbitrary and baseless decision-making is not supposed to happen. Still, sometimes it does. Court is peopled by humans and humans can be biased, arbitrary, and capricious. When judicial decision-makers make arbitrary decisions, however, you have an opportunity to make your case against them. In court, you can fight back.

When a jury issues a verdict for which there is no support in the record, you can ask the court to enter *judgment notwithstanding the verdict*, or JNOV. Again, different standards prevail across different jurisdictions, but there are some similar general principles.

In federal court, for instance, you have to show that, even when giving your opponent the benefit of the doubt regarding the evidence, the facts and inferences nonetheless point so "strongly and overwhelmingly" in your favor that reasonable people couldn't come to a contrary conclusion.

Many states follow a similar analysis. In Ohio, for instance, a court must grant a JNOV if "upon construing the evidence most strongly in favor of the party against who the motion is directed, it finds that upon any determinative issue reasonable minds could come to but one conclusion" against that party. Likewise, in California, a JNOV motion "may properly be granted only if it appears from the evidence, viewed in the light most favorable to the party securing the verdict, that there is no substantial evidence to support the verdict." If the evidence is conflicting or if several reasonable conclusions could be drawn, the court must deny the JNOV motion. Importantly, the court can't "weigh evidence," "draw inferences contrary to the verdict," or "assess the credibility of witnesses." The court will, however, review the whole record so as to determine whether the verdict has a reasonable basis.

Company X built an apartment complex featuring an outdoor swimming pool.

The complex was located in a city that required outdoor pools to be equipped with a self-locking gate in order to prevent access to the pool by unaccompanied children. The ordinance applied to anyone who "owns" or was "in possession of" premises that include an outdoor swimming pool.

Company X hired Contractor 1 to build a fence around the pool. Contractor 1 claimed that Company X hadn't ordered a self-locking gate. Contractor 1 also claimed that Company X had breached certain obligations under its contract, including the obligation to pay! (Contractor 1 maintained that Company X had written a bad check.)

Company X knew that the complex included families with children, knew that the city required self-locking gates, and also knew that in the absence of such gates, the fence surrounding the pool wouldn't close automatically.

Company X didn't install the self-locking gate but it did order that the gate be wired shut. Company X also posted signs prohibiting use of the pool. Still, people were unlatching the fence and using the pool anyway.

Company X then entered in an agreement with Company Y in which Company Y would take over management and control of the property. Company Y wouldn't acquire the title for several months.

Company Y had representatives who lived in the complex; who knew that the self-closing gate was required and hadn't been installed; and who had also been instructed by the health department to keep the pool closed until the gate was installed.

Company Y also knew that the pool was being used, but took no action to install the self-locking gate. According to Company Y, Company X had advised it that the self-locking gate was on order from a source hundreds of miles away. (The gate also was available from a local store.)

After the gate was ordered but before it arrived, Little Girl fell into the pool.

Little Girl lost consciousness and was hospitalized. She later recovered.

Her parents sued Company X and Company Y.

The jury returned a verdict against Company X . The jury let Company Y off the hook.

The plaintiffs weren't satisfied with this outcome. They moved the trial court for judgment notwithstanding the verdict.

The court held that the negligence of Company Y wasn't the proximate cause of the injury.

"Proximate cause" means legal cause. It's a much narrower type of causation than, for instance, a politician might use to justify something.

> The appellate court reversed, holding (among other things) that the plaintiffs should have received a JNOV as to Company Y's liability.
>
> The ordinance specifically applied not just to owners of premises with outdoor pools (Company Y didn't own the property yet) but also to those in possession of such premises (which Company Y was). According to the court of appeal, implicit in the jury's verdict was a finding that Company X's violation of the ordinance was the proximate cause of the accident—in fact, there was no evidence of any other cause. Company Y was in possession and control of the complex; knew that children might wander into the pool area; and was subject to the ordinance on the same terms as Company X.
>
> The jury had let Company Y off the hook, but upon review of that decision the court held there was no substantial evidence that could support that conclusion.
>
> The violation of the ordinance was the cause of the injury.
>
> Company X was subject to the ordinance and violated it. Company Y also was subject to the ordinance and violated it; and there was no substantial evidence excusing the violation.
>
> In other words, where the violation by one defendant was the proximate cause, a violation arising from the same set of facts and giving rise to the same harm, would be too.

Getting the court to overrule a lower court determination, whether by judge or jury, can require that you essentially revisit the entire case and reengage with all that evidence that was flying so fast and furiously at trial. If you want to argue that there was no substantial evidence, you're going to have to take the time to dig into the record so as to prove it. What was the testimony the other side offered against you? What were the worst and most damning documents used against you? Are you prepared to explain why, even if all that evidence is given its best spin, you're still entitled to a judgment?

Sometimes you may be faced with a situation where the decision-maker, whether jury or judge, seems to hang its hat on a hook made of really thin cobwebs, ignoring the big, brass hooks all around it. In that case, you'll still have to do the work of explaining why using cobweb supports makes no sense when there are much stronger materials available. You'll also have to explain just how and why the brass works better.

In other words, if the judgment against you was based on just the scantiest of evidence, you can take the opportunity to argue to the court that better, stronger facts were available that should have carried the day.

BigStore hired Pentague to do some work on its premises. As Pentague walked to the part of the facility where he was to do the work, he used a tunnel that had a slippery floor. BigStore employees were also unloading boxes in the tunnel and stacking them along both sides, obstructing access to handrails.

Pentague slipped and fell in the tunnel.

Pentague then sued BigStore, alleging that BigStore failed to keep the tunnel safe and that it failed to warn him against the dangers the tunnel posed.

In order to prevail under the theory of liability he was asserting, Pentague had to show that he did not have actual knowledge of the danger.

Pentague testified at trial that even though he knew about the tunnel's slippery floor, he didn't know how dangerous it was. He also testified that even though he saw the boxes, he didn't realize they were blocking access to the handrails on each side of the tunnel until he entered it. He admitted, however, that he noticed the floor was slippery as he entered the tunnel. His coworker, who was accompanying him on the job, also testified that he noticed the boxes as he entered the tunnel and that he warned Pentague about the tunnel's slippery floor as they entered. All of this happened before Pentague fell.

The jury ruled that the accident was 65% BigStore's fault and 35% Pentague's fault.

The trial court granted BigStore a JNOV, finding that the evidence demonstrated that Pentague did have actual knowledge of the dangerous condition, and thus couldn't recover.

The court of appeal reversed, holding that the evidence regarding Pentague's knowledge of the dangers was "ambiguous."

The state supreme court reversed, concluding that any inference that Pentague was unaware of the dangers posed was unreasonable. According to the Court, the evidence was clear that he was.

That little cobweb of evidence on which the decision-maker may have based its decision against you can't carry the day against the big, solid pieces of brass you may have offered. Still, you'll have to do the work of explaining why that brass is as strong as it is.

Consider also the journey of this BigStore case. Someone got a jury verdict because he claimed that a wet staircase with boxes on it, which prevented access to handrails, wasn't a danger of which he was aware. The court said, *of course you were aware of it!* The appellate court said, *well, maybe he wasn't really.* The state supreme court said, *of course he was!*

You may not have BigStore's money or resources to fight a case like this. You may not have a lawyer who will take your case the distance like Pentague did. Just be aware of how wild the journey can be even if you win (or lose) something that seems "straightforward."

Almost nothing in court is "straightforward." Your injury, of whatever type, may be obvious, at least to you, or it may arise from circumstances you find painful to relive. Still, you may *have* to relive them—at least through court filings as you make the expensive journey to finality.

Dan was dying. Before he passed, he and his partner, Sam, went to a funeral home to make arrangements for his service. Dan's final wish was to be cremated. Upon his cremation, the funeral home was to release his ashes to Sam. They were explicit about not wanting a religious ceremony of any kind. Instead, they wanted a party.

Dan died. His mother released the body to Sam, who gave it to the funeral home.

Instead of releasing Dan's ashes to Sam, the funeral home instead performed a Christian religious service on Dan's remains and then scattered them at sea.

The funeral home never turned over any remains to Sam, as Dan had requested.

The funeral home had agreed not to contact Dan's family about the mishandling of the ashes until Sam instructed them to do so.

That didn't happen. A representative from the funeral home contacted Dan's mother and sister and told him that even though Sam wanted a party instead of a religious service, they had done the religious service and scattered the ashes. The funeral home representative also told them that Sam was unable to attend the service because he was sick.

Sam, Dan's mother, and Dan's sister sued the funeral home for negligence; mishandling of dead bodies; and breach of fiduciary duty.

The funeral home was able to get a number of the claims dismissed on the pleadings.

Then, after Sam, Dan's mother, and Dan's sister filed a motion for reconsideration, some of their causes of action were reinstated.

They went to trial. It ended in *mistrial.*

They went to trial again. They sought compensatory damages, attorney fees, costs, and $500,000 in punitive damages.

The jury awarded $175,000 in compensatory damages to Sam; $62,500 in compensatory damages to Dan's mother; and $5,000 in compensatory damages to Dan's sister. It concluded that the funeral home had acted with malice, oppression or fraud; in other words, the plaintiffs had met their burden with respect to establishing an entitlement to punitive damages.

They met their burden, yes.

The jury awarded each of them punitive damages—in the amount of $1 each.

Both sides then filed requests for a judgment notwithstanding the verdict and a new trial. The motions were denied.

The funeral home appealed. It claimed that Dan's partner, Sam, couldn't recover because he wasn't a close relative; that Dan's mother and sister couldn't recover because they weren't "direct victims of their negligent conduct" as they weren't the intended recipients of the ashes (nor was it planned that they would attend the ceremony Sam was planning); and that the emotional distress damages were excessive.

Ultimately, the court of appeal rejected the funeral home's arguments, but only after explaining the substantial evidence that existed to support the damages awarded to Dan's partner, mother, and sister. Sam was depressed and withdrawn, among other things. Dan's mother, too, was depressed. In examining the JNOV motion, the court took pains to review the evidence to see if there was substantial support for the jury's verdict. There was. Defending that win, however, involved taking time to restate what may seem fairly obvious.

What You Should Know: Motion for a New Trial

Like a motion for reconsideration, a motion for a new trial requires that you meet certain specific procedural requirements, which vary across jurisdictions.

There are, however, a number of similarities across jurisdictions in the various bases for seeking a new trial: excessive verdicts; misconduct by the lawyers or the jury; a claim that the judge made a critical mistake admitting or excluding certain evidence—these are just a few examples.

EXAMPLES OF SOME OF THE REQUIREMENTS FOR A NEW TRIAL IN DIFFERENT JURISDICTIONS

Federal Court
- the verdict is against the weight of the evidence;
- the damages are excessive;
- the trial was unfair;
- problems with evidence that was introduced or rejected;
- the jury received the wrong instructions;
- to prevent an injustice.

New York
- the verdict is contrary to the weight of the evidence,
- it's in the "interest of justice" ("Interest of justice" includes situations where you believe the trial court made mistakes regarding the admission of evidence; or gave the jury bad instructions; misconduct; newly discovered evidence, and surprise);
- the jury cannot agree.

Texas
- The damages are "manifestly too small or too large."

Ohio
- Irregularity in the proceedings of the court, jury, magistrate, or prevailing party, or any order of the court or magistrate, or abuse of discretion, by which an aggrieved party was prevented from having a fair trial;
- Misconduct of the jury or prevailing party;
- Accident or surprise which ordinary prudence could not have guarded against;
- Excessive or inadequate damages, appearing to have been given under the influence of passion or prejudice;

- Error in the amount of recovery, whether too large or too small, when the action is upon a contract or for the injury or detention of property;
- The judgment is not sustained by the weight of the evidence; however, only one new trial may be granted on the weight of the evidence in the same case;
- The judgment is contrary to law;
- Newly discovered evidence, material for the party applying, which with reasonable diligence he could not have discovered and produced at trial;
- Error of law occurring at the trial and brought to the attention of the trial court by the party making the application;
- "For good cause shown," which is committed to the "sound discretion of the trial court."

California

In order to demonstrate a basis for getting a new trial, you normally have to show that there was either:
- An irregularity in the proceedings;
- Jury misconduct;
- Accident or surprise;
- Newly discovered evidence;
- Excessive or inadequate damages;
- Insufficiency of the evidence; or
- An error in law.[1]

As you can see, it's not just a matter of making vague claims about how unfair the trial was; how the judge seemed biased against you and your lawyer in ways you can't specify; how you could tell from the jurors' body language that they weren't really paying attention when your side put on its case—you get the idea. All of these may have been true, and your gut feelings and common sense judgments may indeed be onto something. Still, unless you can find a way to justify those gut feelings with facts that bring your case within one of the specified categories for getting a new trial, you may just have to live with that bad feeling in your gut.

Also, you must stay on your guard.

You're in trial. Your opponent submits a piece of evidence that they never turned over in discovery. It's something for which you specifically asked. When you made the request, your opponent claimed they had nothing like it. Then, they sprung it on you at trial—and it clearly made a difference in the case. The jury found against you and now you owe this lying d***bag money. You are definitely going to move for a new trial on this basis.

Here's the thing: unless you objected to this evidence at the time of trial or made an issue about it then, you may be out of luck. Some grounds for seeking a new trial require that you demonstrate that you raised or objected to the issue during the course of the proceedings. If you think that something went or is going wrong, you have to make an issue of it when you still have the chance; you can't just wait and see what happens, and then try to get the court to correct it afterwards.

Be prepared to demonstrate that you did all you could with respect to the issue, whether it's proving that you were diligent in your efforts to obtain evidence; that you made timely objections to the admission or exclusion of evidence that was important or unduly prejudicial; or that you made a record of those facts which, taken together, constitutes the type of "injustice" you believe warrants having the first case thrown out. If you didn't complain about it at the time, you may have to show a very good reason for not having done so. If you don't, the court may consider the issue waived.

Of course, whenever there are rules and standards in court, you will find variations in how different courts interpret them. Don't make any assumptions about how they'll be applied in your case, and don't think I'm making any predictions or trying to encourage you to make one decision rather than another, either. If there weren't so many different ways of seeing things, there wouldn't be lawsuits and there wouldn't be lawyers. How your case will fall within the parameters of these rules is something only you and the legal professionals advising you can determine, since the application of the rules will depend on the particular facts of your case. One of the reasons that I'm writing this book is that I want to give you a sense of the various uncertainties that exist.

Still, in order to give you a general sense of what these standards can mean, here's an example of how California interprets the rules:

Irregularity in the Proceedings
This is a catch-all which can include anything from misconduct by counsel, the judge or the jury to any other matter that might have violated a party's right to a fair trial.

There is a collision in the store parking lot between driver C and driver H. The parties involved dispute whether it was accidental or intentional.

C claims he hit H's vehicle only slightly and it was unintentional.

H claims the collision was violent and resulted from C's parking-lot rage. H, the spouse of a law enforcement officer, calls the police.

C is arrested and charged with a crime.

His case goes to trial and he is acquitted of all charges. He then brings an action against the city for false arrest, false imprisonment, malicious prosecution, violation of civil rights, conspiracy, negligence, and infliction of emotional distress. His wife also brings an action for loss of consortium— i.e., being deprived of the benefits of her marital relationship.

C exercises a peremptory challenge to a potential judge, who we'll call Judge No 1.

Again, a peremptory challenge is when you seek to exclude a judge (or juror) from your case simply because you don't want them there—although remember, you can't base a peremptory challenge on race or gender.[2] Maybe the challenge is based on the judge or juror's history or background with respect to certain kinds of matters or some other issue, but you don't have to explain and you don't have to cross your fingers and hope that the judge agrees with you. But you're only allowed a limited number of these challenges.

Judge No. 2 is assigned to the case. The city moves for nonsuit on the ground that H's declaration provided probable cause for C's arrest and prosecution.

A "nonsuit" is like a demurrer. If you file one, you're essentially arguing that even if everything the complaint alleges is true, those allegations are insufficient to support a cause of action. In this case, the nonsuit was based on the city's argument that it was entitled to rely on the contents on H's police report when it arrested and charged C.

Judge No. 2 grants the motion.

C subsequently learns that Judge No. 2 had a conversation with Judge No. 1 about the case. C moves for a new trial on this and other grounds.

Both judges admit to the conversation. Judge No. 2 disclosed that prior to granting the nonsuit motion, he had discussed with Judge No. 1 the law and procedures that might be applicable to the case. Judge No. 2 stated that Judge No. 1 had not advised him how to rule and that his decision granting the nonsuit was the result of his own research and analysis. He also stated that he wasn't aware that Judge No. 1 had been disqualified when they spoke.

Judge No. 1 confirmed that he didn't try to tell Judge No. 2 how to decide the case. He also disclosed another conversation with Judge No. 2 that took place prior to the hearing on C's motion for a new trial. In that conversation, the only subject discussed was scheduling a court reporter for the new trial and the shortage of court reporters.

C challenges Judge No. 2 "for cause." He contends that Judge No. 2's conversation about the case with Judge No. 1 should disqualify him from the matter as well.

Judicial Council Judge disqualifies Judge No. 2. The disqualification is effective as of the time of the conversation with Judge No. 1. Even if Judge No. 2 wasn't actually aware of the disqualification, the information was in the court file. Judicial Council Judge concludes that a reasonable person would entertain doubts about the judge's objectivity.

Judge No. 2 ruled on the city's nonsuit motion *after* he had the conversation with Judge No. 1. He ruled on the nonsuit motion at a time when he was actually disqualified from the matter.

H and C's parking lot crash case is just one example. Again, it would be wrong to assume too much about your situation just based on these facts. The thing to keep in mind is that there are loads of details you have to confirm when you're making this kind of motion; again, it's not enough simply to throw a bunch of stuff at the wall. You have to lay out in painstaking detail why the irregularity is one that denied you a fair process.

Jury Misconduct

Jury misconduct can include all sorts of behavior—from ignoring the judge's instructions, to discussing the case with third parties, to deciding a case by chance. (Remember, "chance" is arbitrary!)

Jurors are trying to agree upon a damages verdict in an automobile accident case. There is a wide disparity among what the jurors think is appropriate: some want to award $1, others $100,000.

You never know how people are going to see things. Remember, these are people who all were considering the same set of facts!

The jurors agree to be bound by the average of the 12 separate amounts they each think appropriate, and to abide by that number without further discussion.

This is not okay. Deciding upon an amount by chance, or simply agreeing to be bound by an average of various conclusions, without further discussion examining the basis for those conclusions, is an improper "quotient" verdict. If the jurors are agreeing to be bound by a calculation that results from numbers about which they have no information (a particular juror will know what *her* estimate is but isn't taking the time to deliberate about the fairness of the estimates provided by others) this is little better than arriving at a verdict by chance.[3] (It would not be misconduct, however, where the jurors discuss their various conclusions with one another and then arrive at an average after they've deliberated about the basis for their decisions.) Going to court may, in fact, be a "roll of the dice" in terms of your having very little certainty about what will happen there, but no one is actually supposed to roll the dice when making decisions about your case.

Accident or Surprise

This means more than just being "shocked" by adverse testimony that you should have anticipated, or inadvertently forgetting to mention something in court that you think might have made a difference. Instead, you usually have to show some unexpected condition or situation that arose through no fault of your own and against which you couldn't have protected by being reasonably careful.

Was the source of the "accident" something unexpected? Were you in part to blame? Could you have prevented it by being more careful? Or did the other side spring something on you that resulted in an unfair outcome?

Newly Discovered Evidence

The trial is over. Since then, however, you came across some old hard drives that contain emails about which you'd completely forgotten.

(Your computer died a year before and you got a new one. You never uploaded your old data.) The emails prove that the other side lied. It's new evidence! You may get another bite at it.

Not so fast. You've already heard about LoLo Corp., who had to bury its opponent's perjury because it only learned of it in a separate proceeding (and the court said LoLo couldn't use it to contradict the false testimony given in the original proceeding).

So remember, even if you discover something new, you'll first have to make sure it's admissible. Otherwise, you can't get it before the court.

There's more. It's not enough simply to have discovered new evidence; you also have to show that it is not redundant with other evidence already put forward; that it's likely to change the result; and that you couldn't have discovered it before.

Not that you *didn't* discover it—but that you *couldn't* have discovered it, even if you'd been *reasonably diligent*. Claiming that you couldn't have discovered evidence when it was somehow in your possession, custody, or control, for instance, but you just didn't take the time to look at it, could set you up for an expensive failure. Maybe the court will conclude that you should have found that old hard drive sooner. Or, maybe the court will excuse your failure to produce it.

Plus, you also have to show that the evidence would likely result in a different outcome. This is a high standard. To meet it, you'll need to demonstrate that the new facts would have changed the outcome, even in the face of other adverse evidence against you.

Excessive Damages

LoLo Corp.'s path to justice was through a claim of excessive damages.

Juries have discretion to award damages, but there are limits to their power. If you're hit by a verdict that you think goes beyond all fairness and reason, then you may have the option of seeking a new trial on this ground, too.

Excessive damages are a basis on which litigants who find themselves on the wrong end of highly punitive verdicts, for instance, frequently seek to undo those results. Punitive damages are a function of the jury's conclusions regarding how bad certain conduct is; they are available when conduct is malicious, grossly negligent, or done with intentional disregard of your rights. They are intended to punish. For that reason, they can easily traverse the distance from *"This makes sense, given the horrible thing you did, and you will have to find a way to pay it, however inconvenient that may be"* . . . to . . . *"We are just going to come up with the highest number we can because we hate you and think you suck."*

A punitive damage award, however, isn't "excessive" just because you'll have a very hard time paying it. There are factors the court will consider in making the determination.

STANDARDS FOR EVALUATING THE SIZE OF A PUNITIVE DAMAGE AWARD

1. The reprehensibility of the defendant's conduct.
2. The proportion of the punitive damage award to the compensatory damage award (compensatory damages are those intended to compensate you for your actual loss, as opposed to punishing the defendant). There are some general guidelines for determining whether a punitive damage award is disproportionate to the compensatory award, but they operate more like general guidelines instead of hard and fast rules.
3. The wealth of the defendant.[4]

Insufficiency of the Evidence

Moving for a new trial on the basis of insufficiency of the evidence essentially requires that you mount a wholesale attack on the case the other side put on against you. You have to do far more than explain why the court should have adopted your view of things instead of your opponent's. It requires that you demonstrate that your opponent didn't put forward enough evidence to support the verdict in the first place. You have to show that the evidence can't reasonably form a basis for the judgment.

Error in Law

Perhaps the judge gave the jury the wrong instructions, which led it to decide your case on erroneous legal grounds. "Error in law" means that the judge made a mistake in the law applicable to your case.

What You Should Know: Appeals

I'm going to appeal all the way to the Supreme Court.

No, you most likely will not.

(FYI, the U.S. Supreme Court hears only a small percentage of the cases that litigants seek to appeal. For the October 2019 term, for instance, the Supreme Court granted only sixty-eight *Petitions for Certiorari*. This is out of the 7000–8000 petitions that are filed each term.)

Some of the cases on which I've relied to explain the various standards for JNOVs and new trials are decisions by appellate courts. When someone loses one of those motions, they can appeal. You can appeal any final judgment of the trial court. (There are also certain limited circumstances where you can appeal "interlocutory" orders—orders that the court issues before the case is over.[5])

An appeal, however, is not a "do-over." In the court of appeal, you will not have the opportunity to testify, or have your lawyer call witness, or do anything except listen to your lawyer (or do it yourself) talk about the things that happened at trial and the law that is applicable to your dispute. You can't present new evidence that you didn't present at trial (although you can challenge the fact that the trial court didn't give you a chance to introduce evidence that you contend might have been helpful to your case).

Your appeal should pinpoint precisely what it is you believe the trial court or jury got wrong.

Everything! They didn't listen! Just reverse it because they really messed up!

This won't work. You have to be able to explain to the court specifically what the mistake was, and why you believe it was a material factor in your obtaining a negative result at trial.

It's not enough to show a mistake, but you usually also must show that the mistake was one that altered the course of things in a significant way. (This is in contrast to a mistake that a court will consider to be "harmless error." Harmless error essentially means *sure, something happened here that shouldn't have happened, but there was so much other evidence justifying your loss that we aren't going to upset the apple cart. In the scheme of things, it's not such a big deal.*)

What Does the Court of Appeal Do?

The way the court of appeal evaluates the case depends on what it is you believe went wrong before the trial court.

What You Should Do: Know Exactly *What* and *Why* You Are Appealing

Did the jury believe someone you contend was a liar? Did the judge make a mistake in admitting a piece of evidence that you believe may have biased the jury against you?

These are questions that go to the issue of who the judge or jury found to be credible. Courts of appeal reason that with respect to credibility issues, the trial judge is in a better position to make appropriate judgments than the appellate court is. After all, the trial judge was the one who observed the witnesses firsthand whereas the court of appeal has only the record of what happened at trial. The trial judge lived it. Besides, if the court of appeal gave every case a fresh bite at the apple, a trial would be nothing more than a formality and our already expensive and interminably long system of civil litigation would be even more so. When you are challenging a question of fact, the court of appeal will review the trial court's decision for an *abuse of discretion* or *clear error.*

The court of appeal, however, is not always so deferential.

An appeal may be based on the claim that the trial court made a mistake regarding the law instead of a mistake involving the facts. An example of this would be if the judge gave the jury the wrong instructions about the law applicable to the facts of your case. When you're bringing a claim, there has to be some law or rule to which the facts you allege apply; the interpretation and explanation of that rule is key to how the decision-maker will evaluate those facts. If the judge gives the wrong instruction, he may have misstated the law to the jury.

Here's an example to help you better distinguish between legal and factual questions in a case: You argue that the rally or demonstration that you've organized is protected by the First Amendment; the other side says no such protection exists because they own the park. The issues of how many people were present at the rally; whether you complied with the park's rules regarding the obtaining of permits; and who said what during the speeches, would be questions of fact to which the "clear error" standard applies. Whether the First Amendment applies to those activities taking place in the park, however, would be a question of law, requiring *de novo* review.

What do these standards—*clear error, abuse of discretion, de novo*—mean? What do you have to show if you want to convince the court of appeal that the trial court got it wrong?

Clear Error

To prove clear error, you have to show that while there may be some evidence to support the lower court's finding, a review of the entire record will leave the appellate court with "the definite and firm conviction that a mistake has occurred." Don't ask the court of appeal to substitute its judgment for the trial court—it can't do that—and if the evidence in the record is such that it could have gone either way (and it went against you), you'll have an uphill battle if you want the court of appeal to reverse course.

You are applying for a job as a statistician in an aeronautics company. You have a degree in statistics; you used to teach statistics; and you have another degree in aeronautics. There was only one other applicant for the job—a high school math teacher ten years your junior. You are a woman. The math teacher is a man.

A panel of interviewers questions you during the application process—four men and one woman. You find the interview strange. Your interviewers asked how your husband felt about you working; they query whether your young children would suffer as a result of your long hours; whether the high-stress environment would adversely impact your family life; plus, they point out that since you're still relatively young (and given all the advances in modern science), you might still be able to have another child. *Are you sure you're going to be in it for the long haul?*

You aren't surprised when, following the interview, the committee, by a vote of 4–1, gave the job to the male math teacher (the woman on the committee was your lone vote of support). You may not be surprised, but you are mad. (You don't care if they call you an *Angry Woman*. You don't like having people throw little rocks in your eyes.)

You bring a lawsuit against the company, claiming gender bias. You win.

John, who owns the company, is horrified by this decision. He testified that he has the highest regard for women, that he built the company from scratch while living with his mother and sister, and that he paid for his sister's education as she pursued her Ph.D. He and the company have been involved in numerous civic and charitable organizations that promote issues important to women and girls, including equality in the workplace. What's more, John's assistant, a woman, testified that he had always treated everyone with kindness and respect and never showed bias toward anyone.

You win your lawsuit and John is furious.

Could the trial court have seen the facts John's way? Sure. But it didn't.

John wants to make a case for why the court of appeal should reverse the trial court's decision, but he must show more than just that there is an interpretation of the evidence under which he would have won. He has to leave the court with the "definite and firm conviction" that a mistake has taken place.

The job of the reviewing court isn't to find a factual basis for the alternative position; it's to determine whether the findings were so without support as to leave a "definite and firm conviction" that a mistake happened.

John is unable to do this and so the trial court decision must stand.

A mistake isn't just a mistake because you lost. A mistake might be what happens when the judge ignores uncontradicted evidence, or makes findings in their decision that something wasn't in the record when it actually was, for example.

Abuse of Discretion

A judge "abuses their discretion" when they act arbitrarily, ignoring the evidence in the record and coming up with a result that isn't supported by it.

This, again, is one of the reasons why there are so many (expensive) pre-trial fights before you actually have the main event: each side wants to make sure that they have in the record as many favorable facts as possible, and that they exclude all the unfavorable ones they can. Then, if things *don't* go their way, they can lead the appellate court through a roadmap of facts in the record that demonstrate why they believe the trial court got it wrong.

De Novo

While the appellate court must defer to the trial court's findings of fact, it is obligated to engage in an independent review of the law at issue. In some circumstances, an appellate court will review even the facts independently to determine whether those facts are sufficient to meet the legal standard.[6]

> You write an op-ed piece against a local politician, who you consider to be nothing more than a shady grifter. In particular, you attack his policy for awarding government contracts, which conveniently seem always to be awarded to his relatives and cronies. Your recent piece was particularly vicious, catching the politician's eye and raising his ire. He sues you for defamation. Since he is a public figure, he has to show not only that the things you wrote about him weren't true (and it turns out, some of your facts were wrong), but also that you had "actual malice" when you wrote them.

The fact that your op-ed was inaccurate may not, in itself, be sufficient to prove malice. The court's de novo review of the case requires that it review the record to determine whether what you did meets the legal standard of malice. Reviewing the facts to determine whether they meet a legal standard is sometimes necessary in order to determine whether that standard is satisfied. "Malice" requires more than simply failing to dot your i's and cross your t's. (Of course, this is different from intentional efforts to avoid seeking the truth, which can support a finding of malice.)[7] "Our profound national commitment to the free exchange of ideas"[8] means that judges, "as expositors of the Constitution,"[9] must engage in an independent review of the record. In other words, the reviewing court isn't obligated to defer to what may be the trial court's reasonable interpretation; instead, it is obligated to engage in an independent review so as to determine whether the applicable legal standards have been met.

Sometimes the distinction between legal and factual questions isn't so clear cut. You might be appealing something that is a mix of both, in which case you'll need to present evidence sufficient to meet the different standards that apply.

Whether you appeal depends on what makes sense for you and your case. Do you have the resources? Can you *not* afford to let a lower court decision stand? Do you want to just be done with it? Do you need to go forward so as to vindicate a right important to you?

Or, you may be in a situation where you've won but the other side appeals. You might end up right back where you started.

Fauzia Din's husband was in Afghanistan. She was a naturalized citizen living in the U.S. He wanted a visa to come to the country so they could live together, as married people like to do. His visa was summarily denied. He was not provided a reason, and she couldn't get an explanation, either.

She filed a complaint for declaratory relief in federal court, asking that the court declare that she, as a U.S citizen, had a constitutional interest in her marriage, which would enable her to challenge the denial of her husband's visa.

A complaint for "declaratory relief" is when the plaintiff asks the court to declare the rights of the parties, as opposed to asking that the other side pay money, or do or refrain from doing something. (You can seek declaratory relief in addition to seeking other things, too.)

The trial court dismissed the complaint. The court of appeal reversed. The government appealed to the U.S. Supreme Court.

In a 5–4 decision, the Supreme Court reversed. Then three of the Justices (Justices Scalia, Roberts, and Thomas) found that there was no constitutional interest at issue in her case. Two of the Justices (Kennedy and Alito) found that the Court didn't need to answer the question of whether "a citizen has a protected liberty interest in the visa application of her alien spouse." Four of the Justices (Breyer, Ginsburg, Sotomayor, and Kagan) concluded that Din had a procedural due process right to know why her husband's visa was denied.

Five of the Justices held that even if the government had a burden to provide due process, the government had met its burden. (Justices Scalia, Roberts, Thomas, Kennedy, and Alito joined in that portion of the opinion.) Four of the Justices disagreed. (Justices Breyer, Ginsburg, Sotomayor and Kagan joined in the dissenting opinion.[10])

She lost at trial; she won on appeal; and then she lost again. In litigation, you can't always be certain that your victory will stick.

A LOSS MIGHT BE SOMEONE'S WIN

In the later case of *Trump v. Hawaii*,[11] for instance, the Supreme Court cited *Din* for the proposition that a "person's interest in being united with his relatives is sufficiently concrete and particularized to form the basis of an Article III injury in fact." (This refers to the concept of *standing*, something else you have to consider before going to court. "Standing" refers to whether or not you've actually been injured by whatever it is you're seeking to challenge in your lawsuit; if it isn't a legally defined injury to *you*, then you don't have any standing to bring the lawsuit and thus can't proceed in court.)

Just because you've got a judgment in your case doesn't mean the fight is over. There are post-trial motions, and appeals to consider, and bringing or defending against them requires that you be familiar with the rules. It's not as easy as just asking for a do-over because you think the judge or jury got it wrong. You have to explain why that "wrong" is something that the appellate court can fix, and why the law and the facts in your case justify that intervention.

TO SUM UP . . .

- Winning or losing your case at trial may just be the first step. You may end up making or defending against post-trial motions, which will require you and your attorneys to pinpoint precisely where you think the trial court got it wrong, if you lost your case.

- In a similar vein, you can't get too secure in your win because there's always a chance that a higher court might see things differently. It's precisely because of this uncertainty that it really can make sense to look for an out-of-court resolution, even if the wind seems to be blowing in your favor.

- The court likely won't just change its mind without you providing it a very good reason. If you want it to change course, you'll have the burden of reciting those parts of the evidence and the law that you believe mandate a reversal, and you'll have to explain why the court made a mistake.

- Your explanation will have to fall into one of certain specified categories in order to get some relief from the verdict. It's usually not enough simply to relitigate your case in the same way.

- The same is true of your appeal. The appellate court will give greater deference to the trial court's factual findings and its decisions regarding trial management issues (such as the admission or rejection of evidence, for example) than it will to the trial court's interpretation of the law. That doesn't mean that an appellate court won't review the facts, but it will usually do so in the course of determining whether they are sufficient to satisfy a legal burden.

- Oh, and you know what? It's never too late to work it out.

10

WHEN YOUR OPPONENT IGNORES YOUR WIN

Don't Assume Compliance with Court Orders Comes Without a Fight

Perhaps you got your judgment and it is final. Maybe the other side didn't appeal. Maybe they appealed and lost. *Finally*, you may be saying to yourself. *Finally. Now I just have to cash the check.*

Maybe not.

What You Should Know:
When They Just Don't Pay

You worked for Orsel, a singer, for years and considered yourself a loyal and faithful employee.

Unfortunately, Orsel wasn't as loyal and had the unfortunate habit of not paying you for your work. You are forced to sue Orsel for unpaid wages.

Orsel decided simply to ignore the lawsuit. You obtain a default judgment against her of more than one million dollars. Now, you have a legal basis to put a lien on Orsel's bank accounts!

When you serve the subpoenas on Orsel's bank, however, you discover that she has closed all of her accounts.

Unfortunately, this isn't uncommon.

Even if you win, getting your money can be hard. Sometimes people just won't pay, regardless of what the court decision is. Remember, some people end up in court because they either don't care about anyone's rules but their own, or they had the misfortune of engaging with someone who falls into this category. Don't assume a court judgment will change that. If you want to get your money, you may have to open up an entirely new front in your battle.

It's hard to get precise statistics on how many judgments go uncollected because not everyone who doesn't get paid necessarily is going to make a record of it. One company that is in the business of selling judgments did a study in one New York court and came back with some pretty staggering results—of the $10,029,585,129 in judgments that were awarded over an 18-year period (from 1996 to 2014), $8,159,894,817 remained uncollected as of the time that the company published its data. Eighty-one percent of judgments in that court over that period went uncollected.[1]

That seems crazy. It can cause one to question the point of bringing the lawsuit in the first place.

I'm not suggesting that the numbers are necessarily that high in other jurisdictions. Still, irrespective of where you file your lawsuit, it can be really tough to get your money.

STILL LEFT HANGING

Some of the litigants who are most in need of court to protect or vindicate their rights can find themselves unable to collect or enjoy the benefits of their litigation victory.

One janitorial worker still hadn't received any payments five years after her employer was hit with a $1.7 million judgment for wage theft against her and other workers. Another employer owed $300,000 and paid nothing. The "successful" litigant in that case was fighting cancer and living on Social Security income.[2]

What You Can Do: Getting Your Money

First, recognize that you may have to spend even more to get some back. If you're among those litigants with few to no resources with which to chase your opponent down, your judgment may be worth little more than the paper on which its printed. It may even be worth less—some paper is expensive.

In any event, if you're able to move forward you may have some work to do.

You may have to file papers instructing that money be paid to you directly from your opponent's bank accounts or other assets. You'll need some basic information first, such as the name of the entity that holds their assets (are they held personally or in a business name?) and the banks where they have accounts. In an age where people can move money with a key stroke and business entities can conceal their owners beneath multi-layered creations that can take

a lot of time and money to dissect, you may spend a lot of time trying to get to the bottom of things.

The steps you have to take to collect will vary depending on your
jurisdiction. Here's an example of what you have to do in California:

Biding Your Time

In the normal case, you'll wait a certain period of time until the
judgment is final. In California, that's thirty days from the time it is
entered—*not from the time you go to court.* Note that because of the
heavy burdens under which many courts work, it may take a while
for your judgment actually to be entered.

Remember to check the statute of limitations for collecting judgments
in your jurisdiction. (In California, it's ten years—and you're entitled to
ten percent interest on the unpaid amounts a year. Plus, if you renew the
judgment each year, you're entitled to compounded interest, which
means that in year two, for instance, you'd be entitled to interest on both
the principal and the interest that's owed from year one.)

Ask Questions

You can request a Debtor's Examination. To start this process, there
is usually a court form you can file (in California, it's the Application and Order to Produce Statement of Assets and Appear for Examination). You can then attend that examination and learn what
assets the defendant has.

After you know more about the defendant's assets, you can then
file what's known as a Writ of Execution—another form that you can
obtain from the court. You have to file a separate writ for each
county where the defendant has assets that you want to attach. You'll
need to pay a processing fee and also a service fee to the sheriff in
order to have the writ served.

Finding the Goods

You can levy the defendant's bank accounts or you can attempt to garnish their wages. If it's a bank levy, the sheriff can collect from the bank

and send the money to you. If it's a wage garnishment, you can garnish up to twenty-five percent of the defendant's total pay until you are paid. You can also file and record an Abstract of Judgment in order to put a lien on any real estate the defendant owns. In order to record the judgment, you file the abstract with the court that issued it, have the abstract certified, and then take the certified abstract to the office of the county reporter in the county where the judgment debtor owns property. Then you can record the abstract and put a lien on the debtor's property.

Enforcing your judgment may mean spending even more time and money trying to get the money your opponent already owes you. When you're fighting in court, it sometimes may feel like the fight never ends.

Harriet obtained a judgment against Jefferson for the money he owed her.

Before the trial started, during it, and after it was over, Jefferson repeatedly insisted that he had no intention of paying.

He wasn't lying. He had no intention of paying. But Harriet did an asset search and discovered that he had a Rolls-Royce. He'd put the car in his deceased ex-wife's name and claimed it had no engine.

About two months after the judgment, Harriet filed for a *writ of execution* on the judgment. The writ had instructions to the sheriff requesting that he "levy upon" Jefferson's car—in other words, that he take it.

The deputy went to Jefferson's home to get the car. Jefferson wasn't home but the car was in the garage. The deputy then advised Harriet's lawyer that because the car was in the garage, she would have to obtain a *private place order.*

Harriet's lawyer then filed a motion with the court seeking a private place order, which she received. The deputy went to the home to obtain the car; Jefferson first attempted to deter them, but since the order gave the deputy the right to use force (provided there was no substantial risk of death or serious bodily harm), Jefferson relented and the deputy removed the vehicle. The Rolls Royce was sold at auction and Harriet received the proceeds.

Another option is to hire someone to pursue the judgment on your behalf, in exchange for their taking a percentage of the recovery. It can save you the time and hassle of trying to track down your opponent and/or their assets.

You may have other options too. In California, for instance, if the dispute involved a motor vehicle accident, you can seek to have the defendant's license suspended. If it involved the rendering of professional services, you can seek to have the defendant's license to do work in that field suspended.

When you finally receive all the money you are due, you then must file an Acknowledgment of Satisfaction of Judgment.

What if your opponent files bankruptcy? File a proof of claim as soon as you can, so you can get in line with the rest of the defendant's creditors. A judgment that you thought would be a game changer can become virtually uncollectible if the defendant files for bankruptcy, another factor that sometimes can incentivize parties to resolve things before a case gets too far down the road.

Collecting your judgment can be a fight. Some of the information you need to get your money may be known to you as a result of the discovery you did in the earlier part of the case—information about where the defendant lives, for instance, which is usually provided in "form" and "special" interrogatories, can help you pinpoint other assets that they may have from which you can collect. Don't be surprised, however, if after your case you have to engage in even more factfinding in order to ensure you get what you're owed.

What You Should Know: Contempt

Courts aren't always indifferent when litigants ignore their orders. Of course not. It's just that in order to obtain the enforcement you need, you may have to invest more of your time and money.

> You win a judgment in a case you brought in California. The other side lives and does business in New York. When you win, your opponent doesn't seek to stay the judgment.

Remember, a "stay" is a request you make to the court to delay implementation of an order. You may have to explain why you believe you're entitled to the stay, unless the court stays the order automatically.

> You know your opponent has assets and accounts in New York, so you subpoena their bank information. You have to file papers with a New York court in order to issue the subpoena on the bank. The New York court issues a subpoena.
>   Your opponent doesn't care and ignores it.
>   You move for an order seeking to have them found in contempt.

If someone is found "in contempt" of court, that means that they aren't doing what the judge ordered. If you're seeking to enforce a monetary judgment this strategy may not always be available,[3] but it is a way to gain additional force and support for other types of orders.[4]

> The New York court grants the contempt motion and orders them to comply.
>   They refuse.

Seriously?

Seriously. So you move for contempt again. The judge holds them in contempt, again.

Ok. So now you're good, right? Now you have *two* contempt orders.

No, you are not good. The other side ignores the order again—at least, they ignore that part of it that requires them to turn over the financial information you're seeking. Meanwhile, they are appealing the underlying judgment in California.

Is your opponent allowed to pick and choose how and when they will show up and acknowledge the power and force of court? *Pay attention to me court, I want to appeal! But forget you court, I do what I want!*

No, your opponent is not supposed to do this. It's not supposed to work this way. In some jurisdictions, courts have applied the *doctrine of disentitlement* to dismiss appeals where the appellant hasn't complied with something they're supposed to do.[5]

Making your win matter can be a struggle and it can open up entirely new rounds of battle with your opponent. You may have to work pretty hard to make your victory actually mean something as your win may not be the end of your fight. Your opponent may think that continuing to fight you (or just running away from you) is cheaper than paying. Or, to put a less cynical spin on it, it may truly be the case that your opponent has nearly gone broke fighting you and may not have much left with which to pay. The threat of bankruptcy can be a big incentive to working things out.

I've said over and over again that you should try to do this anyway (I promise you I'll say it again before we're done here). Now you may better understand why.

TO SUM UP . . .

- Don't assume your opponent will voluntarily comply with the court order to pay you. Unfortunately, many don't. As is true of many parts of the legal process, you may be the only one who cares to do anything about violations of court orders.
- Make sure you familiarize yourself with the collection processes in your own jurisdiction. There are often many

hoops through which you have to jump, and if you're going to have to go through the work of getting what's owed to you, try to make sure you don't end up spending time on things that don't gain you the relief you're seeking. You've already been through a lot!

- Understand that your opponent can make collection difficult, if not impossible, by declaring bankruptcy. If this happens, you'll end up having spent a lot of time and money just to be another creditor waiting in line to be paid.

- I'm a broken record but I don't care. *It's never too late to try to work it out.*

PART V

Finding an Escape Hatch

Court really can be hell so if you can, you should try to avoid it.

—Me, to You, right now.

11

SOLVING YOUR PROBLEM AND AVOIDING COURT

"This Sounds Nuts and I Want to Avoid Court. Tell Me How."

If you go to court, it's usually because you and/or your opponent were looking for something. Resolution. Relief. A decision that will give you some sort of satisfaction. I've tried to point out how costly your pursuit of that satisfaction might be.

Sometimes people prepare to square off in court without making any attempt to resolve things between themselves first. Some fights seem to proceed with a momentum all their own. In Chapter 1, I mentioned some of the tactics that can result in what I called "Buying a Front Row Ticket to the Litigation Circus": ignoring someone; approaching them in a way that leaves little room for resolution; just being a jerk. Things can snowball quickly.

The reason I'm discussing alternatives to litigation at the end of the book is because I wanted first to give you some sense of what you can expect as you go through the process. To be sure, it is an incomplete sense, as it doesn't even begin to include everything you might encounter. So much of what you may endure will depend on the specifics of your own case. (Frankly, I don't know what a book attempting to cover *all* parts of court process even would look like. Unless you're a legal professional or someone exploring the issue for their own professional benefit and edification, I hope you never have need for such a book.)

I simply wanted to give you a sense of the kinds of things that might happen when you're fighting in court. I want you to know about the twists and turns that can arise, depending on your circumstances. Court is much more difficult and uncertain than people sometimes expect and that difficulty can arise for reasons that they similarly don't expect. One of the only certainties in court is its uncertainty, so don't be too sure about anything: not about whether the justice in your position will be as apparent to the decision-maker as it is to you; not about whether you'll be able to tell the story in its fullest form; not about whether the other side will be held accountable for the unbelievable shenanigans that cost you time and money for no good reason. Yes, you showed up in court to get a fair resolution. No, you are not certain to get it.

You might want to consider other methods of resolving your fight. You can start thinking about this well before anyone decides to go to court. In fact, if you end up in court, you'll have additional opportunities to do it again. The judge may even order you to try.

Do not be too quick to dismiss other alternatives. They might save you time, money, and sanity—plus, they might create an opportunity for you to obtain a resolution that better suits your objectives than the result you could obtain in a court judgment. The whole point of your court fight is to get some relief from the troubling thing or situation that brought you to court in the first place. Court, for any variety of reasons, may not be the best place to do that. If you win you may get *something*, maybe, but that "something" may cost you more in time, money, or other resources than the fight is worth. Or, it may not even come close to remedying the situation that caused the fight in the first place, because, for example, of the limits on the types of relief you can get.

There are different types of alternative dispute resolution that might be available. You should consider them.

What You Can Do: Mediation

In a mediation, each side has an opportunity to explain its position and to try to reach agreement with the other side. In some instances, you may be able to devise a resolution that is more favorable than the relief available to you in trial.

The mediator can't force you to do anything. They can, however, point out the weaknesses in your case and the strengths of the other side's. Your opponent will get the same treatment. Is there an opportunity for you and your opponent to avoid a long and drawn out court process? Perhaps.

A mediation can take place almost anywhere the parties agree to do it, although you will want to ensure that it's conducted in a location that ensures the confidentiality of the proceedings and that will allow each party retreat to (or remain in) their separate corners.

Prior to starting, the mediator may ask that each side submit briefs that explain its position and why they believe they're in the right. To be sure, this adds more time and expense to your case; it can be a good investment, however, as it educates the mediator in advance about the key aspects of your dispute. Then, when everyone shows up for the mediation, their time can then be used more efficiently.

Unlike in court, you don't have to share your mediation brief with the other side and parties often don't. Court pleadings—which are shared with your opponent—are sometimes intended to signal to the other side that you are truly committed to showing the world that they are indeed devil's spawn. In other words, sharing your true thoughts about each other when you're trying to find your way out of a lawsuit sometimes can be counterproductive. Just because you're trying to settle a case doesn't mean that you've abandoned the view that your opponent did something terribly and horribly wrong—but the purpose of the mediation process is to speed up the process by which you can be done with each other, and to do it at less expense than a court fight might entail.

You also can share items with the mediator that you specifically want to keep from the other side; additionally, your and your opponent's communications during the mediation are confidential and can't later be used against you in the event you don't settle. Still, you and your lawyer generally should have an understanding about the nature and scope of information you intend to disclose. Even if it can't be used against you later, information learned is information learned. There's nothing to prevent your opponent from attempting to acquire new material about you or the case or embarking upon a change in strategy based on something new that they learned during the mediation. Should you later end up in court, you may not want to give the other side an opportunity to tarnish what you believe to be your silver bullets.

Sharing some information with the mediator (and only the mediator) can be an opportunity to hear someone else's perspective—someone who isn't "on your team" but who isn't antagonistic to you either—on your case. It may be that someone who is more removed from the matter than you are thinks that some of your "silver bullets" are more like silver-plated bullets, or maybe just tin bullets, or maybe they're just pieces of plastic that are painted really shiny. The mediator will collect information from the other side too—information that your opponent hasn't disclosed to you—and use what she knows about both positions in an attempt to nudge people into a compromise.

CONFIDENTIALITY AGREEMENTS

Much has been made of the fact that confidentiality agreements can silence victims of demonstrated harms while allowing the perpetrators to continue harmful behaviors. However, this does not mean that the presence of such agreements is always suggestive of guilt. A confidentiality agreement can be an essential part of putting a dispute behind each party, particularly where one or each denies certain of the key claims. People execute them for all sorts of reasons, especially since making an allegation or having it repeated can be damaging and even untrue rumors grow legs quickly. Some allegations may be true; some may contain just a little truth, or a faint whiff of it, or something that might seem *true-like*; and others may be outright lies. Just because people say something happened doesn't mean it's true. (That's the whole point of court process.)

Some jurisdictions are taking action to limit the scope and enforceability of some of these agreements. In California, the Stand Together Against Nondisclosure (STAND) Act, which took effect on January 1, 2019, prohibits confidentiality provisions that prevent the disclosure of factual information related to certain harassment or assault claims.[1] Confidentiality provisions that prohibit a contracting party from testifying about alleged criminal conduct or alleged sexual harassment by the other party or its agents or employees, are also void.[2] Employers also cannot force employees to sign agreements that prevent them from reporting workplace misconduct, including sexual harassment.[3] In addition, the Federal Tax Cuts and Jobs Act amended the Internal Revenue Code to remove tax deductions for sexual harassment settlements that are contingent upon confidentiality agreements.[4]

Sometimes the mediator begins the session by having everyone in the same room at once. There are, of course, upsides and downsides to this. On the upside, it can give you an opportunity to face your opponent and speak to them outside of what might be an over-heated and charged court environment. If you have a lawyer, per-haps they can deliver an opening statement that signals a willingness to come to agreement. The mediation can induce the parties to calm down and do less posturing than they might when they are operating under compulsion of a court process. After that point, it's usually helpful if people retreat to separate corners, with the medi-ator shuttling between as you and your opponent try to hash some-thing out.

By the same token, sometimes you don't need to "come together" in the same room. Maybe there's too much bad blood and too much interpersonal conflict. Maybe the only hope of settling the case is if the parties keep their distance so they can stay focused on resolving matters instead of being distracted by how much they can't stand each other.

Put yourself in these shoes, for a moment:

You're in a dispute with your business partner. While you were giddy with excitement when you began your venture, you've now soured on one another. A lot.

Because you were smart people, however, you have a pretty de-tailed partnership agreement, which limits the circumstances under which you can dissolve the business and provides that the remaining partner must buy out the one departing at a set price. Plus, you both went in with the expectation of a big payout from a deal that is ex-pected to materialize in the near future. In fact, it was the expecta-tion of this big payout that motivated the venture in the first place.

You are really starting to hate each other, and you're both looking for violations of your agreement so you can find a way out. You keep focusing on the deal while your alienated partner is busy trying to develop other projects that don't require so much one-on-one con-tact with you.

You gather ammunition for a lawsuit, intending to show your for-mer partner, someone with whom you can't believe you ever were so naïve as to go into business, that they'd better just cut it out and do what you want. (The love is all hate now!) You think you have a basis for devising other claims: misappropriation of funds—what WAS that "client dinner" really about?—and breach of fiduciary duty—is he luring opportunities away from your joint enterprise? You think you have a few things up your sleeve.

Not surprisingly, your former partner is doing precisely the same thing. Perhaps both of you were a little "loose" with things at times. (How dare they lob those accusations at you! Satan's spawn indeed!)

Still, you hate each other now. A lot. You really want out.

You can go to court—which may become necessary—but the remedies available under the partnership agreement are limited: reimbursement of the amount of money invested in the business, plus a set amount of interest. You don't really have that money right now. Not to mention that you're afraid of losing—you are certain you will close that lucrative deal that motivated your wanting to do this thing in the first place, and if you lose the court case you may be shut out of that entirely.

As your dispute wears on, your business suffers. Your current customers notice the tension between you and your partner and want no part of the drama. They're starting to keep their distance. And since your dislike of one another has now turned to rank hatred, it's impossible to make even the most basic decisions without a war. The major deal you're anticipating hasn't materialized yet and if you two keep messing around, it's going to go away, too.

Enter your mediator, someone selected not for their warm and fuzzy demeanor but for their ability to get things done.

In your opening session, you and your partner can explain what each of you thinks has happened in a way that doesn't result in things getting out of control the way they have when you two have tried to communicate recently. You now have a referee. A neutral party.

The mediator reminds you of the realities of the world outside your fight and can help nudge you into an agreement that resolves your "big picture" problem—the need for a professional divorce—while negotiating a solution around your specific business concerns. Perhaps you devise a solution which allows one of you to buy the other out over time; and further allows the departing partner to participate in the non-materialized deal to an extent proportionate with his work on it. You can talk about the "proportions" with the mediator, who will also hopefully help him to realize that your sticking around and seeing the project through should count for something, too. None of these are options that a judge necessarily could order.

Hopefully you realize all of the costs and uncertainties of litigation, and are approaching the mediation with an actual good faith intention to resolve the situation. Still, that doesn't mean that whatever you're claiming happened to you didn't really happen, or that the injury you claim to have endured isn't real; nor does it mean that the person or persons you think responsible for that injury shouldn't be as distasteful to you as you find them. Maybe it's their sheer reprehensibility and your desire to have as little to do with them as possible and move on with your life, that convinced you to try to mediate in the first place. You want to put them in the rearview mirror as soon as possible.

Agreeing to mediate doesn't mean that you have to make up; or that you "forgive" your opponent for that horrible thing you believe they did and for which they haven't apologized. It also doesn't mean *you* have to apologize. It can, however, give you a better sense of some of the challenges you may have in presenting what you believe to be an "airtight" case, and it can also provide a cheaper and less stressful exit from what may be a very bitter and expensive court fight.

One retired judge who now conducts arbitrations and mediations discussed with me a *jury mediation* procedure that she has used. In it, individuals from the same community that would make up the jury during the trial of the case listen to the presentation of each side's key evidence, and then deliberate. The deliberations are recorded, and each side then gets to watch. (In particularly large or high-stakes cases, each side may do its own mock jury exercise in order to get a more objective view of the strengths and weaknesses of its case.)

It was a horrible accident. The plaintiffs claimed that the city negligently maintained the highway; the city claimed that the cause of the accident was one of the plaintiffs' negligent driving. The plaintiffs were sure they had a great case—one of the injured parties was a sympathetic student who was studying to become a health care professional. The defendants were sure they had a great case—the accident was caused by one of the plaintiffs' negligent driving. It was a bad driver, not a bad road, that caused the tragedy.

The "mediation jury" listened to the case and then deliberated.

They concluded that each side bore a percentage of fault. After watching the deliberation, the parties settled the case in mediation.

SAYS THE JUDGE/MEDIATOR . . .

One judge who mediates cases describes the process as one where people can reflect upon their dispute in ways that they don't while they're battling it out in court.

I would never have intuited how effective a judge can be in getting parties to focus on resolving a dispute, rather than on winning a fight. The process can be transformative. People who were unwilling to consider settlement, or who were taking most extreme positions, become willing to consider, and sometimes propose themselves, reasonable alternatives. Clients who had been unwilling to listen to the sound advice of their attorney become willing to accept the same information from me. Maybe it shouldn't happen, but it does, time and time again. When I explain to individuals the psychological toll prolonged litigation is likely to have upon them, and how they will constantly be pulled backward in time to a very unpleasant incident, they tend to listen. In fact, the investment of time and emotional energy in the mediation is a learning experience for many people, and it gives them a taste of the pressures of the litigating process.[5]

Mediating your case merely signals that you are looking for an efficient way to resolve your dispute that will keep you both out of court, and it's a method that might result in a better outcome than would be possible if the parties continued litigating. While the mediator can't force you to do anything, she can help you pave the way toward a binding agreement, one in which you may be able to shape and fine tune your resolution to your priorities.

The widow of a professional athlete sues the sports league, claiming they failed to protect players for the type of injuries that killed her husband. As part of a settlement, the league agrees to establish a heatstroke prevention program so as to prevent future tragedies like these.[6]

You may want to consider settlement options even after your trial victory. Remember, a "win" may not signal the end of your case; plus, your lawsuit may be motivated by a desire for nonmonetary resolution.

A mineworker sues an oil well operator for injuries resulting from an oil well blowout. He turns down an eight-figure jury award; instead, he agrees to take an amount less than half of that in exchange for the mine implementing a safety plan.[7]

Even after a case has begun, mediation can help stave off future damage to the parties that might result from the public airing of disputes.

As far as Laverne was concerned, she was a loyal employee who had become aware of what she thought were questionable transactions by the company. She began to drop none-too-subtle hints that she was going to share her concerns with regulatory authorities.

As far as the company was concerned, Laverne was a gossip who based wild tales on half-truths and unsupported assumptions. Plus, they claimed she was mediocre at her job. They didn't think she was worth the trouble she caused.

The company terminated her. She then went public with her claims about corporate irregularities. She brought a "whistleblower" lawsuit, alleging that the company had fired her in retaliation for pointing out its wrongdoing. She aired what she claimed were dirty secrets, with a promise of more to come. The company claimed she was misrepresenting facts to further an extortion. They attacked her as an opportunist.

Things got nasty with the lawyers, too, as each side claimed the other violated any number of court rules.

The court ordered the parties to mediate. The case had become so acrimonious, though, that no one held out much hope that the mediation would accomplish anything. Still, the judge was making them do it.

They never had a joint session. Laverne expressed her frustration with the company's processes and its sullying of her reputation. The company expressed its frustration with what they saw as malicious allegations, ones they claimed she couldn't even prove if she'd tried.

What was important to everyone, however, was that they find a way to shed the dirt that they were each throwing on each other. She wanted to continue to work (albeit somewhere else), free from her reputation being tarnished. The company wanted its business to continue, free from the cloud of salacious media coverage.

From these motivations, a settlement was born, one that addressed each party's respective interest in moving on and trying to recover from the brutal messiness of the dispute.

Sometimes when the litigation is complicated, a mediation can get rid of at least part of it. It doesn't mean that you have to resolve every single thing, but at least you can resolve something, which can make any subsequent proceedings less complicated.

You fall down in the building. The building was owned by Company A but Company B was responsible for maintaining it. Each claimed that the other was responsible for your injuries.

The parties go to mediation, where your lawyer convinces the two companies to pay you a certain amount which they will split equally, and then to sue each other for reimbursement based on who was at fault.

So while it didn't all "go away," the mediation was able to significantly whittle down the issues. (At least now you're out of the case.)

Remember, even though the mediation can't force you into an agreement, once you make one, you're bound by it just like any other contract. **Read it before you sign.** The standard for getting out of a settlement is the same as that of any other agreement. You'll have to show fraud, mistake, duress, or some other legally valid basis for why you shouldn't be held to the agreement's terms. Simply rethinking your agreement or believing you made a mistake isn't the type of legally relevant "mistake" that will warrant canceling your deal. A court will presume you've read and that you understand the agreement if it says you did, so make sure you do.

Sometimes the mediation can lay the groundwork for a resolution that comes later.

You and Plaintiff Pickle are really far apart. Pickle thinks she's entitled to, as you see it, "the world." She slipped and fell. People fall. You don't even think she's hurt that badly, although you admit that you should be responsible for something. You think she's just being greedy and getting carried away.

You have a number in mind. Pickle does too. So now, you have a low-end number—yours—and Pickle's through-the-roof demand to consider. You manage to whittle her down a bit. She manages to get you to cough up more money. You still, however, don't have an agreement.

But you have a range that starts at your low-end number and ends at Pickle's higher-end request. You agree to take that range to the arbitrator and let her decide—after hearing the parties' positions on the case and discussing their evidence, the arbitrator makes a decision on damages that falls within your and Pickle's range.

You have much more control over how to resolve your dispute when you sit down and negotiate with your opponent. By the way, *arbitration* was an element of the dispute resolution procedure in the last example, and we'll discuss that in more detail next.

What You Can (and in Some Instances, *Must*) Do: Arbitration

Arbitration is another type of dispute resolution procedure. In it, the parties choose an arbitrator—or panel of arbitrators—to resolve their dispute. The arbitrator is neutral, like a judge; however, unlike a judgment in court, an arbitration award may not always be appealed to a court. (If the arbitrator's decision is *binding*, it may be appealed only on very narrow grounds. If it's *non-binding*, the parties can take another shot at their fight in court.)

Arbitrators are subject to strict rules regarding impartiality and objectivity, and the conduct of the arbitrator must comport with basic requirements of due process. When the arbitrator issues an award, a party still must take the judgment to court to have it entered and enforced, unless the losing side decides to comply voluntarily.

Arbitrations can proceed at a much quicker pace than a court fight. For instance, in an arbitration, the parties can agree upon more streamlined discovery procedures. If the parties are arbitrating pursuant to an agreement, they can decide (with the arbitrator) what information—in terms of witnesses, documents, and other evidence—each side needs from the other. If the parties aren't able to come to an agreement, the arbitrator can decide upon the fair parameters of discovery. The arbitrator also can award attorneys' fees in the event that either side engages in bad faith tactics.

A retired judge who now arbitrates cases told me about a pretty difficult litigant who appeared to have very little respect for the process. The litigant blew off depositions and hearing dates at the last minute, driving up everyone's costs and fees. (You understand that when you pay your lawyer to do something, and that thing doesn't happen, you don't necessarily get your money back. Your lawyer will never get that time back. In court, time really is money.) In that situation, the arbitrator awarded attorneys' fees. It didn't take as much time to do that as it would have in court.

Arbitrators also can award a full range of damages, including punitive damages.[8] Still, although there is no hard and fast rule, arbitration awards tend to be smaller than jury verdicts.[9]

Arbitration has its detractors. Decisions by the U.S. Supreme Court have expanded the right of employers and large companies to require consumers and employees to submit their disputes to binding arbitration rather than going to court, and the terms of these agreements have dramatically limited the ability to bring class actions and to seek other types of relief.[10] Some have also raised concerns about the professional proximity between arbitrators and the civil defense bar (those lawyers who typically or often represent corporations or employers in disputes with consumers and employees). Still, the arbitrator is required to be neutral, and a failure to abide by that standard could invalidate the arbitration proceedings.[11]

CLASS ACTIONS

Ever get one of those notices about a pending lawsuit involving something you bought, letting you know you're about to get a credit or a coupon or something like that? That is a *Notice of Class Settlement* advising you that you're a member of the group of people on whose behalf the named plaintiffs brought the lawsuit. You and the group are *similarly situated*—perhaps because all of you purchased the product or service that the lawsuit targets—which means that everyone in the group can participate in the settlement. Alternatively, you can opt-out of the class and bring a lawsuit on your own.

In a case involving a very large class, for example, a settlement might include a credit from the defendant in some amount. Maybe it will include a coupon or voucher for some other product or service the defendant provides.[12] Perhaps it will include a cash payment.

Some suggest that it's only the lawyers who benefit from class actions.[13]

That reasoning, however, doesn't fully acknowledge the impact that some class actions have had in vindicating important rights where not enough money was at stake to justify the cost and burdens of bringing a lawsuit. Some class actions have targeted and resulted in remedies for allegedly widespread discriminatory practices in lending and hiring, for instance.[14]

If you are arbitrating because of an agreement to do so, the agreement must be one that satisfies the principles ordinarily applied to all contracts—it must not be the product of fraud or duress, for example. If it is, a court can invalidate the requirement to arbitrate on the same grounds that it can any other agreement.[15] An arbitration must also comply with minimum due process requirements.[16]

It wouldn't be fair to say that every arbitration is simply a procedure where those with fewer resources are waterboarded into bad deals. The procedure can be efficient and effective for many of those who choose to go that route.

It would be fair to say that enforcing and upholding the broad use of arbitration limits the access that many litigants will have to court process. For defenders of arbitration, however, that is precisely the point.

What You Should Do: Be Careful Before You Thumb Your Nose at Their Offer

Parties can seek to settle a case at any point before judgment and even afterward. Sometimes, however, if it looks like things are going poorly, one side might be more incentivized to resolve things than it was prior to going to court. The converse is true, too. When someone thinks a case is moving in their direction (perhaps the judge has made favorable rulings regarding the admission of evidence or other matters, for example), they might be inclined to dig in their heels.

Nothing in court is certain except for the uncertainty, so I recommend not getting too comfortable.

In some jurisdictions, rejecting a settlement offer can be costly, especially if you move forward and obtain a less favorable verdict at trial.

Helen sued the manufacturer of a beauty product, claiming that an ingredient in it had contributed to her cancer. She rejected the company's settlement offer but recovered at trial far less than the company offered.

The company then sought to recover its costs, which Helen clearly couldn't pay.

Her inability to pay was irrelevant—she rejected an offer that was higher than the verdict she received, and she was now going to have to pay the price for that.

You may be liable for fees incurred from the time the settlement offer is presented to you until the time you received the less favorable judgment (or just lost outright).

This is by no means a complete list of the alternative dispute resolution procedures that are available to you. There are mini-trials; combinations of different procedures; and other informal mechanisms for resolving your dispute. You have a lot of control and flexibility—much more so than you do in court. Trying to resolve your dispute outside of the courtroom could give you an opportunity to avoid the grip of the Litigation Hydra. You may be very glad you did.

TO SUM UP . . .

- Recognize that there are times when it may be in your best interest to cut the cord on your fight and look for a way out. Keep in mind that your "way out" could include coming up with a resolution that's better than what you could have devised in court.

- Explore the different methods of alternative dispute resolution (ADR), and see if there is something that works for and resonates with you and your case. Don't assume that ADR is a one-size-fits-all approach. Think about coming up with a size that works for you and that will result in coming to an agreement with which you can live.

- Be mindful of the fact that rejecting the other side's settlement offer can, in some jurisdictions and under certain circumstances, result in your being liable for their costs.

- And, for the last time, please remember that *it's never too late to try to work things out.*

A FINAL WORD

This book couldn't begin to cover all of the ups and downs in litigation. I hope it gives you some flavor, however, about some of the uncertainties and challenges in the process.

For a venue where justice and fair play are supposed to reign, court sometimes might feel like a madhouse. While court fights are supposed to be those where everyone has a voice and a chance, using that voice and getting that chance can require a substantial investment of your time and resources. Knowing why some things happen as they do can be one step in making it feel a little less mad.

Sometimes the threat of litigation is enough to make a problem go away, but perhaps the threat may not be enough.

Sometimes people go to court without trying to resolve matters in other ways. I highly discourage that approach.

As I said at the outset of this, I don't know you or your fight, should you happen to be in one. But it's often the case that court shouldn't be your first stop if you're looking for ways to resolve a dispute. If you do have to be there, don't let its rules and rhythms intimidate you or throw you off your game. Be prepared not only to make the best case you can, but also to choose a path for your case that is comfortable for you. Make it *your* case.

Good luck.

GLOSSARY

abstract of judgment A written summary of a judgment.

abuse of discretion A standard of review used by an appellate court to review certain lower court decisions.

abuse of process The tort of misusing legal procedures for unjust purposes.

accident or surprise One of the grounds for granting a new trial. The term refers to unexpected circumstances that arise through no fault of a party that deprive that party of a fair trial.

acknowledgment of satisfaction of judgment A court form that a creditor completes and files with the court once she receives the full payment of judgment.

affirmative defense A defense that would reduce or eliminate a defendant's liability even if the allegations against her are true.

Anti-SLAPP Motion to dismiss A motion that someone can file to dismiss a Strategic Lawsuit Against Public Participation (SLAPP). Many states have passed anti-SLAPP statutes enabling this type of motion to counter the chilling effect that SLAPP suits have on speech.

appeal Formal review process of a lower court's decision by a higher court.

appellate court Hears and reviews cases decided by lower (trial) courts.

arbitration Method of alternative dispute resolution. In arbitration, parties agree in advance (of a contract or an event) that an independent arbitrator, instead of a judge, will decide any dispute that might arise.

bifurcation With respect to trials, when the matters at issue are separated into two parts and tried separately.

binding Having legal enforceability.

burden of proof The duty of a party to prove an allegation. Burden of proof includes burden of production, which requires that the party produce enough evidence to substantiate the claim, and burden of persuasion, which requires the party to meet a certain standard of proof.

challenges for cause Requests to eliminate a prospective juror for a specific reason such as bias or inability to serve properly and fairly.

circumstantial evidence Evidence where an inferential step is required to connect the evidence to a certain conclusion. This stands in contrast with direct evidence.

clear and convincing evidence Intermediate standard of proof that requires a party to prove that their claim is *far* more likely than not to be true. This standard is higher than "preponderance of evidence" but lower than "beyond all reasonable doubt." It is applied in some criminal and civil cases where significant liberty and property interests are at stake.

clear error Deferential standard of review by a higher court of a trial court's finding of fact. The appellate court would only overturn the lower court's factual determinations if they were manifestly wrong.

coercing party The party that presures the other party into more favorable terms for the former at the latter's expense.

compensatory damages Damages awarded to a plaintiff to compensate for her injury or loss with the view of making the victim whole again. This is also known as actual damages.

competent evidence Evidence that is relevant to proving the issue at hand and is legally admissible.

confidentiality agreements Contracts in which a party promises to not disclose certain confidential or proprietary information; also known as nondisclosure agreements.

contingency fee A fee arrangement with an attorney in which a client pays only upon achieving a successful or specified result.

counterclaims Defendant's claims against the plaintiff in the same proceeding.

damages The amounts of money awarded to the wronged party.

de novo review Standard of review that applies when an appellate court reviews questions of law, with little deference to the lower court's legal judgment and application.

debtor's examination   A post-judgment tool that allows a creditor to investigate a debtor's finances under oath and in court.

declarations   Sworn written statements.

declaratory relief   A form of relief wherein the court issues an official statement about the status of an issue without ordering an injunction or damages.

defamation   The tort of speaking or writing falsehoods about someone and tainting her reputation.

default judgment   A court judgment rendered against a party in the absence of that party.

demurrer/motion to dismiss   A request to throw out a case because the allegations, even if true, do not give rise to a sufficient pleading of a cause of action.

depositions   A discovery device where witness testimony is taken under oath.

direct evidence   Evidence that requires no inference in proving a claim. This stands in contrast with circumstantial evidence. An example of direct evidence is eyewitness testimony.

discovery   Pre-trial process where each party can obtain facts and evidence from the other. Examples of discovery devices are interrogatories, requests for document production, and depositions.

due process   The constitutional requirement that a legal proceeding occur according to established fair procedural rules in order to safeguard individual rights.

duress   The improper coercion of a party, with the aim of forcing that party into conditions to which they would not ordinarily consent.

error in law   Mistake in the way a court applies the law to a set of facts, as opposed to errors in the fact-finding itself.

evidence   Factual basis that serves to substantiate a legal claim.

ex parte   "Of one party." Refers to proceedings and orders that are heard outside of regularly noticed motion practice.

exhibit   A piece of evidence in a proceeding.

extortion   Unlawful exaction of benefits through coercion, blackmailing, and similar threats and tactics.

false light invasion of privacy   Type of privacy tort where a person is subject to unflattering publicity that places that person in a "false light" in the public's eyes.

final judgment   Ultimate decision by a court with regards to a dispute, after which only the execution of the judgment remains. However, a litigant can choose to appeal a final decision of a court to another court above it.

form interrogatories   Written requests for answers in the discovery process. Form interrogatories differ from special interrogatories in that the requesting party can select from a menu of pre-formulated questions.

fraud   An intentional deception so as to gain unlawful benefits.

free will   Ability to choose a course of action without constraint and act on that choice. The assumption of free will underlies concepts of criminal culpability: if a person knew what she was doing, then absent overt coercion, she must have chosen to do it and should be held culpable for the act.

garnish   To obtain a court order requiring a third party holding the debtor's money, such as the debtor's employer, to set aside some of the debtor's property, such as wages, to satisfy the judgment due to the creditor.

general denial   Statement in response to a complaint that denies all allegations thereof.

good faith basis   Reasonable and non-frivolous basis for a certain argument or action.

hearing date   Date on which a hearing is set to take place.

hearsay evidence   Out-of-court statements recited in court to prove the veracity of a certain assertion. Hearsay evidence is usually not admissible.

insufficiency of the evidence   A basis for an appellate court to reverse a lower court judgment because the evidence in the record was not enough to support a conclusion.

intentional infliction of emotional distress   Tort that involves extreme and outrageous deliberate acts that result in severe trauma and mental suffering for the victim.

irreparable harm   Permanent and irreversible harm that neither money nor any post-hoc remedy can sufficiently cure.

issue sanctions   Sanctions that result in the resolution of certain facts or claims in the opposing party's favor.

judgment notwithstanding the verdict   Decision by a judge to overrule or modify a jury verdict.

jurisdiction   The authority of a court to decide a certain matter involving particular persons. Jurisdiction includes personal jurisdiction, which is the authority of a court over a defendant, and subject matter jurisdiction, which is the authority to hear a certain kind of claim.

jury mediation   When both parties present their respective cases to a group of recruited jurors that simulate the juror pool in the venue of choice.

lawsuit   Legal dispute to be resolved in courts.

liability   Legal responsibility for certain actions or events.

libel   Written defamation, as opposed to slander, which is spoken defamation. Like other types of defamation, libel involves publishing falsehoods that cause reputational harms to a victim.

limited jurisdiction   The authority of a court to hear a narrowly defined set of cases.

For example, all U.S. federal courts are courts of limited jurisdiction because they can only hear constitutionally or statutorily authorized cases.

litigation privilege   A type of immunity from liability for certain statements made in connection with litigation.

malice   Wrongful intent to harm another. Malice is an element in certain crimes, like first-degree murder or arson.

malicious prosecution   Tort that allows the victim of bad-faith lawsuits and other abuses of court processes to claim damages against the offending party.

mediation   Out-of-court alternative dispute resolution mechanism involving the assistance of an independent third party to resolve disputes.

meritorious defense   A defense that addresses the merits of the case rather than resting on technical or procedural objections.

mini-trial   A private proceeding where the parties each present their case with the goal of achieving a settlement.

misappropriation   Intentional unlawful deprivation of another's property.

mistrial   When a jury cannot agree upon a verdict, or when a defect or misconduct occurred in the proceeding that rendered the trial unfair.

motion   Formal request supported by arguments directed at a court.

motion for a new trial   Request for a decision to be overturned or a verdict to be set aside and for the matter to be tried all over again because of an egregious problem in the process.

motion for a protective order   Request for the court to order protection of one side from harmful actions by the other side.

motion for judgment notwithstanding the verdict   Request for a judge to reverse or modify the jury's verdict based on factual or legal insufficiency underlying that verdict.

motion for reconsideration   Request for the court to modify its final judgment.

motion in limine   Motion to exclude or include evidence, to be heard not with the jury present.

motion to compel   Request for the court to order the opposing party to take an action.

motion to quash   Request for the court to declare a subpoena or service of process invalid or to suppress a piece of evidence.

newly discovered evidence   Evidence which may have existed during the trial but which could not, through the exercise of reasonable diligence, have been discovered then, constituting one basis for getting a new trial.

non-binding   Having no legal enforceability.

nonsensica   Nonsense!

nonsuit Court's dismissal of a case either at the request of the plaintiff or after the court finds that the plaintiff had failed to plead a case. Voluntary nonsuit is usually without prejudice.

notice of class settlement A notification to all class members about a class action settlement and its terms.

passion and prejudice An improper basis for a jury verdict, indicating that a jury has made its decision based on an emotional response rather than the evidence.

pattern or practice The existence of established practices or policies giving rise to improper conduct, as opposed to isolated instances of that conduct.

payment An affirmative defense to liability. In other words, if one has already paid what one owes, one is no longer liable.

peremptory challenge The procedure for removing certain potential jurors from the pool without having to provide a reason for doing so.

perjury Crime of intentionally lying or making a misrepresentation under oath.

petition for certiorari A request for an appellate court to review a lower court's decision.

preliminary injunction An order entered by a court to compel a party to take an action or refrain from taking an action during the pendency of the trial and/or before a final decision on the merits, usually to prevent irreparable harm while the case is being decided.

preponderance of the evidence A standard that requires a party to present evidence sufficient to demonstrate that their position is more likely to be true than not true.

prima facie Sufficient evidence to demonstrate the existence of an issue in the first instance.

private place order A court order that permits a sheriff to enter into premises and seize property to satisfy a debt.

pro bono Legal representation that is free-of-charge.

probable cause Reasonable belief that police must have before obtaining a warrant for arrest, arresting, searching, or seizing property in connection to a suspected crime. This is also the standard that a grand jury must meet to indict.

probative value Degree to which evidence can prove or disprove a claim or make it more likely or less likely than not to be true.

process server Someone who serves legal notices and paperwork to notify a party of the proceeding.

proximate cause Event that is deemed legally sufficient to be considered a cause of an injury.

punitive damages A monetary award meant to punish the wrongdoer and deter future misconduct.

record   The evidence and arguments that have been made and submitted in a court proceeding.

registered agent   The person or entity that receives legal process on behalf of a business.

release   A legal device in which one party consents to free the other of some or all legal liabilities.

request for relief   Request for the court to decide the rights and liabilities of those involved in a lawsuit.

requests for admission   A discovery device wherein a party sends a set of statements to the other party with the request that the recipient admit or deny the statements.

res judicata   A legal principle that bars relitigation of an already-decided matter.

retainer agreement   A contract between an attorney and her client.

ripe   With respect to a case, it refers to the fact that the matter is ready to be adjudicated.

sanctions   Punitive measures that a court can order to discipline litigants and their attorneys for engaging in improper conduct and tactics during a proceeding.

service of process   Transmission of legal notices and papers to parties to a suit.

similarly situated   Plaintiffs in a class action who share a similar legal problem and who possess similar characteristics, experiences, or circumstances.

special interrogatories   As distinguished from form interrogatories, written questions specifically formulated by the requesting party to solicit specific information from the opposite side.

standing   The legal requirement that the plaintiff have a sufficient interest in the issue before the court in order to bring the case.

statute of frauds   Legal requirement that certain agreements need to be written down to be effective.

statute of limitations   Window of time during which a particular claim related to an event must be brought after the event transpired.

subpoena   An element of court process requiring an individual to give testimony or to produce certain evidence.

summary judgment   Pre-trial procedure in which a case is resolved because there are no outstanding questions of material fact.

temporary restraining order (TRO)   Short-term court order to protect one party from the other, usually until the next hearing or the next issuance of another TRO or a permanent order.

tolled   Temporary stopping of the clock for a statute of limitations.

undue influence   A party's power and control over another party such that the latter may not be able to freely consent to terms set by the former.

GLOSSARY

unlimited jurisdiction   Legal authority for a court to hear any kind of claim within its geographical domain; also known as general jurisdiction.

vacate   An appellate court vacates a decision when it cancels the decision so that it no longer has legal effects.

vexatious litigant   Person who keeps bringing frivolous, meritless suits, often to harass the court or another party.

voir dire   Preliminary examination of prospective jurors, conducted by counsel or a judge, for the purposes of mounting challenges for cause or peremptory challenges.

writ of execution   Order by a court to enforce its judgment, typically involving a sheriff taking possession of a debtor's property to satisfy the judgment on behalf of a creditor.

writ petition   Request to a higher court to compel the lower to take an action as an extraordinary remedy.

ACKNOWLEDGMENTS

This is my first book. It happened because of the tireless support, friendship, and encouragement of many people who I'm lucky enough to have in my life.

My career has been bookended by two incredible judges, each of whom has made her own impact on the law and our expectations of it.

The first is my very first boss out of law school, Judge Dorothy Wright Nelson of the U.S. Court of Appeals for the Ninth Circuit. As one of her law clerks, her vision of justice shaped me and her commitment to conflict resolution inspires me. I serve on the board of the Western Justice Center, an organization she founded that is committed to promoting her vision of peaceful conflict resolution. It *is* possible. She remains my greatest mentor and my very dear friend.

The second is my current boss, Judge Judy Sheindlin. She is the same dynamic woman in person that you see on TV. What you haven't seen is the guidance she's provided me as I've embarked upon my own journey of adjudicating cases on television and learning this new world.

Thank you, Judy, for the opportunity you provided me and for everything you've done to make it a fun one.

CBS has been my television home for the last seven years. Thank you for the platform and thank you to Nicole Harris-Johnson for taking a look at this while you were homeschooling your kids.

Thanks also to my friend Susan Campos, an incredible writer who looked at very early drafts of what this book ultimately became and who provided the type of thoughtful criticism that smart friends who love you will provide. Susan introduced me to my agent, Joelle Delbourgo, who helped fine-tune this project into something more focused than my internal musings and who helped me develop it into a marketable work. Thanks also to Mitch Langberg and William Archer, both of whom gave me the benefit of their review and advice. Alexis Crump—thank you for steering me toward William. You're a muse to your own hubby author (Douglas Davis, *Yoga, A Love Story*) and a great friend to me. Love you sis.

Keli Lee, thanks for the socially distanced study session and for dinner during my last night of proofreading. Friendship is a real thing.

Keith Wallman, Emily Hillebrand, and the team at Diversion are the perfect combination of patience, professionalism, and good-natured humor. I appreciate having found a home for this project at Diversion and thank you for the time and effort you have put into this.

There are a number of lawyers and friends who contributed their stories to this project. I won't mention them all individually here, but they know who they are, and they also know that I am incredibly grateful to them for sharing their stories with me. In terms of providing me the detailed feedback that every lawyer lives for, special thanks go to my friend Mark Flagel, a power attorney who pursued his own writing career and whose review made these pages better; and also to my Sister-in-Spirit Kalpana Srinivasan, another magnificently smart lawyer and all-around brilliant person whose thoughts and notes were spectacularly helpful. More Disneyland for us, Kalpana. One day.

Then there's my BFF of more than thirty years, Melanie Miller, who did her thing by providing her usual careful read. (What are best friends for if not to read your first book?) Your friendship has been a constant—you never fail and you don't lie—and you are one of the smartest people I know, on top of being an artist whose work puts me in a good mood. Plus, best friendship.

I've had help from some amazing research assistants, including Catherine Joyce and Gayton Gomez. Thank you for helping me get this off the ground—your research was invaluable. To Hong Tran, who joined me as a third-year Yale Law student and helped me cross the finish line, you have a brilliant future ahead and I'm honored to have had the chance to work with you. Thank you for your tireless dedication.

To my personal assistant, Kris Embrey—thanks for helping to organize my research and congratulations to you on your own writing career.

To my parents—thanks for always being proud of me and for letting me know that. I am lucky and grateful to have been born to you two. You are the best of everything and you are a great example of winning.

To my husband, Randy, thank you for being an early reader and thoughtful critic; thank you for keeping me company when I felt like I had no words left and couldn't re-read another page; thank you for making the popcorn to keep my energy up; and especially, thank you for being the brilliant and supportive love of my life. Love you now and always.

NOTES

INTRODUCTION

1. COURT STATISTICS PROJECT, http://www.courtstatistics.org/.
2. Dred Scott v. Sandford, 60 U.S. (19 How.) 393 (1857).

CHAPTER ONE

1. Harris v. Forklift Sys., 510 U.S. 17, 114 S. Ct. 367 (1993).
2. Cal. Lab. Code § 2699.3(a)(2)(A) (requiring exhaustion of administrative remedies for claims of Labor Code violations, including unpaid wages); *Filing a Lawsuit*, EEOC, https://www.eeoc.gov/employees/lawsuit.cfm ("If you plan to file a lawsuit under federal law alleging discrimination on the basis of race, color, religion, sex (including pregnancy, gender identity, and sexual orientation), national origin, age (40 or older), disability, genetic information. or retaliation, you first have to file a charge with the EEOC.").
3. 28 U.S. Code § 1332(a).
4. *Family Law: Clarification of Rules Regarding Service and Posting of a Summons and Forms of Pleading SPR* 13-20, JUD. COUNCIL CAL., https://www.courts.ca.gov/documents/SPR13-20.pdf.
5. See, e.g., Tex. Civ. Prac. & Remedies Code § 171.088
6. See, e.g., Federal Tort Claims Act, 28 U.S.C. § 1346; Bivens v. Six Unknown Named Agents of Fed. Bureau of Narcotics, 403 U.S. 388, 91 S. Ct. 1999 (1971).

7. See, e.g., California Tort Claims Act, Cal. Gov't Code § 900 et seq.; 42 U.S.C. § 1983.

8. McMillian v. Monroe County, 520 U.S. 781, 784 (1997).

9. Harlow v. Fitzgerald, 457 U.S. 800, 814 (1982), quoting Gregoire v. Biddle, 177 F.2d 579, 581 (2d Cir. 1949), *cert denied,* 339 U.S. 949 (1950); see also Pearson v. Callahan, 555 U.S. 223 (2009) ("Qualified immunity balances two important interests—the need to hold public officials accountable when they exercise power irresponsibly and the need to shield officials from harassment, distraction, and liability when they perform their duties reasonably.").

10. Zadeh v. Robinson, 902 F.3d 483, 498 (5th Cir. 2018) (Willett, J., concurring).

11. Wellness Int'l Network, Ltd. v. Sharif, 575 U.S. 665 (2015) (resolving a four-year jurisdictional contention regarding a final judgment on an alter ego claim by a bankruptcy court); Stewart Org., Inc. v. Ricoh Corp., 487 U.S. 22 (1988) (deciding a four-year long venue dispute); *Ex parte* De Vega, 65 So. 3d 886 (Ala. 2010) (adjudicating a three-year-long venue dispute).

12. Lujan v. Defenders of Wildlife, 504 U.S. 555 (1992).

13. Wellness Int'l Network, Ltd. v. Sharif, 575 U.S. 665 (2015) (resolving a four-year jurisdictional contention regarding a final judgment on an alter ego claim by a bankruptcy court); Stewart Org., Inc. v. Ricoh Corp., 487 U.S. 22 (1988) (deciding a four-year long venue dispute); Ex parte De Vega, 65 So. 3d 886 (Ala. 2010) (adjudicating a three-year-long venue dispute).

14. Emily Alpert Reyes, *Gov. Brown Signs Bill Cracking Down on L.A. 'Veto' for Homeless Housing,* L.A. TIMES (Sept. 27, 2018) https://www.latimes.com/local/lanow/la-me-ln-homeless-housing-letter-20180927-story.html.

15. See, e.g., Neal v. Farmers Ins. Exch., 21 Cal. 3d 910, 928, 582 P.2d 980, 990 (1978) ("[E]ven an act of considerable reprehensibility will not be seen to justify a proportionally high amount of punitive damages if the actual harm suffered thereby is small."); Little v. Stuyvesant Life Ins. Co., 67 Cal.App.3d 451, 469–470, 136 Cal.Rptr. 653 (1977) ("[A]though there is no fixed ratio by which to determine the propriety of a punitive damage award, punitive damages should bear a reasonable relationship to the compensatory damages awarded.").

16. Fuentes v. Perez, 66 Cal. App. 3d 163 (1977) (reversing lower court's jury award for emotional distress caused by roofer's actions); Mason v. Mercury Cas. Co., 64 Cal. App. 3d 471 (1976) (affirming lower court's judgment notwithstanding the verdict in favor of the insurer).

17. *Am. Rd. Serv. Co. v. Inmon,* 394 So. 2d 361, 365 (Ala. 1980).

18. See, e.g., Cal. R. Court r. 8.1115(a).

19. ROBERT TIMOTHY REAGAN ET AL., FED. JUD. CTR., CITING UNPUBLISHED OPINIONS IN FEDERAL APPEALS 66, 107 (2005). See also Anastasoff v. United States, 223 F.3d 898, 904 (8th Cir. 2000), *vacated by* 235 F.3d 1054 (8th Cir. 2000) (rehearing en banc where the court declined to answer the general question of precedential value of unpublished opinions since the case had become moot) (criticizing the practice of unpublishing opinions as creating "an underground body of law good for one place and time only" and that by unpublishing, courts effectively declare to lawyers that we "may have decided this question the opposite way yesterday, but this does not bind us today, and what's more, you cannot even tell us what we did yesterday").

CHAPTER TWO

1. Black's Title, Inc. v. Utah State Ins. Dep't, 1999 UT App 330, ¶ 10, 991 P.2d 607, 611.

2. Klapprott v. United States, 335 U.S. 601, 69 S. Ct. 384 (1949) (reversing lower court's default judgment in denaturalization case); Emily Badger & QuocTrung Bui, *In 83 Million Eviction Records, a Sweeping and Intimate New Look at Housing in America*, N.Y.TIMES (Apr. 7, 2018), https://www.nytimes.com/interactive/2018/04/07/upshot/millions-of-eviction-records-a-sweeping-new-look-at-housing-in-america.html (reporting on widespread evictions due to default judgment); Laura Beil, *As Patients Struggle with Bills, Hospitals Sue Thousands*, N.Y. TIMES (Sept. 3, 2019), https://www.nytimes.com/2019/09/03/health/carlsbad-hospital-lawsuits-medical-debt.html (reporting on wage garnishments and mortgage liens that result from default judgements).

3. United States v. Mcafee, 8 F.3d 1010, 1015 n.2 (5th Cir. 1993).

4. United States v. Donathan, 65 F.3d 537 (6th Cir. 1995).

5. United States v. Holland, 22 F.3d 1040, 1047 (11th Cir. 1994).

6. Howard Cohen, *Florida Pair's Quarter Pounder with Cheese Lawsuit Against McDonald's Is Over*, MIAMI HERALD (Nov. 6, 2018), https://www.miamiherald.com/news/business/article221203945.html#storylink=cpy.

7. Aila Slisco, *Tennessee Man's Lawsuit Against Popeyes For Running Out of Chicken Sandwiches Goes to Trial*, NEWSWEEK (Oct. 28, 2019), https://www.newsweek.com/tennessee-mans-lawsuit-against-popeyes-running-out-chicken-sandwiches-goes-trial-1468241. Case completion details are obtained from https://tennesseecasefinder.com/

8. See e.g., United States Fid. & Guar. Co. v. J.D. Johnson Co., 438 So. 2d 917, 919 (Fla. Dist. Ct. App. 1983) ("[N]on-final order denying summary judgment is not appealable."); Bell v. Harmon, 284 S.W.2d 812, 814 (Ky. 1955) ("[S]ound reasoning supports the conclusion that an order *denying* summary judgment should not be reviewed on appeal"); State ex rel. Redden v. Willamette Recreation, Inc., 54 Or. App. 156, 160 634 P.2d 286, 288 (1981) ("An order denying summary judgment is not appealable."); Olson v. Faculty House of Carolina, Inc., 354 S.C. 161, 168, 580 S.E.2d 440, 444 (2003) ("[T]he denial of a motion for summary judgment is not appealable, even after final judgment."); Hernandez v. Ebrom, 289 S.W.3d 316, 326 (Tex. 2009) ("[I]t is settled in both state and federal court that the denial of a motion for summary judgment may not be challenged on appeal from final judgment following trial.").

9. See e.g., Bristol v. Vogelsonger, 21 Conn.App. 600, 609, 575 A.2d 252 (1990) (reviewing "an exceptional case where, after the denial of the summary judgment motion, the movant parties were not afforded the opportunity to have a full trial on the merits"); Anderson v. Hopkins, 400 N.W.2d 350 (Minn. Ct. App. 1987) (reviewing lower court's denial of a summary judgment motion based on qualified immunity and remanding for reconsideration); Transatlantic, Ltd. v. Salva, 71 S.W.3d 670 (Mo. Ct. App. 2002) ("In certain circumstances, the denial of a party's motion for summary judgment can be reviewed when its merits are completely intertwined with a grant of summary judgment in favor of an opposing party").

10. See, e.g., Dzack v. Marshall, 80 Nev. 345, 393 P.2d 610 (1964) (issuing a writ of

mandamus compelling lower court to essentially reverse its denial of petitioner's motion for summary judgment).

11. See, e.g., Levy v. Cohen, 19 Cal. 3d 165, 137 Cal. Rptr. 162, 561 P.2d 252 (1977) (reversing lower court's judgment for plaintiff because prior bankruptcy court order for defendant was res judicata).

12. See, e.g., Cal. Civ. Code §1624; Secrest v. Sec. Nat'l Mortg. Loan Tr. 2002-2, 167 Cal. App. 4th 544, 84 Cal. Rptr. 3d 275 (2008) (finding that a forbearance agreement fell under the statute of frauds and was unenforceable).

13. Maurer v. Bernardo, 118 Cal. App. 290, 5 P.2d 36 (Dist. Ct. App. 1931) (affirming lower court's judgment that the action to enforce a note was untimely as the statute of limitations had expired counting from the day the note became due).

14. See e.g., Mele v. Cerenzie, 40 Wash. 2d 123, 241 P.2d 669 (1952) (affirming lower court's finding that written agreement between property seller and broker was unenforceable when broker induced agreement by fraud).

15. See e.g., Rau v. Von Zedlitz, 132 Mass. 164 (1881) (affirming lower court's finding that a debt repayment agreement was unenforceable because the debtor was subjected to undue influence by threats that her marriage would be thwarted, her husband arrested, and their situation publicized in newspaper).

16. Weinberg v. Baharav, 553 S.W.3d 131, 134 (Tex. App. 2018).

17. See, e.g., Wash. Rev. Code §§ 9A.56.130(1), 9A.04.110(28)(d) (defining extortion to the second degree to include making threats of criminal prosecution).

18. See Pliskin v. Radians Wareham Holding, Inc. (In re ICPW Liquidation Corp.), 600 B.R. 640, 669 (Bankr. C.D. Cal. 2019); Aurora Bank v. Hamlin, 609 S.W.2d 486, 488 (Mo. Ct. App. 1980); GRE v. MME, 531 S.W.2d 772, 773 (Mo. App. 1975); *Baharav*, 553 S.W.3d at 134; Galusha v. Sherman, 105 Wis. 263, 277-78, 81 N.W. 495, 500 (1900).

19. See e.g., Scottsdale v. Plitt-Theatres, Inc., 1999 U.S. Dist. LEXIS 7785 (N.D. Ill. 1999); Farm Credit Bank v. Dorr, 250 Ill. App. 3d 1 (5th Dist. 1993).

20. Alcan Forest Prods., LP v. A-1 Timber Consultants, Inc., 982 F. Supp 2d 1016, 1037 (Al. 2013), quoting Comment (b) to the Restatement (Second) Contracts Section 261.

21. See, e.g., Morin v. Innegrity, LLC, 819 S.E. 2d 131 (S.C. Ct. App. 2018).

22. See, e.g., Cal. Civ. Code § 1511.

23. For example, New York's CPLR 4547, Pennsylvania's 225 Pa. Code § 408, Texas Rules of Evidence Rule 408, California Code, Evidence Code - EVID § 1152, and Florida Statutes 90.408 make evidence of negotiation discussion like offers and compromises inadmissible.

24. See e.g., Co. Rev. Stat. § 13-17-202(1)(a)(II) (2017); Miller v. Hancock, 410 P.3d 819 (Co. Ct. App. 2017), ¶ 32; Golz v. State Farm Mut. Auto. Ins. Co., 2011 WI App 114, 336 Wis. 2d 475, 801 N.W.2d 349; American Motorists Ins. Co. v. R & S Meats, Inc., 190 Wis.2d 196, 526 N.W.2d 791 (Ct. App. 1994); *Court of Appeal: Can't Deny Costs Based on Losing Party's Meager Resources*, MET-ROPOLITAN NEWS (Aug. 10, 2018), http://www.metnews.com/articles/2018/alfaro081018.htm.; *Teenage Boys Molested by AA Sponsor; $10,000 CCP 998 Offer. $6.5 Million Verdict. San Diego County*, JURY VERDICT ALERT, https://www.juryverdictalert.com/jury-verdicts/item/sexual-abuse/doe-v-pacific-health.

CHAPTER THREE

1. COURT STATISTICS PROJECT, www.courtstatistics.org.
2. U.S. District Court Eastern District of California's Standing Order in Light of Ongoing Judicial Emergency in the Eastern District of California (Feb. 3, 2020).
3. Letter from the Judicial Conference of the United States to the House Appropriations Committee, April 28, 2020.
4. *Fact Sheet: New Judgeships*, JUD. COUNCIL CAL. (Dec. 2018), https://www.courts.ca.gov/documents/fact-sheet-new-judgeships.pdf.
5. Cara Bayles, *As Judicial Ranks Stagnate, 'Desperation' Hits the Bench*, LAW360 (Mar. 19, 2019), https://www.law360.com/articles/1140100/as-judicial-ranks-stagnate-desperation-hits-the-bench.
6. Joint Statement Before Comm. On the Judiciary, House of Rep., *Examining the Need for New Federal Judges* (June 21, 2018).
7. Jeneski v. Myers, 163 Cal. App. 3d 18 (1984).
8. Davenport v. Blue Cross of California, 52 Cal. App. 4th 435 (1997).

CHAPTER FOUR

1. Aebra Coe, *Like It Or Not, Law May Open Its Doors To Nonlawyers*, LAW360 (Sept. 22, 2019), https://www.law360.com/articles/1201357/like-it-or-not-law-may-open-its-doors-to-nonlawyers (discussing steps taken in this direction by Arizona, California, D.C., Illinois, New Mexico, Utah, and Washington).
2. Debra Cassen Weiss, *Can a Nonlawyer Judge Send You to Jail? Supreme Court is Asked to Hear Case*, ABA J. (Dec. 15, 2016), http://www.abajournal.com/news/article/can_a_nonlawyer_judge_send_you_to_jail_supreme_court_is_asked_to_hear_case.
3. 2020 Cal. R. Court r. 8.883.
4. Model Rules of Prof'l Conduct r. 1.4 (Am. B. Ass'n 1983).
5. Cal R. Prof. Conduct, r. 3-500 & 3-510 (emphasis added).
6. Model Rules of Prof'l Conduct r. 1.6(b) (Am. B. Ass'n 1983).
7. See, e.g., Defendant A. v. Idaho State Bar, 2 P.3d 147 (2000).
8. Call v. Czaplicki, No. 09-6561 (RBK/AMD), 2010 U.S. Dist. LEXIS 75916 (D.N.J. July 28, 2010).
9. Nail v. Husch Blackwell Sanders, LLP, 436 S.W.3d 556 (Mo. 2014).

CHAPTER FIVE

1. LAURENCE BAUM, THE SUPREME COURT (13th ed.) 43 (2019).
2. 418 U.S. 683 (1974).
3. Id. at 715.
4. A.B.A., STATE ADOPTION OF REVISED MODEL CODE OF JUDICIAL CONDUCT (rev. Mar. 5, 2012).
5. See e.g., A.L.A. Schechter Poultry Corp. v. United States, 295 U.S. 495 (1935) (reversing a conviction of a violation of the Live Poultry Code, which exceeded proper executive power).
6. United States v. Johnson, 170 F.3d 708, 719–20 (7th Cir. 1999).
7. Town of Greece. v. Galloway, 573 U.S. 565, 134 S. Ct. 1811 (2014).
8. Denver Area Educ. Telcoms. Consortium v. FCC, 518 U.S. 727, 116 S. Ct. 2374 (1996); see also FCC v. Fox TV Stations, Inc., 567 U.S. 239, 132 S. Ct. 2307

(2012) (holding that the FCC's change in policy gave Fox no notice that fleeting expletives or nudity in its shows was indecent); CBS Corp. v. FCC, 663 F.3d 122 (3d Cir. 2011) (finding FCC's sanctioning of the brief display of breasts during a Super Bowl halftime show arbitrary and capricious under the agency's current exemption for fleeting nudity).

9. See, e.g., Serrano v. Priest, 557 P.2d 929 (Cal. 1977); Edgewood Indep. Sch. Dist. v. Kirby, 777 S.W.2d 391 (Tex. 1989); Rose v. Council for Better Educ., Inc., 790 S.W.2d 186 (Ky. 1989); Abbot v. Burke, 575 A.2d 359 (N.J. 1990); Tenn. Small Sch. Sys. v. McWherter, 851 S.W.2d 139 (Tenn. 1993); McDuffy v. Sec'y of the Exec. Office of Educ., 615 N.E.2d 516 (Mass. 1993). District of Wilkinsburg v. Wilkinsburg Educ. Ass'n, 667 A.2d 5 (Pa. 1995).

10. Model Code Jud. Conduct r. 4.1 (Am. B. Ass'n 1990) r. 4.1 (AM. B. ASS'N 1990), https://www.americanbar.org/groups/professional_responsibility/publications/model_code_of_judicial_conduct/.

11. Id., r. 1.3.

12. Id., r. 4.1.

13. Id.

14. Id.

15. Caliste v. Cantrell, No. 18-30954, 2019 U.S. App. LEXIS 26288 (5th Cir. Aug. 29, 2019).

16. Ian Urbina, "Despite Red Flags, Judges Ran Kickback Scheme for Years," N.Y. TIMES (Mar. 27, 2009), https://www.nytimes.com/2009/03/28/us/28judges.html.

17. James Halpin, *Ciavarella Prison Term Up for Debate*, THE CITIZEN'S VOICE (Mar. 20, 2020); Michael R. Sisak and Michael Balsamo, Associated Press, Kids-for-Cash Judge Released From Prison Over Virus Concerns," The Philadelphia Inquirer (June 23, 2020),https://www.inquirer.com/news/pennsylvania/kids-for-cs-michael-conahan-20200623.html.

18. In civil cases where the amount in controversy is below a certain amount, or where certain types of non-monetary relief are sought, there is no right to jury trial.

19. Batson v. Kentucky, 476 U.S. 79 (1986); J.E.B. v. Ala. ex rel. T.B., 511 U.S. 127 (1994).

20. See, e.g., Simon v. San Paolo U.S. Holding Co., Inc., 35 Cal. 4th 1159, 1187, 29 Cal. Rptr. 3d 379, 399, 113 P.3d 63, 80 (2005) ("[W]hen, as in the present case, the reprehensibility of the defendant's conduct is relatively low, the state's interest in punishing it and deterring its repetition is correspondingly slight. Here, neither the interest in deterrence nor San Paolo Holding's substantial wealth can conceivably justify enforcing the jury's award of $ 1.7 million for a false promise that caused only a $ 5,000 injury.").

21. See, e.g., Fazzie v. Steinberg, No. JKB-15-1730, 2018 U.S. Dist. LEXIS 155035 (D. Md. Sep. 11, 2018) ("[E]ven if contributory negligence theoretically might be applicable to injuries like Mr. Fazzie's, the evidence in this case is insufficient as a matter of law to warrant an instruction."); Diehl v. Butts, 255 Va. 482, 499 S.E.2d 833 (1998) (finding jury instruction on contributory negligence inappropriate because "admissible evidence of record simply did not permit a jury to find that Mr. Dunlap neglected his health after Dr. Butts' alleged negligent treatment").

CHAPTER SIX

1. *Privacy Protections in State Constitutions*, NAT'L CONF. ST. LEGISLATURES (Nov. 7, 2018), https://www.ncsl.org/research/telecommunications-and-information-technology/privacy-protections-in-state-constitutions.aspx.

2. Adlerstein v. S. Nassau Cmtys. Hosp., 109 Misc. 2d 158, 164, 439 N.Y.S.2d 605, 610 (Sup. Ct. 1981).

3. Cal. Code Civ. Proc. 1985.3(g), 1985.6(f)(1); Fla. Stat. 934.24.

CHAPTER SEVEN

1. Helvering v. Taylor, 293 U.S. 507, 55 S. Ct. 287 (1935) (superseded by statute on the unrelated issue of burden of proof) (affirming appellate court's reversal of tax commissioner's arbitrary and excessive determination of plaintiff's taxable income).

2. Concept Automation v. United States, 41 Fed. Cl. 361 (1998).

3. Lee McIntyre, *Flat Earthers, and the Rise of Science Denial in America*, NEWSWEEK (May 14, 2019), https://www.newsweek.com/flat-earth-science-denial-america-1421936.

4. Addington v. Texas, 441 U.S. 418, 424, 426 (1979).

5. See, e.g., Humana Inc. v. Forsyth, 525 U.S. 299, 313 (1999); Nev. Rev. Stat. § 42.005(1).

6. Herman & Maclean v. Huddleston, 459 U.S. 375, 390 (1983).

7. Santosky v. Kramer, 455 U.S. 745 (1982) (finding that clear and convincing standard was required for termination of parental rights hearings); Woodby v. INS, 385 U.S. 276 (1966) (requiring clear and convincing standard for deportation cases); Schneiderman v. United States, 320 U.S. 118 (1943) (requiring government to prove by clear and convincing evidence of its claim before revoking a person's certificate of citizenship).

8. In re Bennett, No. 09-65528-fra7, 2012 Bankr. LEXIS 3127, at 5 (Bankr. D. Or. July 9, 2012).

9. Zander v. Workforce Safety & Ins., 2003 ND 194, ¶ 11, 672 N.W.2d 668, 671.

10. Tex. Dep't of Cmty. Affairs v. Burdine, 450 U.S. 248, 252-53, 101 S. Ct. 1089, 1093 (1981) ("[T]he plaintiff has the burden of proving by the preponderance of the evidence a prima facie case of discrimination.").

11. Comcast Corp. v. Nat'l Assn. of African American-Owned Media, 140 S.Ct. 1009 (2020).

12. Desert Palace Inc. v. Costa, 539 U.S. 90 (2003).

13. See, e.g., DERRICK BELL, RACE, RACISM AND AMERICAN LAW (1970).

14. See, e.g., Richard A. Posner, *On Hearsay*, 84 FORDHAM L. REV. 1465, 1467 (2015) ("Essentially it is a report by one person of what some other person said or wrote. If I say that someone told me it's going to rain this afternoon, my statement is hearsay (I am "saying" what I "heard" = "hearsay"). Hearsay is presumptively inadmissible in a trial because the source of a hearsay statement (repeated by a witness at the trial) is a nonparty to the litigation. He is the person from whom the witness heard the statement that the witness wishes to repeat in court, and ordinarily that nonparty source is unavailable to be cross-examined.").

15. Fed. R. Evid. 803.

CHAPTER EIGHT

1. See, e.g., Mass. Gen. L. Ch. 186, § 14 (fee-shifting statutes relating to rental disputes); Alaska R. Civ. P. 82; Wis. Stat. §§ 814.025, 809.25(3) (2003); Tex. Civ. Prac. & Rem. Code § 38.001 (West 2017).
2. Cal. Civ. Code § 47.
3. Id; Ohio Rev. Code § 4113.71(B); "*New California Law Extends Defamation Privilege to Communications Related to Sexual Harassment Claims and Investigations,*" NAT'L L. REV. (Jul. 27, 2018), https://www.natlawreview.com/article/new-california-law-extends-defamation-privilege-to-communications-related-to-sexual.
4. Halliday v. Ctr., 2016 Me. Super. LEXIS 22, 4-5 (citing Bean v. Cummings, 2008 ME 18, P. 1, 939 A.2d 676, 677).
5. Fed. R. Civ. P. 11; Cal. Code Civ. Proc. 128.7.
6. Oren Royal Oaks Venture v. Greenberg, Bernhard, Weiss & Karma, Inc. 42 Cal.3d 1157, 1168, 232 Cal. Rptr. 567, 7.28 P.2d 1202 (1986); Hardick v. Homol, 795 So. 2d 1107, 1111 n.2 (Fla. 5th DCA 2001) (citation omitted); Lynn v. Mc-Cormick, 2017 NY Slip Op 06169, 153 A.D.3d 688, 60 N.Y.S.3d 316 (App. Div. 2nd Dept.) (citations omitted); Martin v. Trevino, 578 S.W.2d 763, 769 (Tex. Civ. App. 1978) (citing J. C. Penney Co. v. Gilford, 422 S.W.2d 25, 31(Tex. Civ. App. 1967)); Preiser v. MacQueen, 177 W. Va. 273, 279, 352 S.E.2d 22, 28 (1985) (quoting Glidewell v. Murray-Lacy & Co., 124 Va. 563, 571, 98 S.E. 665, 668 (1919)).
7. Bidna v. Rosen, 19 Cal. App. 4th 27 (1993).
8. Bertero v. National General Corp. 13 Cal.3d 43, 50, 118 Cal. Rptr. 184 (1974) (citations omitted); Alamo Rent-A-Car v. Mancusi, 632 So. 2d 1352, 1355 (Fla. 1994) (citations omitted); Texas Beef Cattle Co. v. Green, 921 S.W.2d 203 (Tex. 1996) (citing James v. Brown, 637 S.W.2d 914, 918 (Tex. 1982)); Truman v. Fidelity & Casualty Co. of New York, 146 W. Va. 707, 123 S.E.2d 59 (1961) (citation omitted).
9. Seldon v. Lewis, Brisbois Bisgaard & Smith, LLP, 2012 NY Slip Op 32867(U), ¶ 6 (Sup. Ct.).
10. *Id.* (quoting Part 130 of the Rules of the Chief Administrator); Tavella v. Tavella,2006 NY Slip Op 565, 25 A.D.3d 523, 812 N.Y.S.2d 38 (App. Div. 1st Dept.).
11. *Tavella,* 25 A.D.3d at 524-25.
12. Walters v. Hometown Bank N a, 2014 Tex. Dist. LEXIS 8454, 31-32.

CHAPTER NINE

1. See Montgomery Ward & Co. v. Duncan, 311 U.S. 243 (1940); Cal. Code Civ. Proc. 657(1); N.Y. C.P.L.R. Law § 4404; Ohio R. Civ. Proc. r. 59; Tex. R. Civ. Proc. r 320.
2. Batson v. Kentucky, 476 U.S. 79 (1986); J.E.B. v. Ala. ex rel. T.B., 511 U.S. 127 (1994).
3. See, e.g, Chronakis v. Windsor, 14 Cal. App. 4th 1058, 18 Cal. Rptr. 2d 106 (1993).
4. Neal v. Farmers Ins. Exch., 21 Cal. 3d 910, 928, 582 P.2d 980, 990 (1978).
5. 28 U.S.C. §§1291 & 1292.
6. Bose Corp. v. Consumers Union, 466 U.S. 485, 511 (1984).
7. See, e.g., Harte-Hanks Communications v. Connaughton, 491 U.S. 657 (1989).

8. Id.

9. Bose Corp. v. Consumers Union of United States, Inc., 466 U.S. at 510-11 (1984).

10. Kerry v. Din, 576 U.S. 86, 135 S. Ct. 2128 (2015).

11. Trump v. Hawaii, 138 S. Ct. 2392 (2018).

CHAPTER TEN

1. *Uncollected Judgments May Add Up to $ Trillions*, JUDGMENT MARKETPLACE, https://www.judgmentmarketplace.com/blogs/53 ("Judgment Marketplace has recently started a new program that gathers statistics from courthouses around the country to discover the scale of the problem of unpaid judgments. Unfortunately, it's often difficult to compile these statistics, as many courthouses do not have advanced record keeping systems").

2. Eli Wolfe, *'We're Being Robbed': Wage Theft in California Often Goes Unpunished by State*, KQED (Oct. 16, 2019) https://www.kqed.org/news/11780059/were-being-robbed-california-employers-who-cheat-workers-often-not-held-accountable-by-state

3. See, e.g, In re Estate of Bonham, 817 A.2d 192, 195 (D.C. 2003) (quoting Bahre v. Bahre, 248 Ind. 656, 230 N.E.2d 411 (Ind. 1967)) ("[R]efusal to discharge a money judgment is not contempt of court and cannot be punished as a contempt of court."); Jou v. Adalian, No. 09-00226 JMS-BMK, 2015 U.S. Dist. LEXIS 13786, at *2 (D. Haw. Feb. 5, 2015) ("[C]ontempt proceedings are, without more, an improper means of collecting a pure money judgment."); London v. London, 149 Ga. App. 805, 256 S.E.2d 33 (1979) (holding that lower court erred in finding failure to pay constituted contempt of court).

4. See, e.g, 6th Ward/Crowley Gravity Drainage Dist. v. Benoit, 17-82 (La. App. 3 Cir 10/04/17), 229 So. 3d 590 (finding judgment of contempt was properly entered when owner refused to comply with consent order to clear the drainage for parts of his building). See also EEOC v. Local 580, Int'l Ass'n of Bridge, Etc, 1988 U.S. Dist. LEXIS 14205 (S.D.N.Y. Dec. 15, 1988) (finding a union in contempt of court for not complying with terms of a consent judgment); SEC v. Bilzerian, 131 F. Supp. 2d 10 (D.D.C. 2001) (finding that incarceration for contempt of order to disgorge profits warranted). Similarly, in Missouri, statutory grounds exist for civil contempt based on failure to perform pursuant to a judgment (but not for failure to pay). Rutter v. Bugg (In the Estate of Downs), 300 S.W.3d 242, 246 (Mo. Ct. App. 2009).

5. California courts recognize this doctrine. So do courts in Massachusetts, New York, New Jersey, North Dakota, South Carolina, and Virginia. See, e.g., Yousif v. Yousif, 61 Mass. App. Ct. 686, 814 N.E.2d 14 (2004); Matter of Allain v. Oriola-Allain, 2014 NY Slip Op 07151, 123 A.D.3d 138, 995 N.Y.S.2d 105 (App. Div. 2nd Dept.); Matsumoto v. Matsumoto, 171 N.J. 110, 792 A.2d 1222 (2002); Johnson v. Johnson, 2012 ND 31, 812 N.W.2d 455; Scelba v. Scelba, 342 S.C. 223, 535 S.E.2d 668 (Ct. App. 2000); Moscona v. Shenhar, 50 Va. App. 238, 649 S.E.2d 191 (2007). Tennessee has used it in juvenile delinquency proceedings (State v. Kelley, No. M2011-02758-COA-R3-JV, 2012 Tenn. App. LEXIS 785 (Ct. App. Nov. 9, 2012)).

CHAPTER ELEVEN

1. Cal. Code Civ. Proc., § 1001.

2. Cal. Civ. Code § 1670.11.

3. Cal. Gov't Code 12964.5.

4. 131 Stat. 2054, Pub. L. 115-97, Dec. 22, 2017.

5. Dan Aaron Polster, "The Trial Judge as Mediator: A Rejoinder to Judge Cratsley," MEDIATE, (Mar. 2007), https://www.mediate.com/articles/polsterD1.cfm.

6. Mike Pankow, *League Settles with Stringer's Wife*, CHICAGO TRIB. (Jan. 27, 2009), http://articles.chicagotribune.com/2009-01-27/news/0901260958_1_kelci-stringer-korey-stringer-heat-illness-prevention-program.

7. *Plaintiff Turns Down $30 Million*, DALLAS MORNING NEWS (Dec. 2, 1997).

8. Mastrobuono v. Shearson Lehman Hutton, 514 U.S. 52, 61 (1995) (holding that the National Association of Security Dealers' Code of Arbitration Procedure P3741(e) and an NASD manual suggest that arbitrators can award "damages and other reliefs," which may consist of punitive damages as a remedy).

9. Joseph Garrison, *The Bottom Line on Arbitration vs. Jury Awards*, CT. L. TRIBUNE. (Feb. 23, 2004), https://www.law.com/ctlawtribune/almID/900005402545/ (citing studies of arbitrations between 1999 and 2000 where "the median award in a non-civil rights case was about $13,000, the mean about $31,000" while in courts, "the median was $69,000 and the mean was $462,000"). Note that the difference is negligible for higher-paid employees in non-civil right cases. *Id.* See also EMPLOYMENT CLASS AND COLLECTIVE ACTIONS: PROCEEDINGS OF NEW YORK UNIVERSITY'S 56TH ANNUAL CONFERENCE ON LABOR 851 (David Sherwyn & Samuel Estreicher, eds., 2009) (stating that arbitration awards tend to be smaller than jury verdicts).

10. Epic Sys. Corp. v. Lewis, 138 S. Ct. 1612 (2018) (limiting employee class actions); AT&T Mobility LLC v. Concepcion, 563 U.S. 333, 131 S. Ct. 1740 (2011) (holding that California law requiring class arbitration for consumer contracts is pre-empted by the Federal Arbitration Act).

11. See e.g., Int'l All. of Theatrical Stage Emps., etc. v. Laughon, 118 Cal. App. 4th 1380, 1381, 14 Cal. Rptr. 3d 341, 342 (2004) (holding that the arbitrator's failure to disclose prior disqualifying employment was grounds for vacation under Cal. Code Civ. Proc. § 1286.2(a)(6)(A)); Burlington N. R.R. v. TUCO, 960 S.W.2d 629 (Tex. 1997) (vacating arbitration award when neutral arbitrator exhibited evident partiality in failing to disclose referral from firm of non-neutral co-arbitrator).

12. In a Vibram USA Inc. settlement over its FiveFingers shoes, $3.75 million fund was divided among countless claimants such that each person received just $8.44, even though the payout was originally expected to be $20 and $50. The First Circuit thought the underpayment was still fair. Ann Bucher, *Appeals Court Upholds Vibram FiveFingers Class Action Settlement*, TOP CLASS ACTIONS (Jan. 7, 2016), https://topclassactions.com/lawsuit-settlements/lawsuit-news/300292-appeals-court-upholds-vibram-fivefingers-class-action-settlement/. Papa John's settled for $16.5 million in class action suit over its spam text advertising. Each eligible class member was to receive $50 and a free pizza coupon. Sarah Mirando, *Papa John's Agrees to $16.5m Text Spam Class Action Settlement*, TOP CLASS ACTIONS (May 20, 2013), https://topclassactions.com/lawsuit-settlements/lawsuit-news/4146-papa-john-s-agrees-to-16-5m-text-spam-class-action-settlement/.

13. MAYER BROWN LLP, DO CLASS ACTIONS BENEFIT CLASS MEMBERS? AN

EMPIRICAL ANALYSIS OF CLASS ACTIONS, INSTITUTE FOR LEGAL RE-FORMS, https://www.instituteforlegalreform.com/uploads/sites/1/Class_Action_Study.pdf.

14. *CFPB and DOJ Order Ally to Pay $80 Million to Consumers Harmed by Discriminatory Auto Loan Pricing*, CONSUMER FIN. PROTECTION BUREAU (Dec. 20, 2013), https://www.consumerfinance.gov/about-us/newsroom/cfpb-and-doj-order-ally-to-pay-80-million-to-consumers-harmed-by-discriminatory-auto-loan-pricing/. See also Butler v. Home Depot Inc., GBDH, https://gbdhlegal.com/cases/butler-v-home-depot/ (detailing a case where a court awarded "$87.5 million and extensive injunctive relief including a seven year compliance period in which Home Depot made significant changes to its personnel practices nationwide to ensure equal employment opportunities for all employees and to increase the number of women in sales and management positions"). The money was spread among 17,000 employees and 200,000 unsuccessful applicants so the individual payout was small. Butler v. Home Depot, Inc., No. 3:94-cv-4335 (N.D. Cal. Jan. 14, 1998); *FedEx Settles Race Bias Class Action for $55 Million*, INS. J. (Aug. 15, 2017), https://www.insurancejournal.com/news/national/2007/08/15/82685.htm (detailing FedEx racial discrimination settlement where the settlement was less as the attorneys' fees and costs divided by the large class (23000 members) would be small but where FedEx was forced to eliminate its discriminatory Basic Skills Test for employees).

15. Kindred Nursing Centers Ltd. P'ship v. Clark, 137 S. Ct. 1421, 1426, 197 L. Ed. 2d 806 (2017) (quoting *Concepcion*, 563 U.S. at 339) ("A court may invalidate an arbitration agreement based on 'generally applicable contract defenses' like fraud or unconscionability, but not on legal rules that 'apply only to arbitration or that derive their meaning from the fact that an agreement to arbitrate is at issue.'"); Ramos v. Westlake Servs. LLC, 242 Cal. App. 4th 674, 195 Cal. Rptr. 3d 34 (2015) (affirming lower court's voiding of an arbitration agreement on grounds of fraud because the Spanish translation of the agreement lacked the arbitration clause); Wofford v. M. J. Edwards & Sons Funeral Home Inc., 490 S.W.3d 800 (Tenn. Ct. App. 2015) (invalidating arbitration agreement for unconscionability because it was vague and one-sided and there was unequal bargaining power).

16. Wells v. S. Airways, Inc., 616 F.2d 107, 110 (5th Cir. 1980) (internal citations omitted) ("Arbitration is a quasi-judicial function, and we have construed the Railway Labor Act to require proceedings before System Boards of Adjustment to comport with due process. . . . Bias or hostility on the part of any member of a System Board sufficient to amount to a denial of due process in the arbitration is sufficient to invalidate an award by that Board"). In one case, an appellate court held that the arbitration proceeding violated due process when a party was not allowed to present expert testimony and cross-examine witness for the opposing side. Crawford v. Sanwardeker, Case No. CA-8288, 1992 Ohio App. LEXIS 303 (Ct. App. Jan. 21, 1992).

INDEX

ABOUT THE AUTHOR

Tanya Acker received her B.A. at Howard University and graduated from Yale Law School in 1995. Straddling legal work in government and private practice, Acker served as judicial law clerk to the Honorable Dorothy Wright Nelson on the Ninth US Circuit Court of Appeals, worked at the Office of the White House Counsel and the Civil Rights Division in the US Department of Justice, and also for private law firms. She received the ACLU's First Amendment Award for work on behalf of the homeless and she serves on the boards of various organizations dedicated to providing legal and community services. You can catch her every day on the Emmy-nominated show, *Hot Bench*. You can also hear her on her podcast, *The Tanya Acker Show*. She lives with her husband, Randy, and her dog, Max, in Los Angeles, California.